# THE CAMBRIDGE COMPANION TO
## ALEXANDER POPE

Alexander Pope was the greatest poet of his age and the dominant influence on eighteenth-century British poetry. His large oeuvre, written over a thirty-year period, encompasses satires, odes and political verse and reflects the sexual, moral and cultural issues of the world around him, often in brilliant lines and phrases which have become part of our language today. This is the first overview to analyse the full range of Pope's work and to set it in its historical and cultural context. Specially commissioned essays by leading scholars explore all of Pope's major works, including the sexual politics of *The Rape of the Lock*, the philosophical enquiries of *An Essay on Man* and the *Moral Essays*, and the mock-heroic of *The Dunciad* in its various forms. This volume will be indispensable not only for students and scholars of Pope's work, but also for all those interested in the Augustan age.

PAT ROGERS is DeBartolo Chair in the Liberal Arts at the University of South Florida.

THE CAMBRIDGE
COMPANION TO
# ALEXANDER POPE

EDITED BY
PAT ROGERS

CAMBRIDGE
UNIVERSITY PRESS

# CAMBRIDGE
## UNIVERSITY PRESS

University Printing House, Cambridge CB2 8BS, United Kingdom

Cambridge University Press is part of the University of Cambridge.

It furthers the University's mission by disseminating knowledge in the pursuit of education, learning and research at the highest international levels of excellence.

www.cambridge.org
Information on this title: www.cambridge.org/9780521549448

© Cambridge University Press 2007

First published 2007

*A catalogue record for this publication is available from the British Library*

ISBN 978-0-521-84013-2 Hardback
ISBN 978-0-521-54944-8 Paperback

# CONTENTS

ILLUSTRATIONS

# NOTES ON CONTRIBUTORS

PAUL BAINES is Professor in the School of English, University of Liverpool. His publications include *The House of Forgery in Eighteenth-Century Britain* (1999), *The Complete Critical Guide to Alexander Pope* (2000), *The Long Eighteenth Century* (2004), several articles in the *Oxford Dictionary of National Biography*, and a number of articles on poetry, crime, and punishment in the early eighteenth century. His biography of the rogue bookseller Edmund Curll, co-written with Pat Rogers, appeared in 2007.

LAURA BROWN is John Wendell Anderson Professor of English at Cornell University and author of *Fables of Modernity: Literature and Culture in the English Eighteenth Century* (2001), *Ends of Empire: Women and Ideology in Early Eighteenth-Century English Literature* (1993), *Rereading Literature: Alexander Pope* (1985), and *English Dramatic Form 1660–1760: An Essay in Generic History* (1981), as well as co-editor, with Felicity Nussbaum, of *The New Eighteenth Century: Theory-Politics-English Literature* (1987).

HELEN DEUTSCH is Professor of English at UCLA and the author of *Resemblance and Disgrace: Alexander Pope and the Deformation of Culture* (1996), and *Loving Dr. Johnson* (2005), as well as co-editor of *Defects: Engendering the Modern Body* (2000). She has recently returned to Pope's work as one of the focuses of a new book project on gendered subjectivity, embodiment, and intimate literary forms such as the essay and the verse epistle.

HOWARD ERSKINE-HILL is a Fellow of Pembroke College, Cambridge, and a former Professor of Literary History in the University of Cambridge. He is a Fellow of the British Academy. His many works include *The Social Milieu of Alexander Pope* (1975) and an edition of Pope's *Selected Letters* (2000). He has also written *Poetry of Opposition and Revolution: Dryden to Wordsworth* (1996) and, with Eveline Cruickshanks, *The Atterbury Plot* (2004).

DAVID FAIRER is Professor of Eighteenth-Century English Literature at the University of Leeds. His most recent book is *English Poetry of the Eighteenth Century,*

*1700–1789* (2003). He is also the author of *Pope's Imagination* (1984), *The Poetry of Alexander Pope* (1989), and editor of *Pope: New Contexts* (1990), *The Correspondence of Thomas Warton* (1995), and the first complete printing of Warton's *History of English Poetry* (1998). With Christine Gerrard he has edited *Eighteenth-Century Poetry: An Annotated Anthology* (second edition, 2004).

CATHERINE INGRASSIA is Professor of English and Associate Dean for Academic Affairs at Virginia Commonwealth University. Her books include *Authorship, Commerce and Gender in Eighteenth-Century England: A Culture of Paper Credit* (1998), *"More Solid Learning"; New Perspectives on Alexander Pope's* Dunciad, co-edited with Claudia Thomas (2000), and *A Companion to the Eighteenth-Century Novel and Culture*, co-edited with Paula R. Backscheider (2005). She is also the editor of Eliza Haywood's *Anti-Pamela* and Fielding's *Shamela* (2004), and a past editor of *Studies in Eighteenth-Century Culture*.

MALCOLM KELSALL is Professor Emeritus at Cardiff University. His principal publications in the field of architectural and landscape iconography are *The Great Good Place: The Country House and English Literature* (1993), *Jefferson and the Iconography of Romanticism: Folk, Land, Culture and the Romantic Nation* (1999), and *Literary Representations of the Irish Country House: Civilisation and Savagery Under the Union* (2003). He has taught at the universities of Cardiff, Exeter, Oxford and Reading and has been visiting Professor at Hiroshima, Paris, and Wisconsin, and International Scholar in Residence at the Center for Jefferson Studies, Charlottesville, Virginia.

JAMES MCLAVERTY is Professor of English at Keele University. He has written widely on literary and bibliographical topics, including a book on *Pope, Print and Meaning* (2001). He revised and edited for the press David Foxon's lectures on *Pope and the Early Eighteenth-Century Book Trade* (1991), as well as David Fleeman's *Bibliography of the Works of Samuel Johnson* (2000).

DAVID NOKES is Professor of English at King's College London. He has written biographies of Jonathan Swift, John Gay, and Jane Austen, and is currently working on a tercentenary biography of Samuel Johnson, to be published in 2009. He has also written television programmes on Swift and *Frankenstein*, adaptations of *Clarissa* and *The Tenant of Wildfell Hall*, and a novel, *The Nightingale Papers*.

PAT ROGERS is DeBartolo Professor in the Liberal Arts at the University of South Florida, and the author of several books on Pope and his contemporaries, including *The Alexander Pope Encyclopedia* (2004) and *Pope and the Destiny of the Stuarts* (2005). Recent work includes a biography of Edmund Curll (2007), with Paul Baines, and an edition of Pope's major works for Oxford World's Classics (2006).

GEORGE ROUSSEAU has written numerous books, including *This Long Disease, my Life: Alexander Pope and the Sciences* (1968), with Marjorie Hope Nicolson, *Goldsmith: The Critical Heritage* (1974), with Pat Rogers, *The Enduring Legacy: Alexander Pope Tercentenary Essays* (1988), and *The Languages of Psyche: Mind and Body in Enlightenment Thought* (1990). He has also published a trilogy entitled *Pre- and Post-Modern Discourses: Medical, Scientific, Anthropological* (1991), with Roy Porter, *Gout: The Patrician Malady* (1998), *Framing and Imagining Disease in Cultural History* (2003), *Yourcenar: A Biography* (2004), and *Nervous Acts: Essays on Literature, Culture and Sensibility* (2004).

VALERIE RUMBOLD is Reader in English Literature at the University of Birmingham. She is author of *Women's Place in Pope's World* (1989) and of a range of articles on Pope and on women writers of the eighteenth century. Her edition of *Alexander Pope: The Dunciad in Four Books (1743)* appeared in 1999. She is one of the editors, with Julian Ferraro and Nigel Wood, contributing to the Longman Annotated Pope, and is currently working on a volume for the Cambridge Edition of the Works of Jonathan Swift.

STEVEN SHANKMAN is Professor of English and Classics at the University of Oregon. He is the author of *Pope's Iliad: Homer in the Age of Passion* (1983) and *In Search of the Classic* (1994). His edition of Pope's translation of *The Iliad* appeared in 1996. Recent books include, with Stephen Durrant, *The Siren and the Sage: Knowledge and Wisdom in Ancient Greece and China* (2000).

JOHN SITTER is Notre Dame Professor of English at the University of Notre Dame, the editor of *The Cambridge Companion to Eighteenth-Century Poetry* (2001), and author of *Literary Loneliness in Mid-Eighteenth-Century England* (1982), which was awarded the Louis Gottschalk Prize, and *Arguments of Augustan Wit* (1991), other studies of eighteenth-century poetry and satire. He teaches courses in those areas and in modern poetry.

CYNTHIA WALL is Professor of English at the University of Virginia. She is the author of *Poetics of Space: Transformations of Description in the Eighteenth Century* (2006) and *The Literary and Cultural Spaces of Restoration London* (1998), as well as an editor of Pope, Defoe, and Bunyan.

HOWARD D. WEINBROT is Ricardo Quintana Professor of English, and William Freeman Vilas Research Professor in the College of Letters and Science at the University of Wisconsin, Madison. He has published widely on numerous aspects of eighteenth-century texts and contexts. His latest books are *Menippean Satire Reconsidered: From Antiquity to the Eighteenth Century* (2005) and *Aspects of Samuel Johnson: Essays on His Arts, Mind, Afterlife, and Politics* (2005).

BRIAN YOUNG is University Lecturer and Official Student and Tutor in History at Christ Church, Oxford. He is the author of *Religion and Enlightenment in Eighteenth-Century England* (1998), and a co-editor, with Stefan Collini and Richard Whatmore, of two collections of essays, *Economy, Polity, Society* and *History, Religion, Culture: British Intellectual History 1750–1950* (2000), and, with Richard Whatmore, of *Palgrave Advances in Intellectual History* (2006). He is currently engaged in completing a study of Victorian understandings of the eighteenth century.

# ABBREVIATIONS

| | |
|---|---|
| *Anecdotes* | Joseph Spence, *Observations, Anecdotes, and Characters of Books and Men*, ed. J. M. Osborn, 2 vols. (Oxford: Clarendon Press, 1966). |
| *Corr* | *The Correspondence of Alexander Pope*, ed. G. Sherburn, 5 vols. (Oxford: Clarendon Press, 1956). |
| Johnson, *LOP* | Samuel Johnson, *The Lives of the Poets*, ed. G. B. Hill, 3 vols. (Oxford: Clarendon Press, 1905). |
| *Life* | Maynard Mack, *Alexander Pope: A Life* (New Haven: Yale University Press, 1985). |
| *Prose* | *The Prose Works of Alexander Pope*, vol. 1, ed. N. Ault (Oxford: Blackwell, 1936); vol. 2, ed. R. Cowler (Hamden, CT: Archon Books, 1986). |
| Swift *Corr* | *The Correspondence of Jonathan Swift*, ed. D. Woolley, 3 vols. (in progress) (Frankfurt: Peter Lang, 1999–). |
| *TE* | *The Twickenham Edition of the Poems of Alexander Pope*, ed. J. Butt *et al.*, 11 vols. (London: Methuen, 1938–68). |

In the *Imitations of Horace*, vol. IV, *Ep* refers to the *Epistles* and *Sat* to the *Satires*. Unless otherwise indicated, *The Dunciad* is quoted from the A text (1729) in *TE*, vol. V.

1688      Alexander Pope born in the commercial area of the City of London, 21 May. King James II flees to France, prior to accession of William III and Mary.

1692      The Pope family move to Hammersmith, outside London.

1698      Alexander Pope's father acquires house at Binfield, Berkshire, in Windsor Forest: the family in residence there by 1700. While living there, Pope meets older men who will serve as literary mentors, including the retired diplomat Sir William Trumbull, the dramatist William Wycherley and the actor Thomas Betterton.

1702      Accession of Queen Anne. Start of the War of the Spanish Succession (to 1713), with British forces under the command of the Duke of Marlborough.

1703      Isaac Newton becomes President of the Royal Society (to 1727).

1704      Jonathan Swift, *A Tale of a Tub* and *The Battle of the Books*. Marlborough and the allies gain a spectacular victory over the French at the battle of Blenheim.

1705      Alexander Pope's first surviving letters. Close friendship with Trumbull, a neighbour in the Forest. Has begun work on his *Pastorals*.

1707      About this time, Pope meets Martha and Teresa Blount, members of the Catholic gentry; Martha was to become his closest woman friend for the rest of his life.

1708      Final stone laid on St Paul's cathedral, designed by Sir Christopher Wren.

1709    *Pastorals* and other early work published.

1710    In the wake of the divisive Sacheverell affair, the Tories gain power under Robert Harley (later Earl of Oxford) and Henry St John (later Viscount Bolingbroke), who become important supporters of Pope. Swift begins his *Journal to Stella* (to 1713). George Frideric Handel arrives in London and helps to initiate a fashion for Italian opera.

1711    *Essay on Criticism*. Addison and Steele begin *The Spectator*, runs until 1713 (Pope is an occasional contributor). South Sea Company launched under the aegis of Oxford. Marlborough dismissed as commander as part of Tory moves to end the war.

1712    First version of *The Rape of the Lock* in two cantos. *Messiah* appears in *The Spectator*.

1713    Pope publishes *Windsor-Forest*, celebrating end of the War of the Spanish Succession. Addison's *Cato*, with prologue by Pope. By now Pope is familiar with the Scriblerus group, including Swift, John Arbuthnot, Thomas Parnell and John Gay. He also is in contact with the leading ministers, Oxford and Bolingbroke. Contributes to Steele's *Guardian*.

1714    The full *Rape of the Lock* appears in five cantos. Death of Queen Anne; succession of George I. The Tories lose power and Whigs dominate national politics for the rest of Pope's life.

1715    *The Temple of Fame*. First instalment of the *Iliad* translation, issued by subscription. Bolingbroke flees to France. Jacobite rising led by the Old Pretender, James Francis Edward Stuart. Pope friendly with Lady Mary Wortley Montagu (later a bitter enemy). John Gay, *The What d'ye Call It* (comedy on which Pope and Arbuthnot may have given assistance).

1716    Rising put down. Pope family forced to leave Binfield, in the wake of anti-Catholic legislation, and move to Chiswick, outside London. Pope becomes familiar with members of the court of the Prince and Princess of Wales. John Gay, *Trivia*. Some of Pope's earliest brushes with the rascally publisher, Edmund Curll, initiating a lifelong war of words.

1717    Death of Pope's father. Collected *Works* published, containing *Eloisa to Abelard, Elegy to the Memory of an Unfortunate*

*Lady*, and other new poems. Farcical comedy written by Pope, Gay, and Arbuthnot, *Three Hours after Marriage*, performed to a mixed reception.

1718    Pope leases house at Twickenham, his home for the rest of his life. Death of his Scriblerian colleague Parnell.

1719    Daniel Defoe, *Robinson Crusoe*, part 1, admired by Pope.

1720    Last instalment of the *Iliad*. South Sea Bubble, a major financial crash which has widespread political and social effects.

1721    Pope brings out edition of Parnell's poems. Robert Walpole attains power and serves as prime minister until 1742, frequently incurring the criticism of Pope.

1722    Death of Marlborough, unlamented by Pope.

1723    Pope's edition of the Duke of Buckinghamshire's works. Jacobite plot involving Pope's friend Atterbury discovered; the bishop exiled to France. Pope's in-laws implicated in Waltham Blacks affair, a politically charged crime spree in Berkshire and surrounding counties. Death of Sir Christopher Wren, admired by Pope.

1725    First instalment of the *Odyssey*. Edition of Shakespeare. Bolingbroke returns from exile and settles not far from Pope's home.

1726    Translation of the *Odyssey* completed. Swift visits England and stays with Pope. *Gulliver's Travels* published. Voltaire begins three-year exile in England, where he will meet both Pope and Swift.

1727    First two volumes of *Miscellanies* published, including work by Pope, Swift and other Scriblerians. Swift's final visit to England. Death of George I. His son George II ascends the throne, with Caroline as consort. *The Craftsman* begins as a weekly journal of the opposition to Walpole. Death of Newton.

1728    *The Art of Sinking*, written largely by Pope, published in third volume of *Miscellanies*. *The Beggar's Opera*, by John Gay, performed and scores a major hit. First version of *The Dunciad* in three books.

1729      *The Dunciad Variorum* published, with fuller apparatus and annotation. Edmund Curll, *The Curliad*, one of many ripostes. Swift, *A Modest Proposal*.

1730      Colley Cibber, a frequent butt of Pope, appointed Poet Laureate. Throughout the coming decade Pope grows more closely involved with the opposition to Walpole's government, enjoying friendship with the "Patriot" leaders who stood against the influence of the court. *The Grub-street Journal* begins its career (to 1737), supporting Pope's stance in literary politics and satirizing his enemies.

1731      *Epistle to Burlington.* Death of Defoe.

1732      *Miscellanies*, fourth volume. Death of John Gay. Death of Atterbury. Hogarth, *The Harlot's Progress*.

1733      First of the *Imitations of Horace* published (to 1738). *Epistle to Bathurst. Essay on Man*, epistles I–III published. Death of Pope's mother.

1734      *Essay on Man*, epistle IV published. *Epistle to Cobham.*

1735      *Epistle to Arbuthnot*, followed by death of Arbuthnot. *Epistle to a Lady*. Second volume of Pope's *Works*. Curll's edition of Pope's *Letters* (publication engineered by Pope).

1737      *Epistle to Augustus* published. Authorized edition of *Letters*. Death of Queen Caroline. Theatrical Licensing Act increases government control over new plays. Samuel Johnson, *London*.

1738      *Epilogue to the Satires* brings the imitations of Horace to an end. Samuel Johnson, *London*, praised by Pope.

1739      Swift's *Verses on the Death of Dr Swift* first published.

1740      Pope's health grows worse. Samuel Richardson, *Pamela*, Part I.

1741      *Memoirs of Scriblerus* published under Pope's direction.

1742      Fourth book of *The Dunciad* published separately. Henry Fielding, *Joseph Andrews*.

1743      Pope publishes complete version of *The Dunciad* in four books. Fielding, *Jonathan Wild*.

1744    Pope working on deathbed edition of his works. Dies, 30 May. Buried at Twickenham. Johnson, *Life* of Richard Savage (a writer well known to Pope).

1745    Death of Swift. Death of Robert Walpole. Jacobite rising led by the Young Pretender, Charles Edward Stuart.

PAT ROGERS

# Introduction

It would not be quite true to say that Pope has proved a poet for all the ages, if only because some late Victorians thought him safely dead and buried in terms of any active presence in the poetry of their day. Even then, however, Pope refused to lie down, and for the past three hundred years he has shown surprising resilience in the face of condescension, assumed indifference, or outright hostility. Recent generations of poets and critics have joined the scholars in helping to recover some of the ground he had lost. A look at his reputation as it stood 100, 200, and 300 years ago may help to make the point.

In the first quarter of the eighteenth century, Pope had seen his career take off with a series of major poems: *An Essay on Criticism, Windsor-Forest, The Rape of the Lock,* and *Eloisa to Abelard,* which would all be packaged in the sumptuous collection of the poet's *Works* in 1717. Scarcely anyone without a personal grudge then doubted that a poet of the highest excellence had arrived on the scene – in the view of most dispassionate observers, the greatest English writer since Milton and Dryden in the late seventeenth century. A hundred years later, in the first quarter of the nineteenth century, his position had undergone serious challenge, but he remained a potent influence for Wordsworth, and earned the vehement support of Byron:

> Neither time, nor distance, nor grief, nor age, can ever diminish my veneration for him, who is the great moral poet of all times, of all climes, of all feelings, and of all stages of existence. The delight of my boyhood, the study of my manhood, perhaps (if allowed to me to attain it), he may be the consolation of my age. His poetry is the Book of Life.[1]

This may seem hyperbolic, with its calculated reworking of a tag from the Roman moralist Cicero in the second sentence. But a similar tribute came from Byron's contemporary, the essayist Charles Lamb, when he remarked that Pope paid the finest compliments ever devised by the wit of man – "Each of them is worth an estate for life – nay an immortality."[2] Pope's reputation reached its low point in the late 1800s. Then, just a hundred years ago, things began to look up for the poet in the first decades of the twentieth century. His admirers were not critics who set the blood raging today – figures such as Austin Dobson and George Saintsbury, whose learning and love of poetry may be disguised from us by their blimpish personae. But the tide turned between the two world wars, as poets such as Edith Sitwell and W. H. Auden recognized Pope's outstanding technical accomplishments, and scholars such as George Sherburn began to reappraise his legacy. In the heyday of "New Criticism", around the 1940s and 1950s, Pope prospered mightily, enjoying the esteem of writers like Cleanth Brooks and W. K. Wimsatt; and even the ranks of Cambridge could scarce forbear to cheer, as these were represented by influential pioneers of twentieth-century literary analysis such as F. R. Leavis and William Empson. Pope also gained in public recognition through the efforts of modern scholarship, especially the imposing Twickenham edition of his complete poems spearheaded by John Butt from the 1930s to the 1960s, and the massive contributions to Popian study of Maynard Mack right up to the late 1980s.

But that was then and this is now. Against all expectations, Pope has made it into the early twenty-first century with very little, if any, loss of momentum. New approaches in the post-structuralist era have confirmed just how central a place he holds in the narrative of poetic history. Scarcely any critical school has managed to sideline his work: all our new terms and favored concepts turn out to fit Pope's practice with startling precision. It is no accident that so many of the shibboleths of modern criticism repeatedly turn up in the criticism of Pope. Nor, for that matter, that these keywords have come to the fore in this volume. The reason that the *Companion* is organized in part around issues such as identity, gender, the body, the history of the book, crime, and the other, goes back to a simple fact: Pope's work raises these issues in a peculiarly direct and pervasive way. No work of the time adumbrates the concerns of modern feminism more immediately than the *Epistle to a Lady*; no poem dramatizes the march of the literary, journalistic and publishing profession so richly as *The Dunciad*. We should find it hard to name any considerable body of poetry so replete with images of crime and punishment as the *Imitations of Horace*. Few writers have confronted the nature of heroism in the modern world so searchingly as did Pope in his translations of Homer. If there is a single text in the entire canon which brought the topic of consumerism and commodification into the western mind, then it must be *The Rape of the Lock* – as innumerable modern readings serve to confirm. Luxury, politeness, effeminacy, private and public spaces, neuroticism – they all come into question during the course of the *Rape*, in a text that lasts less than 800 lines (you could recite it within the span of a half-hour television programme, with commercial breaks between the cantos.). It is as though Pope had a land line to the twenty-first century and intuited the nature of our modern obsessions.

With his meticulous attention to detail – the tone and texture of words, the sound and syntax of verses, the shape of longer poems – Pope repays the kind of detailed attention that a *Companion* of this sort is designed to provide. A love of Pope starts with a love of words, and it is readily accountable that poets should long have relished the effects he taught himself to achieve. But his work repays close observation on other grounds, for anyone who wishes to explore the recesses of the human heart, or to appreciate the comedy of men and women in their social dance.

## Pope's life

The salient facts of Pope's life are set out in summary form on pp. xiii–xvii above, and later essays in this book explore many detailed aspects of his career. We need to remember first that he did not set out with great advantages: while this does not affect the intrinsic quality of his poems, the fact does reinforce our sense of the great human achievement which his life as a writer represented. He was born a Roman Catholic in 1688, the year that an alliance of political, military and church leaders drove the last Catholic monarch from the English throne. His father, a retired London merchant already well into middle age, had to move his family out of the city because of harsh new measures directed against the papist community under the new monarchs, William III and Mary II. An invalid from his early years, the boy grew up in Windsor Forest, about thirty miles from the centre of the capital. There he developed a taste for poetry, communed with nature in what was then a wholly rural environment, and acquired some elderly mentors, including the retired diplomat Sir William Trumbull, the dramatist William Wycherley, and the actor Thomas Betterton. They encouraged his first literary efforts, culminating in a precociously brilliant set of *Pastorals* organized around the four seasons. Pope may have started on these as early as the age of sixteen, but they did not appear in print until 1709, just before his twenty-first birthday, in a volume of miscellanies put out by the greatest publisher of the age, Jacob Tonson. Having gained attention and started to make a mark in the London literary world, Pope soon followed up with the dazzling epigrammatic wit of *An Essay on Criticism* (1711). These works brought him to the notice of two Whig authors who now dominated the scene, Joseph Addison and Richard Steele, then at the height of their popularity through two innovative journals, *The Tatler* and *The Spectator*. However, Pope was tending to gravitate towards an alternative camp, including his fellow-members in the high-spirited writers' workshop known as the Scriblerus Club, Jonathan Swift and John Gay. This group had close links with the Tory ministry which had come to power in 1710. Pope would maintain an intimate friendship in later years with the leaders of this government, the moderate Robert Harley, Earl of Oxford, and his uneasy colleague in a sometimes uneasy coalition, the mercurial Henry St John, Viscount Bolingbroke. In 1712 came the first version of *The Rape of the Lock*; then *Windsor-Forest*, a work on the long-awaited Peace in 1713 which blends descriptive, historical, and political elements; and finally in 1714 the expanded *Rape*, a mock-heroic poem utilizing all of the young man's accumulated poetic skills. It exhibits wit in language, poise in tone, elegance in its simulation of heroic diction, ingenious parody of epic structure, and devastating powers of social observation.

But Pope's golden youth came to an abrupt halt. In 1714 Queen Anne died, the ministry collapsed, and the accession of the Hanoverian kings left the Tories on the political sidelines for almost fifty years. The unsuccessful Jacobite rising of 1715/16 involved a number of Pope's friends and co-religionists. When the dust settled, Oxford found himself in the Tower of London on charges amounting to treason, while Bolingbroke was exiled in France and stripped of his honours. Swift, too, went into a kind of exile as Dean of St Patrick's Cathedral in Dublin, safely remote from the day-to-day battles of party politics at Westminster. Meanwhile Pope's own family was hounded by the measures taken against Catholics as a result of the Jacobite scare, and they had to leave their cherished home at Binfield for the more humdrum (if not yet suburban) surroundings of Chiswick, to the west of London. For the next few years Pope concentrated on his ambitious plan to transform Homer's epic, *The Iliad*, into a contemporary classic by re-laying its ancient and in some sense "primitive" outline on the template of Augustan poetics. Opinions have always differed about the degree of his success, but there is no doubt of the commercial coup which the translation delivered. Pope negotiated strict terms from the publisher Bernard Lintot, and gained enough subscribers to ensure that he was set up for life. As a result he could disdain patronage by the court in a way that no other considerable writer had managed for a very long time. His position at the head of English letters was further ratified in 1717 when a sumptuous volume of collected poems appeared. This contained a few new items, notably *Eloisa to Abelard*, but for the most part it represented a summation of major poetry written before the death of the Queen.

Pope's own father died in 1717 and not long afterwards he took his aged mother to live with him in a new house in the Thames-side village of Twickenham. Here he was to spend the last quarter-century of his life, and "Twickenham" was to become as familiar an address in the public mind as Gad's

Hill for Dickens or Ayot St Lawrence for Bernard Shaw. Strictly the villa did not embody a new structure but rather two rebuilt cottages, planted on five acres of rented land, and the house was a conscious miniaturization of the great Palladian mansions of the aristocratic friends he had begun to acquire. Pope gave even more attention to the garden, which included a lawn by the riverside and a parcel of land at the back, across the road towards Hampton Court. To connect these two segments Pope built his famous subterranean grotto, and along with the garden's own features and ornaments this served as a personal and family shrine, dedicated to the poetic and political values he held most dear.

In his new "retirement" at Twickenham, Pope continued to work on Homer, having taken on a version of the *Odyssey*, and on Shakespeare, whose works he edited in 1725 with moderate distinction. Around 1722–3 he had been distracted by the fallout from the Atterbury affair, yet another Jacobite plot and yet another banishment of a friend in the person of Francis Atterbury, Bishop of Rochester, and ringleader of the conspiracy. By the later 1720s Pope had gone over a decade without composing a single original poem to rank with the major works of his early twenties. A new burst of energy may have been inspired partly by a renewal of his intimacy with Swift. The Dean paid his only return visits from Dublin in 1726 and 1727, bringing with him some dangerous contraband in the shape of *Gulliver's Travels*, an explosive work whose origins went back to the convivial days of collaborations in the Scriblerus Club. So, too, did *Peri Bathous*, a collective work of Scriblerian fun at expense of bad writers, published in 1728, where Pope took the leading authorial part. Soon afterwards came the first version of *The Dunciad* in three books, a poem long meditated but only recently actualized by Pope. Unlike *The Rape of the Lock*, this leaves its mock-epic plot behind as it portrays the fate of literature and learning in a modern Babylon. Little escapes the torrent of satiric invention as it envelops the court of George II, the ministry of Robert Walpole, the church of cozy latitudinarian divines, the theatrical establishment led by Colley Cibber (an actor–manager and playwright eventually advanced to the throne of the dunces), the world of education and scholarship symbolized by the bullying pedant – as Pope saw him – Richard Bentley, classicist and would-be improver of Milton. At the heart of the plot come the doings of a tribe of so-called dunces, Pope's name for writers, journalists and publishers, whose combined activities threaten to sink literature into a squalid branch of commerce, marketing and scandalous gossip.

The government of Robert Walpole became one of Pope's prime targets in the 1730s, even though the poet and the prime minister appear to have maintained decent personal relations. In the early part of the decade Pope hit a rich vein of form with two series of poems he initiated. First came the *Moral Essays* (1731–35), four richly allusive and skilfully argued discourses on topics such as the use of riches. There followed the *Imitations of Horace* (1733–38), taking on a range of contemporary social issues. Though following the poems of Horace quite closely, Pope injects a vein of sharp localized commentary on individuals, couched in a language that is often spiky and abrasive. Also published in separate instalments was *An Essay on Man* (1733–34), issued anonymously to confuse and distract Pope's critics. It incorporated his most extensive disquisition on philosophic, cosmic, and social themes, and entered into a Europe-wide debate over the nature of the good, the beneficence of nature, and the rôle of the individual in society. For generations it remained one of the poet's most admired and most quoted works, although in recent years the *Essay* has slid towards the margins of most readers' interests. After this there was time only for a revised version of *The Dunciad*, with a new fourth book devoted mainly to some cultural crazes of the day. By 1740 all of Pope's old friends in the Scriblerian gang had passed on, with the lone exception of the distant Swift, who had in any case sunk into senile decay. Pope himself suffered a number of illnesses that ultimately crushed his fragile constitution. He died in May 1744 at the age of fifty-six.

## Summary of essays

Many of the Cambridge Companions to Literature have placed a strong emphasis on readings of individual works written by the author under discussion. This volume by set purpose departs from that scheme, as it is organized topically. There are two main reasons for this decision. First, while there is no shortage of commentary on poems such as *The Rape of the Lock*, the epistles *To a Lady* and *To Arbuthnot*, or *The Dunciad*, it seems desirable to set these well-known works within the context of the full range of Pope's poems. By this means we have attempted to ensure that items such as the *Imitations of Horace* (e.g. *Sat*, II.i) receive their share of notice. We have also been able to give a little more space to the *Essay on Criticism* and the *Essay on Man* – once regarded as central planks in Pope's achievement – than many recent accounts of his work have done. Second, Pope's oeuvre constitutes a kind of sustained enterprise, or magnum opus in which the separate parts make up an interactive system. (Something far less true of writers like Samuel Johnson or Alfred, Lord Tennyson.) The shape of this volume is meant to allow readers to establish fruitful connections between different texts, as these poems are exposed to a shifting light from one essay to another. More than once it happens that the same passage of verse is analyzed by two or three different contributors and we have left it to readers to make their own cross-references and comparisons.

We begin with two essays which examine facets of Pope's literary personality. In recent years writers on the eighteenth century have devoted considerable attention to issues of identity. A neat summation of this concept is provided by Dror Wahrman: "an essential core of selfhood characterized by psychological depth, or interiority, which is the bedrock of unique, expressive individual identity."[3] But students of Pope had begun some time ago to explore the poet's sense of self, in the wake of Maynard Mack's Northcliffe Lectures, delivered in 1972. An essay entitled "'The Least Thing like a Man in England'", reprinted in Mack's volume, *Collected in Himself* (1982), focused interest on Pope's complex response to his medical history. Mack brought to light some of the stratagems Pope devised to cope with illness, along with the shrivelled and invalid body which his ailments had left him.[4] One book that followed up on this lead was Helen Deutsch's *Resemblance and Disgrace* (1996), which went into many aspects of the poet's life as they expressed the limitations of his condition – his deformity, his poor health, his miniaturized stature, his Catholicism, and his exposure to public ridicule through hostile prints and writings. All these things made Pope an outsider in his society, and to some extent a feminized and aberrant individual with reduced agency and authority – a state that his lifetime achievement as a poet could mitigate but not wholly control. In her essay for this volume, Deutsch shows how Pope "transformed his marginality into a source of creative self-reflection, self-possession, and self-legitimation." She also examines the various projections of self which the poet adopted, as "the young would-be libertine and love poet, the dutiful translator and ambitious emulator of the classics, the mature moral arbiter and ultimately the great negator of English satire."

In fact, the privacies of day-to-day existence invade the best known work more often than readers generally recognize. David Nokes, a novelist as well as a critic, has written biographies of Swift, John Gay, and Jane Austen. Here he considers a number of Pope's friends and enemies, such as respectively Jonathan Swift and Edmund Curll, not forgetting ambiguous cases such as Lady Mary Wortley Montagu and Joseph Addison, who moved in and out of favor. For Pope, as Nokes tells us, "the desire to establish around himself a circle of virtuous men, to correspond with constantly, became a vital element in his desire to fix forever the image of his life as a virtuous crusade." Nokes shows, too, how the relationships fed into poems such as the *Epistle to Arbuthnot* and *The Dunciad*.

The two succeeding essays examine the form and style of Pope's verse. His masterly technique, once a favorite topic for critics, has suffered comparative neglect over the past twenty years. John Sitter, author of major studies including *The Poetry of Pope's "Dunciad"* (1971), asks pertinent questions here about the manner in which we should *read* Pope, that is to say aurally, in order to get the right noises sounding in our heads as we encounter the highly polished and regular-seeming texture of his verse. As Sitter points out, "Deciding how to perform a line, if only for our own ears, will require decisions about meaning and psychological emphasis." Sitter emphasizes, too, the varied voices which Pope projects in his work. In allied fashion Cynthia Wall, a critic who has edited *The Rape of the Lock* and has also charted the literal and imaginative spaces of eighteenth-century literature, shows how the structure of the couplet enables Pope to fix meaning and suggest connotations. She argues that "within the strict form of the heroic couplet [in *The Rape of the Lock*] the verbs are wriggling and the images escaping," while *Eloisa to Abelard* "employs the couplet structure and off-rhymes to generate an unremitting pattern of confinement and rebellion that resists final reconciliation." Both these essays show that there are abundant ways to get behind the apparently rocking rhythm and smooth syntax to find the complex inner core of the poetry.

Another development, clearly visible over the last few decades, is a renewed interest in Pope's translations of the two great epics of Homer, *The Iliad* and *The Odyssey*. This process has gone alongside a major revaluation of the output of his great predecessor John Dryden, whose versions of writers such as Virgil, Juvenal, and Ovid have come to seem some of his most significant "creative" works. A major advance in taking the Homeric translations seriously came with R. A. Brower's *Alexander Pope: The Poetry of Allusion* (1959). However, the main starting point for this reappraisal was the appearance of the Twickenham edition of these poems in 1967 (*TE*, VII–X), an enterprise in which Mack again took a leading part. Since then numerous scholars have brought a series of insights to the text of Pope's work. A key figure has been Steven Shankman, both through his book *Pope's "Iliad": Homer in the Age of Passion* (1983), and through his own edition of Pope's translation (1996). In this volume, Shankman reveals the ways in which Pope's experience as a translator affected his entire career, and in which the presence of Homer permeates his oeuvre. Even the mock epics he composed provide a parallel with the aims of the ancient heroic poet, whose "dual achievement of glorifying through poetry and yet at the same time analyzing the sources of psychic and social disorder finds expression in *The Rape of the Lock* as well." Equally, much debate in the recent past has gone on around the nature of Pope's putative "Augustanism," or in broad terms the extent to which he approved of the civilization of ancient Rome, whose major writers served as some of his principal models. Two key documents here are books by Howard D. Weinbrot, *Augustus Caesar in "Augustan" England: The Decline of a Classical Norm* (1978) and Howard Erskine-Hill, *The Augustan Idea in English Literature* (1983), which take rather different approaches and reach different conclusions. In his essay for this volume Weinbrot, author of another well-known study, *Alexander Pope and the Traditions of Formal Verse Satire* (1982), investigates some of the further complexities in Pope's relation to the admired (but not always sacrosanct) masters of ancient poetry, especially Horace. As the essay argues, "Pope learned to compartmentalize and to continue his affection for Greek and Roman literary achievement. In each case, however, he distinguished between often morally or politically unacceptable content, and generally brilliant literary talent that had given pleasure for thousands of years."

From his youth Pope cared greatly for poets of the Elizabethan and Jacobean era, including Edmund Spenser, John Donne, and Ben Jonson. This aspect of his work remains something of a black hole in the critical legacy, and David Fairer's essay here is designed to plug the gap. In addition to writing several studies on Pope, Fairer has carried out extensive work on Thomas Warton, the critic whose *History of English Poetry* (1774–1781) helped to create the canonical eighteenth-century view of earlier literature and on Joseph Warton, brother of Thomas, whose *Essay on the Genius and Writings of Pope* (1756–82) did most to influence the tide of critical taste. In the present volume, Fairer considers a number of ways in which Elizabethan poetry (broadly defined) left its mark on Pope. As his essay illustrates in depth, Pope "valued humanist argument with its sceptical wit and its respect for individual experience and intelligent conscience. But it is clear from his poetry that he also relished another side of Renaissance culture, the rich symbolic language that the Elizabethan world in particular offered him." My own essay on Pope in Arcadia seeks to trace some of the ways in which the poet's use of pastoral reflected his own early experience in rural Berkshire, and to show how this vision of spiritual harmony was shattered by reverses in political and personal life.

Both of the next pair of essays confront the wider public debates which raged in Pope's time. Brian Young has specialized in the intellectual and theological controversies of the early Enlightenment. Here he situates Pope in the crucial matrix of issues which would soon come to be defined as "ideological" in nature. The essay shows how Pope moved from one oppositional stance, associated with his roots in the Catholic community, to one centered on the "Patriot opposition" directed against the Prime Minister Robert Walpole and on the freethinking philosophies of his friend and mentor Lord Bolingbroke. From this exposed position, casting him as a heretic in terms of political and religious norms of his day, Pope was "saved" near the end of his life when William Warburton, "a Whig cleric who subsequently shaped Pope's posthumous reputation," reinterpreted his poems along the lines of Anglican orthodoxy. After this comes an essay by Howard Erskine-Hill, whose many important contributions to the field include *Poetry of Opposition and Revolution: Dryden to Wordsworth* (1996), as well as some widely read studies of the Jacobite climate in which much of Pope's work was performed. Here he turns to the latter half of the poet's career, starting with the Atterbury crisis of 1722–3, and moving into the 1730s, when Pope was associated with the opposition to Robert Walpole, nurtured by the so called "Patriot" ideology. Fixing on William Fortescue, a lawyer who mediated between Walpole and the opposition, Erskine-Hill carries out the most thorough investigation yet attempted of the role that this important figure in Pope's life played in literary politics. The enquiry prompts a wider conclusion about the public and private aspect of the poetry: "As with other aspects of his personality, [Pope's] political identity was made up of many different components, all registered in the subtle modulations of his poetry."

Some wider social and cultural matters occupy the remaining essays. In the first of these Paul Baines investigates an undertow of references to crime and punishment in the poems. Baines, author of *The Complete Critical Guide to Alexander Pope* (2000), has made a special study of this aspect of the age. Starting from the insight that "Punishment was more physical, and more visible, in Pope's day than it is in ours," he reads a number of major texts with an eye for the presence of penal concerns in the texture of the verse, and illustrates some of the ways in which satire especially was construed as an alternative mode of social retribution – Pope's works indeed constituting a "supplement to the public laws." After this Malcolm Kelsall, well known for his work in the field and author of *The Great Good Place: The Country House and English Literature* (1997), analyzes the landscapes and estates which formed a part of Pope's life (often as the object of his own skills as a garden designer, as with his own small villa at Twickenham) and which became the subject of major poems, such as the *Epistle to Burlington*. While there were certainly ideological components within Pope's notion of taste, we should not dismiss the pleasure principle which was also at work: as Kelsall says, "To emphasise the elements of moral allegory in the Popeian landscape is not to deny the keen sensitivity of his eye for natural beauty. It was this exquisite sensibility which led his friends to value his contribution to the planning of greater demesnes."

In the following essay, we encounter another ubiquitous element in the materials which went to make up Pope's imaginative world – money. Catherine Ingrassia, author of relevant studies including *Authorship, Commerce, and Gender in Early Eighteenth-Century England* (1998), places Pope's own monetary history in the context of the Financial Revolution which Britain was undergoing in his lifetime, in the years just before and after the South Sea Bubble of 1720. She then moves on to a detailed survey of the "poetic response," in the shape of the extended treatment of commercial and financial matters in the *Imitations of Horace* and elsewhere. As Ingrassia argues, Pope's success in promoting his Homer subscription, and his skill in taking control of his own literary properties, enabled him to escape the fate of his victims: "Because of his carefully achieved wealth, he does not have to become 'the bard . . . | Who rhymed for hire'." The insights of this essay provide a useful overlap with some of those found in the next section of the volume. This concerns Pope's dealings with the publishing industry of his time, a topic revolutionized by David Foxon's study, *Pope and the Early Eighteenth-Century Book Trade* (1991). The work of editing Foxon's lectures for the press fell to James McLaverty, a leading authority in the area, and author of *Pope, Print, and Meaning* (2001). In his essay for this volume he examines the history of Pope's contacts with publishers such as Jacob Tonson, Bernard Lintot, and Edmund Curll, and discusses the means by which Pope was able to achieve a situation of power within the book industry, unparalleled by any previous writer (and by very few in the succeeding three hundred years). As McLaverty notes, his damaging critiques of mercenary practices in the trade went with an astonishing capacity to use this same trade for his own purposes: "Although, with his attacks on Grub Street, his hostility to individual booksellers, and his sense of the unreliability of print, Pope can be thought of as an enemy to the book trade, few writers made better use of its resources."

Gender is an inescapable issue in modern literary studies, and Pope has proved to be a peculiarly fruitful source of material for critics interested in this subject. Valerie Rumbold, the author of a standard book, *Women's Place in Pope's World* (1989), gives a full account of the manner in which the poet's "work was both energized and constrained by gender." She reveals the conflicting pressures on the poet as he sought to achieve standing in the largely masculine world of letters, while in some ways placed by his personal limitations in a position of feminine dependency (an obvious link exists here to the essay by Helen Deutsch). Yet he was also responsible for some radical and even subversive versions of gender: in her analysis, Rumbold points to poems "explicitly critical of the patriarchal limitations imposed on women, notably *Verses to the Memory of an Unfortunate Lady*, *Eloisa to Abelard*, 'To a Lady with the Works of Voiture.'" These were among the most popular of Pope's work with eighteenth-century women readers, an important segment of the poet's clientele. Another growth subject in recent decades has been the area of medicine and the body, and again Pope happens to provide an especially interesting case study. The founding work here was impressively done by Marjorie H. Nicolson and G. S. Rousseau, with *"This Long Disease, My Life": Alexander Pope and the Sciences* (1968). The essay written for the present volume by Rousseau, a specialist in the interface between literature and medicine, starts from the poet's physical disabilities, and contends that "It is unthinkable that such a 'Carcass' (as he metonymically often referred to his deformed body) would not take a psychological toll on his selfhood and literary identity." This essay connects feelings about identity and the body to developments in neurology, and sees the relevance of medical advances to "a poet of selfhood like Pope, whose infirm body was paradoxically the source of *both* pain and power, blemish and asset." Again this recalls some motifs which came up at the opening of this volume.

The last essay reaches out beyond conventional appraisals of Pope as a representative "Augustan" figure to chart some of the wilder shores of the eighteenth-century imagination. Laura Brown has written widely on the period, including a bravely contentious exercise in "rereading literature," *Alexander Pope* (1985). Here she interrogates the familiar modern notion of the "other" as it emerges in Pope's work. In Brown's formulation, the other focuses primarily on "the representation of women or of indigenous or non-European peoples in literary texts," for instance the passage on the "poor Indian" in the first epistle of the *Essay on Man*. She analyzes this excerpt to bring out the multiple series of "intersecting perspectives on indigenous peoples" which are set in motion by Pope's verse. In the poet's work we find "a rich and pervasive engagement with alterity – an engagement that privileges the unfamiliar, the non-civilized, and the non-European, and that simultaneously evokes an inversion of traditional hierarchy, a destabilization of systems of order or continuity, and a questioning of fundamental assumptions of value and meaning."

Such claims provide a bracing note on which to end a volume of this kind, intended to encourage informed reading, as well as stimulating fresh and unprejudiced thinking about the issues which Pope brings to our consciousness. The contributors all have a deep commitment to understanding his poetry as it speaks to the present age. They do not all share Pope's attitudes, and they certainly do not all agree with one another. What they do have in common is a delight in returning to Pope, as this promotes a renewed engagement with his extraordinary qualities as a poet – his range, his finesse, his articulacy, and his capacity to surprise and disturb.

## NOTES

1. "Observations on 'Observations': A Second Letter to John Murray, Esq." (1821) (first published in Thomas Moore, *The Works of Lord Byron: With His Letters, and Journals, and His Life*, 17 vols. [London: John Murray, 1832–35]).
2. Conversation reported in William Hazlitt, "Of Persons one would have Wished to have Seen" (first published in *New Monthly Magazine*, January 1826).
3. Dror Wahrman, *The Making of the Modern Self: Identity and Culture in Eighteenth-Century England* (New Haven: Yale University Press, 2004), p. xi.
4. Maynard Mack, *Collected in Himself: Essays Critical, Biographical, and Bibliographical on Pope and some of his Contemporaries* (Newark: University of Delaware Press), 1982, pp. 372–92.

# I

HELEN DEUTSCH

# Pope, self, and world

Behold it is my desire, that my adversary had written a book. Surely I would
take it on my shoulder and bind it as a crown unto me.

(Job, xxxi, 35)

I have heard Mr. Richardson relate that he attended his father the painter on a
visit, when one of Cibber's pamphlets came into the hands of Pope, who said,
"These things are my diversion." They sat by him while he perused it, and saw
his features writhen with anguish; and young Richardson said to his father,
when they returned, that he hoped to be preserved from such diversion as had
been that day the lot of Pope.

(Samuel Johnson, *Lives of the Poets*, III, 188)

Alexander Pope, eighteenth-century England's most prominent poet and his
generation's most frequently portrayed celebrity, dominated the emergent literary marketplace as the first self-supporting, non-playwriting professional
author (shrewd enough to rely on an aristocratic coterie of subscribers to
get his start, yet savvy enough to supervise almost every aspect of the publication process), while fascinating his audience as a spectacle of deformity.
Characterizing the life of a wit in the preface to the first published volume of his *Works* (1717) as "a warfare upon earth," and complaining as
a well-established poet and celebrity in his 1735 *Epistle to Arbuthnot* of
"this long disease, my life," which poetry and friendship served to ease,
this protean master of the heroic couplet suffered a war between an excep-
tional mind and a body lambasted as "at once resemblance and disgrace"
of humanity's "noble race." Barely four and a half feet tall when grown, in
Voltaire's words "protuberant before and behind" (current medical science
attributes his deformity to childhood tuberculosis of the spine, otherwise
known as Pott's disease, contracted from a wet nurse, while his contemporaries also considered trampling by a cow and excessive study as potential
causes), socially disenfranchised for his Catholicism, Pope transformed his
marginality into a source of creative self-reflection, self-possession, and self-
legitimation. His life's work was the ultimate couplet of deformity and poetic
form.

Mocked early on as "the ladies' plaything" for the best-selling translation
of Homer appealing to a non-aristocratic and female audience (a serious

attempt at post-Miltonic epic refracted in his mock-heroic mirror *The Rape of the Lock*) that enabled him to declare himself "indebted to no priest or peer alive," Pope began his career as a generic virtuoso, modeling the monument to poetry and his own version of classical authorship of his early *Works* – beginning with his self-proclaimed masterpiece of versification, the *Pastorals* and concluding with an English and Christian version of Ovid's *Heroides*, *Eloisa to Abelard* – after the Virgilian progression from eclogue to epic.[1] By the end of his career, Pope had turned all genres, most importantly epic, into satire, casting himself in the *Epilogue to the Satires* (1738) as a hyper-masculine epic hero rejecting Horatian politeness and embodying solitary moral integrity in an age of beautiful social hypocrisy. Radically conservative in his final nostalgic Tory critique of British economic and imperial progress, fundamentally modern in his exploitation of the book trade, Pope embodied, negotiated, and redefined the ambiguities of his age. Pope had bid farewell to satire in the *Epilogue*, but he returned for one last performance: when the curtain falls at the end of his final poem (revised for half of his career), that grand mock-epic of Grub Street and modern ignorance, *The Dunciad*, and "universal Darkness buries all," Pope's couplet art finally triumphs by envisioning art's destruction.

The genre that distinguishes Pope's art through all its phases is the portrait – whether we consider the irreverent depiction of John Dennis as Appius in the *Essay on Criticism* (585–6), or the vitriolic portrait of Lord Hervey as Sporus, neatly encapsulated in the *Epistle to Arbuthnot* as "one vile Antithesis" (325), or his rival the laureate and famous fop Colley Cibber asleep in the lap of the goddess Dulness (*Dunciad*, III, 1–2). Such portraits stud his work like jewels, complex and often emotionally fraught attempts to capture the complexities of another human being in the couplet's suspended paradoxes. Alexander Pope seemed destined for the margins: he was Catholic at a time of intense social and economic discrimination, of uncertain class origin though possessing great social aspirations, and, most strikingly, in his own words, "the Least Thing like a Man in England" (*Corr*, I, p. 89). Yet he was at the center of a world that we might figure to ourselves as a portrait gallery that featured the poet both as master painter and visual curiosity. His "libel'd Person" and "pictur'd Shape" (*Arbuthnot*, 353) – distorted in carica-ture in cheap printed pamphlets, idealized in neoclassical grandeur in busts, frontispieces, and on mock-ancient medals – circulated throughout the liter-ary marketplace of eighteenth-century London, a teeming and contentious universe which he dominated as "King of Parnassus."

To try to paint Pope's portrait, to consider the relationship of "Pope, self, and world," is to enter into a battle for control of his image originating in the poet's own time but still continuing throughout over two centuries of critical response, in which Pope is marked out from the order his own words construct.[2] These reactions reveal Pope, who took on a variety of guises over the course of his career – the young would-be libertine and love poet, the dutiful translator and ambitious emulator of the classics, the mature moral arbiter, and ultimately the great negator of English satire – as excluded from what he celebrates, or implicated in what he rejects. Whether he is Leslie Stephen's monkey pouring boiling oil on his victims, William Empson's cripple admiring a natural order he cannot enter at the end of the grand georgic vision of empire in *Epistle to Burlington*, Maynard Mack's self-styled "feisty little alien . . . in the country of the normals," or the aspiring bourgeois hypocrite of Peter Stallybrass and Allon White, immersed in the Grub Street culture he disdains, Pope becomes, to use his phrase for Atossa in the *Epistle to a Lady*, one who "is whate'er he hates and ridicules," while doomed to love – like the lovelorn "future Bard" summoned by the grieving heroine of *Eloisa to Abelard* as best suited to "paint" the grief he himself feels – at a distance. Yet the couplet partner to this need to fix Pope, to objectify him and his intent, is career-long changeability: he is as variable and hard to "hit" as the women over whose portraits he puzzles in the opening of *Epistle to a Lady*, which begins with the casually uttered and recollected words of Pope's friend Martha Blount, "Most Women have no Characters at all" (2). In short, Pope's portraits reflect and refract himself. Who is more than he an "Antithesis," split between a "Cherub's face" and a beastly body (*Arbuthnot*, 325, 331)? Who else, like Atossa in *To a Lady* (118), called *his* life "one warfare upon earth"? As this essay will reveal, Pope often employed even more self-conscious and self-referential examples.

If the portrait was Pope's favorite genre, he was – as the proud monument of the 1717 *Works* and the full embrace of the personal voice afforded by the Horatian imitations of the 1730s demonstrate – his own favorite subject. Despite, or perhaps because of his career-long focus on himself, Pope remains one of the most elusive authors in the English canon. This paradox becomes even more complex when we consider the fact of Pope's deformity, which marked him apart from the intricate interrelations of nature and art as his age understood them, "where," as he wrote in his loco-descriptive masterpiece *Windsor-Forest*, "Order in Variety we see, | And where, tho' all things differ, all agree" (15–16). How then are we to understand Pope's insistence on making nature and art identical – both in the *Essay on Criticism*, when Virgil, attempting original poetry, finds that "Nature and Homer were . . . the same" (135), and in the *Essay on Man*'s vindication of the ways of God to man, in which "All Nature is but Art, Unknown to Thee" (I, 289)? Deformity served as Pope's trademark, as key to originality in a career of literary imitation, as proof of self-ownership in a world of economic circulation.[3] In this essay

I shall, as Maynard Mack undertook to do in his late writings on Pope, explore deformity in Pope as a key to subjectivity. The paradox of art and life in Pope's work also articulates the ways in which stigma shaped him as he responded to it, turning blunders into beauties, abjection into the portrait of authority.

Pope provokes readers to expose the painter of portraits accurate enough to imprison their subjects as himself an object marked by an order at once natural and divine, thus confirming their own sense of the world as intelligible and coherent. (We should recall that during this period, physical deformity was still believed to be a sign of divine punishment or warning, as well as the legible index of a corrupt soul, or as Francis Bacon put it "the consent between body and mind" [Essay 44, "Of Deformity," in *Essays and Counsels, Civil and Moral*, {1612}], even as these early modern beliefs were challenged by both the growth of a new science that saw monsters as part of nature, and an emergent sense of personal interiority – one which Pope's psychological portraits helped his culture to imagine – as an invisible depth that belied the body.) Even, or perhaps especially, at the level of the lived body, a body even the poet's own mother believed to be marked by excessive love of literature, Pope's poetry emerges from the intersection of creative imagination and shameful objectification, of self and world, of life and art.

The greatest paradox any reader of Pope must reckon with is that he wants art to embody the truth about himself. Perhaps this is because his body had to bear the burden of so much falsehood. The poet inscribed the words from Job with which we began on the flyleaf of the four volumes of pamphlet attacks he had collected and bound, preserved like the "flies in amber" of trivial enemies he marveled over in the *Epistle to Arbuthnot*, and exhibited in the notes of *The Dunciad* as well as the barrage of proper names that stud his later satire with asterisks. The ugly particulars of these volumes and the satiric responses they provoke serve as our emblem for Pope's will to self-portraiture at all costs: rather than ignore or reject the attacks of his adversaries, Pope displays them as the mark of his distinction, the source of his subjectivity. If these printed assaults were, as Pope claims in the anecdote which serves as this essay's epigraph, his "diversion" – and the portraitist Jonathan Richardson's son glimpses here, in the telling disparity between the poet's statement and his pained expression, a truth consistently on display to Pope's readers – they provoked an art that was profoundly serious play.

Such play in Pope's poetry alternates between satiric self-defense and acts of self-exposure; we can see its rhetorical roots in the poet's early letter to Lady Mary Wortley Montagu, in which Pope flirtatiously imagines, in an effort to move Lady Mary to follow his example: "If Momus his project had taken of having Windows in our breasts, I should be for carrying it further

and making those windows Casements: that while a Man showed his Heart
to all the world, he might do something more for his friends, e'en take out,
and trust it to their handling" (*Corr*, I, p. 353). In his first Horatian imitation,
such transparency exposes the poet's flaws:

> I love to pour out all my self as plain
> As downright *Shippen* or as old *Montagne* . . .
> In me what Spots (for Spots I have) appear,
> Will prove at least the Medium must be clear.
> (*Sat*, II.i, 51–6)

We might read this passage as a prime example of the ways in which Pope
deploys the rhetoric of personal deformity as proof of his universal virtue –
the spots in the medium, like the printed marks on the page, are proof of his
complete self-disclosure and sentimental transparency.[4] But such frankness is
also informed by a tradition of philosophical skepticism of which Horace and
Montaigne are important examples. From this perspective, Pope creates not
complete transparency but rather a paradoxically elusive depiction of what
James Noggle calls "a specially poetic, cleansed, fluid version of himself,
apparent only in contrast with the ordinary self represented as the 'spots' or
personal flaws that appear in it . . . [A] self so cleansed is a nothing, empty
if not for what it bears, virtuous only in invisibility." The ultimate Popean
couplet, as Noggle would have it, holds in tension not deformity and form
but rather the poetic self and any attempts to define it.[5] Pope is never more
elusive, in other words, than when he is telling us everything.

Yet we should also recall that, beginning with the young author's mockery
of the older critic Dennis, or perhaps even earlier with an anecdote recorded
by Joseph Spence of the poet as schoolboy penning a satire on his master and
being beaten for his pains, Pope provoked the attacks that justified a satire
advertised as virtuous self-display. "And with the Emblem of thy crooked
Mind | Mark'd on thy Back, like *Cain*, by God's own Hand, |Wander, like
him, accursed through the Land," ends one lampoon by two of Pope's famous
targets, Lord Hervey and Lady Mary Wortley Montagu (*Verses Address'd to
the Imitator of the First Satire of the Second Book of Horace* (1733), lines
110–12). Branded for life, Pope makes a career out of the indelibility of insult.
What Didier Eribon has recently argued about insult and the formation of gay
identity might equally apply to Pope's life-long effort to rewrite marginality
as authority.[6] Arguing that insult creates a subject who is "destined for
shame," forced to don a mask of otherness that can't be removed, Eribon
sees literature as a field of struggle in which the person objectified by insult
can speak in a self-created voice, thus rupturing the "world as it is" that has

rendered him alien. We might also recognize Pope in Eribon's claim that the internalization of insult creates a melancholy for "normal society" which is articulated as rejection.

Pope's embrace of the "not unpleasing Melancholy" that characterizes his lot at the end of *An Epistle to Arbuthnot* also shades the unrequited love triangles of the *Pastorals* and the sympathetic mirroring of poet and episto-lary heroine in the dark anthropomorphic landscape of the lovelorn Eloisa at the beginning of his career, while animating his unique spin on Horatian retirement of the 1730s. By turning his rented Twickenham estate on the out-skirts of London into a symbol of moral self-possession and freedom from material attachment, Pope transforms the legal ban on Catholics owning property or living within the city limits into a sign of his personal distinc-tion. These qualities also infuse the grand condemnation of British society in his *Epilogue to the Satires* and irradiate the "universal darkness" at the end of *The Dunciad*. We might consider that the great philosophical Opus Mag-num – a unfinished project that included a "system of ethics in the Horatian way" in the form of the four *Moral Essays* (also termed "Epistles to Several Persons"), along with that hybrid of poetry and philosophy, *An Essay on Man* – which crowned Pope's career in the 1730s, arose in part out of a need to justify his satiric attacks on poor scribblers in the 1728 *Dunciad*. We may then realize how even the larger currents of Pope's poetic progress were put into motion by a dynamic of insult and response. Pope, in other words, was constantly aware of himself as framed – as a person whose meaning had already been partially determined by commonplace, burdened by the book of his adversary. This does much to explain his career-long preoccupation with the portrayal of character, in which he would increasingly insist upon "touching persons" with the bite of satire.

When David Garrick, the most famous actor of the eighteenth century, glimpsed Pope at the theatre two years before his death in 1744, he gave us an emblem of this dynamic:

> When I was told . . . that POPE was in the house, I instantaneously felt a palpitation at my heart; a tumultuous, not a disagreeable emotion in my mind. I was then in the prime of youth; and in the zenith of my theatrical ambition. It gave me a particular pleasure that RICHARD was my character, when POPE was to see, and hear me. As I opened my part; I saw our little poetical hero, dressed in black, seated in a side box, near the stage, and viewing me with a serious and earnest attention. His look shot and thrilled, like lightning, through my frame; and I had some hesitation in proceeding, from anxiety, and from joy. As RICHARD gradually blazed forth, the house was in a roar of applause; and the conspiring hand of Pope showered me with laurels.[7]

Haunting this exchange of looks between the poet and the actor, and no doubt informing the "particular pleasure" that Garrick experiences at seeing Pope in the audience for this performance, is the awareness that both are using the same script – that of Shakespeare's *King Richard III*, that most infamous of hunchbacks who defines himself at the outset as unfit for love, "nor made to court an amorous looking-glass":

> Cheated of feature by dissembling Nature,
> Deform'd, unfinish'd, sent before my time
> Into this breathing world scarce half made up –
> And that so lamely and unfashionable
> That dogs bark at me, as I halt by them –
> (*Richard III*, I.i, 19–23)

Richard is the ultimate showman, who by "descant[ing] on [his] own deformity," improvises upon the script that nature has written for him. "Determined to prove a villain," he is also a source of Francis Bacon's influential maxim in his essay "Of Deformity" (the text of which was often quoted in attacks on Pope) that "Deformed persons are commonly even with nature: For as nature hath done ill by them; so do they by nature: being for the most part, (as the Scripture saith), void of natural affection; and so they have their revenge of nature" (Essay 44, *The Essays or Counsels of Francis Bacon* [1612]). The character, the poet, and the actor here unite in a common performance of the body's burden as the source of art.

I want to conclude by pointing briefly to several places in Pope's poetry where, like Richard in a virtuous key, he performs deformity as a self-conscious violation of proper decorum (and here I hark back to the Latin root of the word "decens," both what is fitting and what is ornamental), and as defacement of an earlier self-portrait. Each of these instances unites an early moment in Pope's poetic career with a later one, each offers in the process a revised sense of the poet's relationship to a self that is experienced at once as freeing and unsettlingly elusive.

The first is Pope's epigraph to his imitation of Horace's *Epistle* II.ii: "Ludentis speciem dabit et torquebitur" [he will give the appearance of playing and be turned/distorted/tortured on the rack.] In the context of the Latin original "torquebitur" takes on the neutral meaning of "turn," as the line in full reads "He will give the appearance of playing and turn, as one who now dances the Satyr, now the boorish Cyclops." This elusive play reminds us of the "diversion" of Pope's earlier brand of self-exposure, an artful elusiveness here thematized as performance. Aptly enough, in the body of his English text, Pope translates these lines with a self-conscious quotation from his *Essay on Criticism*, (362–3): "But Ease in writing flows from Art, not Chance, | As those move easiest who have learn'd to dance" (178–9). His italicization of "torquebitur" in the Latin text on the opposite page reminds us of his epigraph, and undermines the youthful *sprezzatura* of his earlier insistence on the invisibility of poetic labor. These ironically quoted lines seem to respond not just to the "you" of the previous line in the poem, who is tricked into thinking good poetry only "Nature and a knack to please," but also to Horace and the younger self for whom emulating the ancients was all. At this moment of self-scrutiny, Pope embraces disease as the pain of a laborious art that refuses to conceal itself, and that in a tacit revision of Horace refuses, at the end of the poem, decorously to abandon the stage of life to the young without judging their folly.

The next is a brief moment in Pope's self-portrait in his last Horatian poem, *Epistle* i.i, a poem that seems to abandon satire for a different kind of moral exemplarity. Housing "with Montagne now, or now with Locke" (26), Pope in his self-confessed changeable folly is at once skeptical of Christian tenets and free-ranging in his thought (Montaigne), while rigorously logical and overly accepting of the proofs of Christianity (Locke). He is also living a continual flux between the active (Montaigne's social criticism) and contemplative (Locke's investigation of the mind),[8] a flux complicated further by the unbalanced contrast between the poet's penchant to "Mix with the World, and battle for the State, | Free as young Lyttelton" (28–9), a prominent Whig opposition statesman, and his habit to "Sometimes, with Aristippus, or St. Paul, | Indulge my Candor, and grow all to all" (31–2). Further dividing his first opposition (between the moderns Montaigne and Locke) with another doublet (balancing ancient pagan Aristippus and early Christian Paul) announcing affinities with both the hedonist philosopher Aristippus, whom, Horace's *Epistle* i.i. (17) tells us, all situations suited due to his infinite adaptability, and his inverse St. Paul, who was "all things to all men" in his unwavering desire to convert them to the true faith, Pope is at once a devout Christian and a pagan sceptic, a self unchanged by circumstance and a chameleon.

This latter intermittent penchant to "indulge my Candor, and grow all to all," is shadowed by Pope's earlier condemnation of Wharton – the first and most powerful portrait in that investigation of the "characters of men," the *Epistle to Cobham*, "Grown all to all, from no one vice exempt, | And most contemptible, to shun contempt" (194–5).[9] The line which concludes this passage from Pope's *Ep*, i.i, "And win my way by yielding to the tyde" (34) completely reverses Horace's original, "I attempt to subject the world to me, not myself to the world." Pope stresses here not his stoical integrity but his ideological and historical fluidity, not his satiric authority but his indistinguishability from the human objects of his condemnation. When at the poem's conclusion Pope's addressee Lord Bolingbroke (the *Essay on Man*'s "Guide, Philosopher, and Friend," and most important influence) interrupts the poet's ruminations with a laugh (a laugh that reminds us of the cruel propensity of the eighteenth-century public to mock cripples), the confident certainties of the *Essay*'s theodicy, in which all aberration is seen as part of the divine order, are rewritten as the subjective inconsistencies that limit all human thought and moral judgment. Pope's status as a moral exemplar, through the essayistic shifts of *Epistle* I.i, comes to rest neither in his satiric righteousness nor his philosophical confidence but rather in his frank consciousness of his own flawed and unknowable self.

Thus we should not be surprised when in one of the most recent critical readings of Pope's *Essay on Man*, one which stresses the poet's self-consciously ironic manipulation of received wisdom throughout a poem too often dismissed as complacent, Helen Vendler pauses over Pope's perhaps most famous and oft-quoted portrait, in which he enlists a dizzying array of echoes from Renaissance literature (most notably *Hamlet*), in its magisterially balanced paradoxes:

> Know then thyself, presume not God to scan;
> The proper study of Mankind is Man.
> Plac'd on this isthmus of a middle state,
> A being darkly wise, and rudely great:
> With too much knowledge for the Sceptic side,
> With too much weakness for the Stoic's pride,
> He hangs between; in doubt to act, or rest,
> In doubt to deem himself a God, or Beast;
> In doubt his Mind or Body to prefer,
> Born but to die, and reas'ning but to err;
> Alike in ignorance, his reason such,
> Whether he thinks too little, or too much:
> Chaos of Thought and Passion, all confus'd;
> Still by himself abus'd, or disabus'd;
> Created half to rise, and half to fall;
> Great lord of all things, yet a prey to all;
> Sole judge of Truth, in endless Error hurl'd:
> The glory, jest, and riddle of the world!
>
> (II, 1–18)

Aptly describing this passage as a kind of divine creation of Man, one that "render[s] graphically the mobility of mind as it operates at full tilt," Vendler goes on to read the lines as Pope's ultimate self-portrait.

Detached from all reference to his own biography, Pope is not, here, the warm friend, the social companion, the scourge of dullards, or the pious son; rather, he is looking at himself in his interior solitude. Before his eyes, in a secular *Ecce Homo*, he places himself: the strange genius-cripple, the frustrated yearner, the inquisitive skeptic, the Catholic deist, the gothic classicist, the ill sensualist, the self-deluding self-satirist, the baffled inquirer, the language-tethered visionary. He is bold enough to think that what he sees in himself can be generalized to the rest of us.[10]

It is testament to the power of Pope's poetry that he is able to write himself, in all of his flawed and labile contradiction, as both human and exemplary. Through the workings of polished art, his unnatural deformity becomes our own.

But this is too neat an ending for Pope, who concluded his career, as we'll recall, on a dramatically oppositional note. We might end our reflections on "Pope, self, and world" by considering the epigraph to the final 1744 version of *The Dunciad*:

> *Tandem* Phoebus *adest, morsusque inferre parantem*
> *Congelat, et patulos, ut errant, indurate hiatus.*
> (OVID.)

[But Phoebus comes to his aid, and checks the monster, ready for the devouring grasp; whose expanded jaws, transformed to stone, stand hardened in a ghastly grin.]

The passage from which these lines are taken reads as follows:

> Here, as the head lay exposed on the alien sand, its moist hair dripping brine, a fierce snake attacked it. But at last Phoebus came, and prevented it, as it was about to bite, and turned the serpent's gaping jaws to stone, and froze the mouth, wide open, as it was.
>
> The ghost of Orpheus sank under the earth, and recognised all those places it had seen before; and, searching the fields of the Blessed, he found his wife again and held her eagerly in his arms. There they walk together side by side; now she goes in front, and he follows her; now he leads, and looks back as he can do, in safety now, at his Eurydice.
> (Ovid, *Metamorphoses*, XI, 70–86)[11]

Here Pope, whose head circulated freely through the visual culture of London, portrays himself with a powerfully self-divided emblem that evokes both satire triumphant and satire disarmed. He is Orpheus, torn to pieces by the Bacchantes he spurned (shades of the Dunces' violent attacks), whose head continued to sing even after being severed from his body. But he is also the monstrous serpent threatening that singing head, whose satire has the power to bite (unlike Sporus in *Arbuthnot*, who can only spit, spew, and "mumble of the game he dare not bite"), frozen for eternity in a pose of attack. Tellingly, Pope chooses to omit the powerful fantasy that follows these lines: a dream of losing the self in union with a beloved, and of falling out of step with the couplet's metre, looking beyond deformity's static and solitary frame.

## NOTES

1. On the *Works* as a monument to love and fame, see Vincent Caretta, "'Images Reflect from Art to Art': Alexander Pope's Collected Works of 1717," in *Poems in their Place: The Intertexuality and Order of Poetic Collections*, ed. Neil Fraistat (Chapel Hill: University of North Carolina Press, 1986), pp. 195–233.
2. For a fascinating overview of this dynamic, see Blakey Vermeule, *The Party of Humanity* (Baltimore: Johns Hopkins University Press, 2001).
3. Helen Deutsch, *Resemblance and Disgrace: Alexander Pope and the Deformation of Culture* (Cambridge, MA: Harvard University Press, 1996).
4. Deutsch, *Resemblance and Disgrace*, pp. 38–9.
5. James Noggle, *The Skeptical Sublime: Aesthetic Ideology in Pope and the Tory Satirists* (Oxford: Oxford University Press, 2001), pp. 147, 154.
6. Didier Eribon, *Insult and the Making of the Gay Self*, trans. Michael Lucey (Durham, NC: Duke University Press, 2004), p. xv.
7. David Garrick, as quoted in Percival Stockdale, *Memoirs of the Life and Writings of Percival Stockdale* 2 vols. (London, 1809), II, pp. 153–4.
8. Brean S. Hammond, *Pope and Bolingbroke: A Study of Friendship and Influence* (Columbia: University of Missouri Press, 1984), p. 121; Thomas E. Maresca, *Pope's Horatian Poems* (Columbus: Ohio State University Press, 1966), p. 179.
9. Dennis Todd, *Imagining Monsters: Miscreations of the Self in Eighteenth-Century England* (Chicago: University of Chicago Press, 1995), p. 257. Todd also elucidates the way in which Pope confuses Horace's orderly oppositions between the active and contemplative lives in this passage, leaving the reader and himself unconvinced of his ability to "project himself effortlessly into opposite extremes," and preparing us for the tonal shift of the next passage (pp. 256–7).
10. Helen Vendler, *Poets Thinking: Pope, Whitman, Dickinson, Yeats* (Cambridge, MA: Harvard University Press, 2004), p. 28.
11. Translated by A.S. Kline, and available at etext.virginia.edu/latin/ovid/ trans/ Metamorph11.html_Toc485520962.

# 2

DAVID NOKES

# Pope's friends and enemies: fighting with shadows

Pope never found it difficult to identify the moral values he defended: "To VIRTUE ONLY and HER FRIENDS, A FRIEND", he proclaimed in the first of his *Imitations of Horace* (*TE*, IV, p. 17), making the claim specific and only the application general. Where others wrestled with the semantics of a precise meaning, Pope had a startling simplicity. "Ask you what Provocation I have had? | The strong Antipathy of Good to Bad" (*TE*, IV, p. 324). His desire to claim a similar authority for his friendships made explicit a tendency enunciated by Swift:

> I have often endeavoured to establish a Friendship among all Men of Genius, and would fain have it done. They are seldom above three or four Contemporaries and, if they could be united, would drive the world before them.
>
> (*Corr*, II, p. 199)

For Pope the desire to establish around himself a circle of virtuous men, to correspond with constantly, became a vital element in his desire to fix forever the image of his life as a virtuous crusade. In his villa at Twickenham everything, from the motto *Libertati & Amicitiae* over the door to the placing of ornaments in the grotto, was designed to give his moral sentiments an outward and visible form.

From the first Pope's versifying abilities were accompanied by a desire to establish friendships less with contemporaries than with men who, though advanced in years and decayed in style, could prove helpful to an aspiring poet. William Wycherley and William Walsh were among the first with whom Pope cultivated a deferential literary manner, praising Wycherley for the brevity of his wit "like those who have most Money, are generally most sparing of either" (*Corr*, I, p. 12), and soothing Walsh by aiming (hopelessly) to become "a Critic by your Precepts, and a Poet by your Example." (*Corr*, I, p. 20). With the patronage of such men he was content to live at Binfield, celebrating the virtues of the spot with Horatian dignity.

Happy the Man, who free from Care,
The Business and the Noise of Towns,
Contented breaths his Native Air,
In his own Grounds.

(*Corr*, I, p. 68)

When, some years later, he came to London and needed a town-companion he fell in with Henry Cromwell, thirty years his senior, who favoured (in no particular order) snuff, nosegays, and ladies of easy virtue. He and Pope played a kind of literary one-upmanship, with Cromwell maintaining his dazzling, if slightly shop-soiled lexicon of Statius, Homer, and ladies of the night, and Pope developing a style of "talking upon paper" about classical literature and domestic dogs.

When writing on his canine theme, Pope could maintain an easy superiority; when the subject came to sexuality he felt more vulnerable. At twenty-three, referring to his friends Martha and Teresa Blount, he said how gladly he would give "all I am worth, that is to say, my *Pastorals* for *one* of their *Maidenheads*, & my *Essay* for the other" (*Corr*, I, p. 137). To his friend John Caryll, he felt able to speak even more frankly and, writing with his wit pared down to cover his embarrassment, he asked for the recommendation of a prostitute.

> If you know One particular Nymph that can carry herself and me, better than usually, whom you can give upon yr word, pray acquaint me, that I may wear her Chain forthwith; I fancy my Size and Abilities may qualify me to Match her Monkey very well.[1]

John Caryll was someone he could always speak to with a minimum of fuss. A few months earlier he told him he was "satisfied in [his] conscience" he had behaved honourably in the troubles over the *Rape of the Lock* and the *Essay on Criticism*. "I dare stand to posterity in the character of an unbigoted Roman Catholic and impartial critic" (*Corr*, I, p. 151). He may, perhaps, have expected his words to carry to John Caryll senior, his oldest friend and fellow Catholic with whom he kept up a closeness that lasted all his life.

By this time he was well embarked upon his London literary career in which the cast lists of friends and enemies have firm, emblematic qualities. John Gay was an impetuous juvenile whose career needed careful supervision and if, in recompense, Gay should assist him, attacking those inveighing against his growing reputation, it was a happy coincidence. In the dedication to *The Mohocks* (1712) Gay delivered a gratuitous snub to the critic John Dennis after he had abused Pope's *Essay on Criticism*: three years later Ambrose Philips was singled out in *The Shepherd's Week* for the same reason. "It is to this management of *Philips*, that the world owes Mr. *Gay's*

*Pastorals*," said Pope, keen to show off his eager disciple's work (*Corr*, I, p. 229). Should this element of partnership ever fail, Gay was there to take the flak: before the opening of *Three Hours after Marriage* Gay boasted of having received the assistance of "two of his friends" (Pope and Arbuthnot) in writing it; when it failed, he alone accepted full responsibility: "I will (if any Shame there be) take it all to myself" (*Corr*, I, p. 388). Not until much later would Gay risk things of which Pope might not approve and Swift's suggestion for "a Newgate pastoral, among the whores and thieves" (*Corr*, I, p. 360) took thirteen years from hint to happening. Gay was always a slow worker.

Throughout the later 1720s Gay's friendship with Pope cooled so much that Swift wrote in 1730, "Mr Pope talks of you as a perfect Stranger" (*Corr*, III, p. 96). But when Gay was on his deathbed in 1732 Pope mysteriously reappeared to reclaim the career he had initiated. He wrote to John Caryll (senior) that he "no sooner saw the death of my old friend Mr Gay, whom I attended in his last sickness (it was but three days), but [Martha Blount] fell very ill, partly occasioned by the shock his death gave her." The phrasing here is ambiguous: George Sherburn comments, tentatively "one must feel that Pope does not here intend to say that he was at Gay's bedside when he died. Possibly Miss Blount was" (*Corr*, III, p. 337). In life, Pope always presented himself as Gay's indispensable friend; in death, he became his trusted curator. "Our poor friend's papers are partly in my hands," he wrote to Swift, "I will take care to suppress things unworthy of him" (*Corr*, III, p. 365). Swift wholeheartedly agreed: "I think it is incumbent upon you to see that nothing more be published of his that will lessen his reputation" (*Corr*, III, p. 361). Gay's merits, suitably refashioned, were proclaimed at Westminster Abbey as the personification of childlike innocence.

> Of manners gentle, of affections mild;
> In wit, a man; simplicity, a child . . .

In the *Epistle to Arbuthnot* he presents Gay as the perfect model of neglected genius.

> Blest be the *Great*! for those they take away,
> And those they left me – for they left me GAY,
> Left me to see neglected Genius bloom,
> Neglected die! and tell it on his Tomb.
> (*TE*, IV, pp. 306–7)

This may not have been the truth about Gay's life; but it was a very important myth for Pope to cling to.

Dennis erupted into Pope's life almost simultaneously with Gay. In May 1711 Pope published his *Essay on Criticism* including these lines:

> But *Appius* reddens at each Word you speak,
> And *stares, Tremendous!* with a *threatning Eye,*
> Like some *fierce Tyrant* in *Old Tapestry.*
>                                                    (*TE*, I, pp. 306–7)

The comments were designed to remind its readers that John Dennis, most famous critic of the age, wrote execrable tragedies (*Appius and Virginia*), uttered extravagant adjectives ("Tremendous!"), and had a violent temper. The jibe is gentle and, given the *Essay's* subject, might have been greater had Dennis simply been ignored. At fifty-three Dennis was the author of numerous well-respected works, but personally was immensely irritable with the tendency to read poetry "as if it were a legal brief" (*Life*, p. 182). Pope's lines evidently irritated him and, a month later, his *Reflections* on the *Essay* appeared displaying both his incisive mind and utter lack of charity. He swatted away a few genuine errors and concluded: "As there is no Creature so venomous, there is nothing so stupid and impotent as a hunch-back'd Toad." He concentrated on Pope's physical appearance, "the very Bow of the God of Love."

> This little Author may extol the Ancients as much and as long as he pleases, but he has reason to thank the good Gods that he was born a Modern. For had he been born of *Graecian* Parents, and his Father by consequence had by Law the absolute Disposal of him, his Life had been no longer than that of one of his Poems, the Life of half a Day.                                    (*Life*, p. 184)

Until Dennis wrote, Pope was essentially an optimistic young man of twenty-three with enormous talent and a keen sense of the world before him. Taunts about his physical shortcomings were laughed off as merely verbal and, though painful, were turned to his advantage. But this very public branding was a reminder for the rest of his life that, for all the mellifluous beauty he created, it was as a "hunch-back'd Toad" that he was known in society. He tried to laugh the attack off, protesting to Caryll that if he'd known Dennis would react so badly "his name had been spared" and wondering at Dennis's fury for lines "which only describe him subject a little to colour and stare on some occasions" (*Corr*, I, p. 121). But he got Gay to pay Dennis back immediately in the dedication to *The Mohocks*, and took the further opportunity afforded by the opening of Addison's tragedy *Cato* for which he wrote the prologue. In his *Remarks* on *Cato* Dennis had complained that the "great success" of this "very faulty Play" foretold the ruin of the stage. Pope seized the opportunity to pay him back in a wicked satire as a careful act of friendship to Addison; but Addison, aware of Pope's growing reputation, asked Steele to write to him wholly disapproving of his "manner of treating Mr *Dennis*." When he thought it "fit to take notice" of Dennis's remarks he would do it in a way "Mr. *Dennis* shall have no just Reason to complain of" (*Corr*, I, p. 184). Gradually Dennis slipped out of focus until, in 1721, Pope sent him a brief note confessing sorrow for the "differences" between them which, his latest editor records, is "to the credit of both men."[2]

With Addison Pope's relationship went in the other direction, beginning in friendship, deteriorating rapidly and leaving an unpleasant aftertaste. Addison – writer, politician and diplomat – had everything his talent and connections could bestow. His writings, from his poem *The Campaign* to his tragedy *Cato*, became the models for correct expression, while *The Spectator* informed his admirers, of both sexes, what to talk about in social situations. From his seat at Button's Coffee House Addison did not dictate but rather (as in Steele's letter above) let his minions do that for him.

> Damn with faint praise, assent with civil leer,
> And without sneering, teach the rest to sneer.
>
> (*TE*, IV, p. 110)

Addison was among Pope's early friends but by the time of *Cato* both were aware the relationship was breaking up, no doubt assisted by Pope's epigram *On a Lady who P-st at the Tragedy of Cato*. Addison made a last attempt, if not to win Pope over, at least to neutralize him. "You gave me leave once to take the liberty of a friend" he wrote, "in advising you not to content yourself with one half of the Nation for your Admirers" (*Corr*, I, pp. 196–7). The final break between them came over the *Iliad*. Late in 1713 Pope desired Addison to "look over" the first book of his translation for which he was canvassing subscriptions; Addison declined having recently, he declared, designed to print a version by Thomas Tickell. This was the first Pope had heard of this rival version, done several years previously, while Tickell was at Oxford; but the printer John Watts noted that though "the first book of the *Iliad* was in Tickell's handwriting" it was "much corrected and interlined by Addison."[3] The first volume of Pope's *Iliad* appeared in June, followed just two days later by Tickell's, but the results of any contest were not long in doubt. Lintot dashed off a note to Pope at Binfield, telling him "Mr Tickles Book . . . is allready condemn'd here and the malice & juggle at Buttons is the conversation of those who have spare moments from Politicks" (*Corr*, I, p. 294).

Addison died in 1719, but Pope's revenge was long and slow. Sixteen years later he contrived, through a network of intermediaries, to leak letters to the pirate publisher Edmund Curll, in order to justify following up with a "corrected" version of his own correspondence in which several letters were revised, re-assigned or fabricated. Awkward phrases were removed and, along with them, awkward or inopportune friends. Before he replaced Theobald's name with Cibber's in his expanded version of *The Dunciad*, Pope went further in his correspondence, trimming the role of Caryll and substituting Addison. One wonders at his sentiments towards both men when he fabricated a snub to Dennis ("he has written against every thing the world has approv'd these many years") in a supposed letter to Addison written *more than twenty years* after the date assigned to it. "So ingeniously done . . . it is Pope's masterpiece in this kind" writes Sherburn (*Corr*, 1, p. 183). When upon the discovery of Caryll's original letters Pope's tactics were revealed it did much to blacken his reputation, which, though understandable, is to be regretted. That he did wrong is certain; that Addison's dealings over the rival *Iliad* were deeply underhand has unfortunately been forgotten.

On the intellectual and financial proceeds from the *Iliad* Pope came to have a wide circle of acquaintances, among them Lord Burlington, with whom he shared architectural visions. For some months in 1717, buoyed up by the excitement of his lordship's extensive renovations of Burlington House in Piccadilly, he thought seriously about building a matching *palazzato* just behind it, "on the same Plan & Front with Lord Warwick's." But the cost of Colen Campbell's proposals ("200 pound above what I am pretty well assured I can build the same thing for") made him think again (*Corr*, 1, p. 516). Gay too had a lively friendship with Burlington, or he did until the *Beggar's Opera*; in January 1732 he wrote innocently to Swift of Pope's searching for his lordship "within whose walls I have not been admitted this year & a half but for what reason I know not" (Swift *Corr*, III, p. 452). Pope maintained a diplomatic neutrality between the two, seeking the advice of Burlington's lawyer, after the banning of *Polly* (sequel to *The Beggar's Opera*), to minimize the dangers to *The Dunciad*. "I could be glad of the decisive opinion of Mr Fazakerly," he wrote, otherwise it might be "impracticable to publish the thing before Mr G.'s and I am grown more prudent than ever, the less I think others so" (*Corr*, III, pp. 4–5).

He was less prudent in some of his friendships and Bolingbroke inspired in him an admiration bordering upon hero worship. Pope described Bolingbroke to Spence as "something superior to anything I have seen in human nature"; noting the appearance of a comet, he speculated that "it might possibly be come to our world to carry him home" (*Anecdotes*, 1, pp. 274–5). Bolingbroke came home at last, to England not to heaven, in 1725 having paid the penance of his vainglorious flourish as the leader of the Jacobite rebels in 1715, and retired to his estate, rechristened Dawley Farm, where he made a show of enjoying the life of bucolic retreat. "I overheard him yesterday," Pope wrote, "agree with a Painter for 200*l.* to paint his country-hall with Trophies of Rakes, spades, prongs" (*Corr*, II, p. 503). It was a painful descent from his meteoric rise to sole control of the government for just four days in 1714: "The Earl of Oxford was remov'd on tuesday, the Queen dyed on Sunday . . . what a world is this, & how does fortune banter us?" (Swift *Corr*, II, p. 47). The world might rebuke him as a dangerously impulsive "man of mercury" but for Pope, Bolingbroke remained an heroic figure living the life of virtue.

After Bolingbroke it was Francis Atterbury, Bishop of Rochester and leader of the English Jacobites, who was captured and imprisoned following the failed conspiracy of 1722. Walpole engineered a show trial for him in the House of Lords at which Pope gave evidence for which he considered his own residence in England might be ended. He wrote to Atterbury in the Tower that he was "every day less and less fond of it," considering "a friend in exile" like "a friend in death, one gone before where I am not unwilling, nor unprepared to follow" (*Corr*, II, p. 167). The Lords voted eighty-three to forty-three for Atterbury's perpetual banishment and on 9 June 1723 a ship bore him to Calais where, waiting unseen in an inn, was Bolingbroke, his exile having just been terminated. "On learning of his presence, Atterbury is reported to have commented, with a grim smile, 'Then I am exchanged!'" (*Life*, p. 402). For both these men Pope put up a certain personal show of defiance, but was nevertheless keen to preserve his good standing with the government. Only a fortnight after the publication of Gay's *Polly* his *Dunciad Variorum* appeared and was presented to the King by Walpole himself, a piece of such good fortune that Arbuthnot commented "Mr Pope is as high in favour as I am affraid the rest are out of it. The King upon the perusal of the last edition of his Dunciad, Declard he was a very honest Man" (Swift *Corr*, III, p. 226). Whatever his claims to the contrary, Pope managed to secure tolerable relations with men of all kinds.

With women, though, he had more difficulty. Bitterly sensitive of his physical appearance he was clumsily defensive, offering an exaggerated old-world gallantry to mask desires which, if exposed, needed just a hint of ridicule to curl up into hate. The woman who most fully exposed these feelings was Lady Mary Wortley Montagu whom Pope first met in 1715, three years after her marriage. Together he, she and Gay composed a set of up-to-the-minute "town eclogues" which ridiculed the fond hopes of several ladies of the court. The smallpox which Lady Mary contracted shortly afterwards seemed to some an appropriate revenge, but it only heightened Pope's admiration. He took what for him was the extraordinary step of exacting physical revenge on Curll, who had published their *Court Poems*, by placing an emetic in his drink and then boasting of it in print. By the summer of 1716, when Lady Mary accompanied her husband as British envoy to Constantinople, Pope was fairly smitten; it needed only her departure for his passion to burst forth in epistolary form. The further away she went, the stronger grew his desire. "I foresee," he wrote,

> that the further you go from me, the more freely I shall write, & if (as I earnestly wish) you would do the same, I can't guess where it will end? Let us be like modest people, who when they are close together keep all decorums, but if they step a little aside, or get to the other end of a room, can untye garters or take off Shifts without a scruple. (*Corr*, I, p. 384).

For two years he addressed Lady Mary with all kinds of erotic whimsy, culminating, on her homeward journey, with a lengthy romantic tribute to the innocent pastoral lovers who were killed in each other's arms by a freak lightning storm near Stanton Harcourt. Where Pope was sentimental Lady Mary was blunt, and she attempted to indicate this difference between them with some answering couplets on the Stanton Harcourt pair.

> Who knows if 'twas not kindly done?
> For had they seen the next year's sun,
> A beaten wife and cuckold swain
> Had jointly curs'd the marriage chain;
> Now they are happy in their doom,
> FOR POPE HAS WROTE UPON THEIR TOMB
> (*Corr*, I, p. 523).

Shortly after her return there was a break between them for which no factual cause has been assigned, though this story, told by Lady Mary's granddaughter Lady Louisa Stuart, offers a kind of explanation:

> At some ill-chosen time, when she least expected what romances call a *declaration*, he made such passionate love to her, as, in spite of her utmost endeavours to be angry and look grave, provoked an immoderate fit of laughter; from which moment he became her implacable enemy.[4]

Though both Maynard Mack and Valerie Rumbold reject this as a factual version of the rift between Pope and Lady Mary, both print it, agreeing that the fit of laughter, if nothing else, accurately pinpoints a sudden switch of tone. Rumbold lists twenty places where Pope attacks Sappho, Lady Mary's literary namesake, with a truly venomous hatred. In his later poems only her friend Lord Hervey (Sporus) is treated with more loathing as an effete, epicene thing.

> Amphibious Thing! that acting either Part,
> The trifling Head, or the corrupted Heart!
> Fop at the Toilet, Flatt'rer at the Board,
> Now trips a Lady, and now struts a Lord.
>
> (*TE*, IV, p. 119)

In this case, however, Lady Mary had the last laugh. Showing a friend around her apartment late in life, she pointed to her commode decorated "with ... the works of Pope, Swift and Bolingbroke" whom she said she had known well: "They were the greatest Rascals" she said, "but she had the satisfaction of shitting on them every day."[5]

This cloacal reference brings us to *The Dunciad* in which Pope settles several literary disputes in similarly excremental fashion. There is Curll, whose victory in the urinating competition of Book II is accompanied by some of the wittiest (and wickedest) notes of the poem. "His rapid waters in their passage burn" (II, 176) is, after several learned pot-shots at emendatory critics "said to be Mr. *Curl's* condition at that time" from which Scriblerus (alias Pope) concludes the word *burn* cannot be correct, for "every lover of our author will conclude he had more humanity, than to insult a man on such a misfortune or calamity, which could never befall him purely by his *own fault*, but from an unhappy communication with another." Lewis Theobald, hero of the first *Dunciad*, published *Shakespeare Restored* in 1726, the year Pope finished editing Shakespeare, making it clear Pope's work had been not only "dull" but also sadly inaccurate. Anointing Theobald as the hero of *The Dunciad* was wickedly appropriate since much of the fun in the poem is at the expense of single letters; his name appears variously as Tibbald, Theobald or even Mr. T for, as the first note reminds us, "the neglect of a *Single Letter*" is no trivial matter, "the alteration whereof ... is an *Atchivement* [sic] *that brings honour*."

The four-book *Dunciad* of 1743 is a very different poem; a vision of chaos not a praise of folly, presided over not by Theobald but by the arch dunce Colley Cibber. Pope had known and mocked Cibber for years, ever since the farce *Three Hours after Marriage* (1717) when he, Gay and Arbuthnot had Cibber, acting Plotwell, say lines reflecting on himself. The two had numerous other spats until, in 1742, Cibber published a sixty-page *Letter ... Inquiring into the Motives that might induce [Mr Pope] in his Satyrical Works, to be so frequently fond of Mr Cibber's name*. In particular, Cibber recalled a drunken evening twenty-five years earlier at a house of "carnal recreation", when

Pope's "little-tiny Manhood" had been tempted by a "smirking Damsel" to essay the "fit of Love". After waiting for a while in an adjacent room, Cibber "threw open the Door upon him, where I found this little hasty Hero, like a terrible *Tom Tit*, pertly perching upon the Mount of Love!" Such was his surprise he "fairly laid hold of his Heels" and dragged him away and, on being upbraided for his action by a noble lord, replied:

> Consider what I have done was in regard of the Honour of our Nation! For would you have had so glorious a Work as that of making *Homer* speak elegant *English*, cut short by laying up our little Gentleman of a Malady, which his thin Body might never have been cured of? (*Life*, p. 779)

Pope took revenge the only way he could and when, a few months afterwards his new *Dunciad* was revealed, Cibber was sitting on the "gorgeous seat" previously filled by Theobald (II, 1).

The greatest literary friend to be associated with Pope is Swift, though. Twenty years his senior, Swift lived most of his life in Ireland which was no doubt very fortunate for their friendship; closer acquaintanceship would surely have ended it, as it ended all Swift's other friendships, even that with Tom Sheridan. The two men first met in 1713 and developed their friendship at meetings of the Scriblerus Club during the last months of the Tory administration. When Swift came over to England in 1726 to deliver *Gulliver's Travels* he stayed with Pope but left when his host grew ill, lest the extravagance of entertaining "if it be only two bits and one sup more than your stint"(*Corr*, II, p. 384) should be more than he could bear. The following year Swift planned a return trip: "Going to England is a very good thing," he wrote, "if it were not attended with an ugly circumstance of returning to Ireland." He came in April, full of hopes, but within weeks these all were ended. He had fraught meetings with Bolingbroke while Walpole confirmed his grip on power and, in September he received a letter containing, he thought, news of his loved companion Stella's death. "The last Act of Life is always a Tragedy at best," he lamented (Swift *Corr*, III, p. 123), stealing away to London and thence to Ireland, leaving Pope a letter which, when he read it made him feel "like a girl". He felt bitterly regretful that Swift "could think [him] self easier in any house than in mine," and threatened to visit Swift in Ireland and act "as much in my own way as you did here in yours". His irritation though soon passed and he wrote in early 1728 promising Swift the dedication of *The Dunciad* and telling him "I believe we should be fit to live together" (*Corr*, II, pp. 447–8, 480).

Once Swift was safely back in Ireland this last became a favourite fantasy; "Would to God we were together for the rest of our lives!" he wrote in

November, which became "I now as vehemently wish, you and I might walk into the grave together" (*Corr*, II, p. 522; III, p. 365) on Gay's death in 1733. Usually these phrases, no doubt sincere, were used to cloak other, more urgent, meanings as when Pope wrote "the Fame I most covet indeed, is that, which must be deriv'd to me from my friendships," accompanying a request for the return of letters which he wished to publish, though without seeming to do so. "Believe me" he wrote in August 1736, "great geniuses must and do esteem one another, and I question if any others can esteem or comprehend uncommon merit" (*Corr*, II, pp. 447–8; IV, p. 28). Swift, bafflingly evasive, used irony to unsettle his English friend and sent him the manuscript of *Verses on the Death of Dr Swift* to be printed in England. Pope was so mystified and embarrassed by the direct "lies" that it contained (for example, "To steal a hint was never known | But what he writ was all his own" being directly stolen from Denham's *Elegy on Cowley*) that he edited out several couplets before forwarding it to the press. The resulting *Verses* sold several thousand copies and he hoped Swift would not "dislike the liberties" he had taken, believing "the latter part of the poem might be thought by the public a little vain."[6] But Swift did dislike them, and insisted on publishing his own, unexpurgated Dublin edition. It must have caused him some amusement, as well as irritation, to have his irony so thoroughly missed.

Throughout Pope's life his closest friends were the Catholic families of the Carylls and the Blounts of Mapledurham. At first it was Teresa whom Pope most affected and wrote playfully suggestive letters to, as for example this, from summer 1717: "I know no Two Things I would change you for, this hot Weather, except Two good Melons" (*Corr*, I, p. 409). In his later life, particularly after the death of his mother, it was Martha (Patty) Blount that he relied upon. It was to her he wrote, a few weeks before his death "I love you upon unalterable Principles" (*Corr*, IV, pp. 510–11). The question of whether these "unalterable Principles" might lead to marriage between these two Catholics was often raised, particularly by Caryll. But Pope denied that he had any special *tendresse* for Patty. "I know myself too well at this age to indulge any," he replied, "and her too well, to expect as much folly in my favour as she shows for her relations" (*Corr*, III, p. 70).

Alongside Swift, though by no means so difficult to please, stood Dr John Arbuthnot with whom Pope came to have a long and lasting friendship. It was to Arbuthnot that Pope not only dedicated his famous verse *Epistle* but addressed important principles of his writing, notably the roles that friends, and enemies, came to play in the construction of his verse. "But sure," he wrote in 1734, it is as impossible to have a just abhorrence of Vice, without hating the Vicious, as to bear a true love for Virtue, without loving the Good. To reform and not to chastise, I am afraid is impossible . . . To attack Vices in the abstract, without touching Persons, may be safe fighting indeed, but it is fighting with Shadows.

(Corr, III, p. 419)

## NOTES

1. *Selected Letters*, ed. Howard Erskine-Hill (Oxford: Oxford University Press, 2000), p. 64.
2. *Selected Letters*, p. 141.
3. Sir Richard Phillips, *Addisoniana* 2 vols. (London: Richard Phillips, 1803), I, p. 167.
4. Valerie Rumbold, *Women's Place in Pope's World* (Cambridge: Cambridge University Press, 1989), p. 143.
5. Rumbold, *Women's Place*, p. 145.
6. *The Correspondence of Jonathan Swift*, ed. Harold Williams, 5 vols. (Oxford: Clarendon Press, 1963–65), vol. IV, p. 133.

# 3

JOHN SITTER

# Pope's versification and voice

Attending closely to how Alexander Pope's versification – how he makes verses – lets us hear the distinctive voices of his poems. Careful listening pays rich rewards. Without it we may have a hard time getting beyond a first impression, like that of Thomas Berger's young protagonist in *Little Big Man*, Jack Crabb. Having spent his childhood among the Cheyenne Indians, Jack is adopted by a clergyman whose high-minded wife decides to civilize him by reading Pope to or perhaps at him:

> She read me some of that man's verse, which sounded like the trotting of a horse if you never paid attention to the words or didn't understand most of them like me. What I did savvy seemed right opinionated, like that fellow had the last word on everything.[1]

This essay attempts to help readers new to Pope hear in his work something more than mechanical monotony and dogmatic pronouncements.

The first step to appreciating Pope's voice is to think of the word as plural: Pope wrote in many voices. He shared with his age a sense of *decorum*, which does not necessarily mean politeness but rather the idea that different occasions call for different kinds of behavior. *Literary decorum* means that various styles are appropriate for various kinds of poetry, just as dress differs according to setting:

> For diff'rent *Styles* with diff'rent *Subjects* sort,
> As several Garbs with Country, Town, and Court.
> (*An Essay on Criticism*, 324–5)

If Pope prized difference, why are we so likely to hear only uniformity? The simple answer is that Pope's variability is initially obscured by the prominence of his heroic couplets. These rhymed, end-stopped units of iambic pentameter (five-stressed lines) are immediately conspicuous for us because poets haven't much used couplets for the last 200 years. But the pentameter couplet Pope favored was familiar to his readers as one of the central

37

forms in English poetry since Chaucer; thus, variations and the construction of an original voice within it were more noticeable than its mere presence. Careful eighteenth-century readers would have been likelier to recognize a difference, for example, between Richard Blackmore's couplet,

> Did not the Springs and Rivers drench the Land,
> Our Globe would grow a Wilderness of Sand,

and Pope's,

> See, thro' this air, this ocean, and this earth,
> All matter quick, and bursting into birth,

than to note merely that both were "heroic."[2] They would have felt, for example, the dogged regularity of Blackmore's lines, each of which marches straight to the rhyme word, as opposed to the interesting tensions within Pope's lines, complicated by caesuras (internal pauses) and parallel phrasing. And they would have noticed the difference between Blackmore's versified truism (if the earth were not wet it would be very dry) and Pope's paradoxical insistence that what might seem empty is full and what might seem dead ("matter") is actually pregnant with life ("quick").

The present-day American poet Hayden Carruth argues elegantly for learning to hear in Pope's poetry the naturalness his contemporaries heard. According to Carruth, the heroic couplet, "which seems to us the height of artifice, was just the opposite in the minds of those who used it." Focusing on John Dryden (1631–1700), Pope's influential predecessor, Carruth makes a strong case for historical imagination:

> Dryden chose the couplet because he thought it the plainest mode available, the verse "nearest prose," and he chose it in conscious reaction against the artificial stanzaic modes that had dominated English poetry during most of the sixteenth and seventeenth centuries. In short, he and his followers thought they were liberating poetry, just as Coleridge and Wordsworth liberated it a hundred years later, or Pound and Williams a hundred years after that. The history of poetry is a continual fixing and freeing of conventions. It follows that these poets, Dryden and Pope, really were engaged in a liberation; and it follows too that we ought always to pay at least some attention to history and fashion, the worldly determinants, in our consideration of any poetry.[3]

Reading historically is in fact unavoidable. No one picks up the work of Pope or Tennyson or Milton mistaking it for contemporary poetry. The task is to expand our sense of history as fully as possible, so that it allows us to engage rather than merely distance the poetic past. Pope's own view of the rhymed verse with which we so fully associate him was disarmingly pragmatic. In his most direct comment on the matter he does not seem to see his choice of the heroic couplet as ideological. He does not seem to see it as the only medium that could adequately reflect his worldview, nor to regard it as intrinsically superior. Later in his career he told Joseph Spence that "I have nothing to say for rhyme, but that I doubt whether a poem can support itself without it in our language, unless it be stiffened with such strange words as are like to destroy our language itself" (*Anecdotes*, I, P. 173). Pope means that the artifice and stylization of rhyme can, paradoxically, allow the poet to be more "natural" – more colloquial – in diction and phrasing than would blank verse, for the writer of unrhymed poetry will feel the greater need to elevate the poem's language to differentiate it from prose. This claim is not exactly the same as saying that couplets are themselves "nearest prose," but it suggests that they may give the poet great freedom to incorporate the language of prose.

Poetry is notoriously difficult to define, but we can describe it as essentially a discourse of parallelism. The most immediate feature of poems is that they are composed in lines, and one line of a poem is parallel to others simply by being a line, usually of about the same length. This feature beckons us to be especially alert to smaller and larger parallels. Smaller parallels include similar words and syllables, tied to each other by devices such as alliteration, assonance, rhyme, and stress. Larger parallels depend on meaning and include grammatical parallelism, simile, metaphor, and other expressions of likeness or unlikeness (antithesis). This interplay of similarities seems to be what the Victorian poet Gerard Manley Hopkins had in mind when he asserted, in a remarkable undergraduate essay, that all poetic "artifice" finally "reduces itself to the principle of parallelism."[4] The couplet is arguably a very elemental form because the pairing of rhymed lines announces so clearly where one line ends and another begins, thus making the similarity of a line to its partner conspicuous and thus highlighting the basic "principle of parallelism" that Hopkins finds fundamentally poetic.

Pope's versification is a chapter – some would say the concluding chapter – in a gradual "refinement" of the pentameter (five-foot) couplet in English poetry. "Refinement" is a misleading term if we take it to mean that Chaucer and Donne were less sophisticated artists than Dryden and Pope, but we can get a good idea of what writers of Pope's day had in mind by "refinement" or "correctness" in formal matters by hearing what one poet who followed Pope, Charles Churchill (1731–64), had to say about one who preceded him, Edmund Waller (1606–87). Looking back from the 1760s, Churchill declared Waller the "Parent of harmony in English verse" because he "In couplets first taught straggling sense to close" (*The Apology*, 363, 365). Churchill means that mid- and late-seventeenth century poets began to bring grammar and versification together, treating the couplet as a syntactic unit. Thus, what we think of now as "heroic couplets" tend to form a complete sentence or independent clause, and usually each line will be end-stopped. Often these self-contained units are vehicles for epigram:

> Hope springs eternal in the human breast:
> Man never Is, but always To be blest . . .
> (*Essay on Man*, I. 95–6)

> True ease in writing comes from art, not chance,
> As those move easiest who have learned to dance.
> (*Essay on Criticism*, 362–3)

(Here the typography is normalized to dispel any "obsolete" flavour.)

A good way to grasp what Pope and his age valued as poetic "ease" is to compare John Donne's manner of writing satire in the 1590s with Pope's modernizations of Donne in the 1730s. Pope revived two of Donne's satires for political as well as artistic reasons (he could invoke the memory of the respected Church of England clergyman as he made potentially dangerous attacks on the government), but his versions of Donne's satires afford a quick comparison of versification and voice. Here is Donne describing various kinds of bad writers, including those who write for the stage:

> One, (like a wretch, which at Barre judg'd as dead,
> Yet prompts him which stands next, and cannot reade,
> And saves his life) gives ideot actors meanes
> (Starving himselfe) to live by his labor'd sceanes.
> As in some Organ, Puppits dance above
> And bellows pant below, which them do move.

The lines are difficult, even for Donne. They are so partly because Elizabethan writers believed that satire should be crabbed and rugged in language and pacing, speaking as they imagined an angry "satyr" would. Donne's parenthetical simile is somewhat obscure as well as sudden. It alludes to the old provision (originally "benefit of clergy") by which a defendant who could read might escape the death penalty; Donne imagines the dramatist as a doomed man prompting another to pass the literacy test. Then he just as quickly imagines him as the invisible bellows of an ornate organ, imparting motion to its visible puppets.

All of this would have been difficult enough in the late seventeenth century; by the early eighteenth century it was growing hopelessly obscure. Pope attempts to make it clearer for an audience further removed from Donne's allusions and assumptions:

> Here a lean Bard, whose wit could never give
> Himself a dinner, makes an Actor live:
> The Thief condemn'd, in law already dead,
> So prompts, and saves a Rogue who cannot read.
> Thus as the pipes of some carv'd Organ move,
> The gilded Puppets dance and mount above,
> Heav'd by the breath th'inspiring Bellows blow;
> Th'inspiring Bellows lie and pant below.
>
> (*Second Satire of Dr. Donne*, 13–20)

Pope initially avoids the abruptness of Donne's courtroom simile by delaying it until the reader at least has a chance to see what it refers to. Then he expands Donne's last two lines to paint a scene he knows the reader may never have viewed and to enact the comically repetitive huffing and puffing of "th'inspiring bellows."

A further comparison illustrates how changes in form may also be changes in voice and point of view. Donne's complaint about the several sorts of bad writers reaches a climax with his denunciation of the plagiarist:

> But hee is worst, who (beggarly) doth chaw
> Others wits fruits, and in his ravenous maw
> Rankly digested, doth those things out-spue
> As his owne things; and they are his owne, 'tis true,
> For if one eate my meate, though it be knowne
> The meate was mine, th'excrement is his owne . . .
>
> (25–30)

In Pope's version, Donne's breathless exasperation becomes cool detachment, more in keeping with the sense Pope and his age had of Horatian satire. Technically, the change depends on making all but the first of Donne's enjambed (run-on) lines end-stopped and syntactically self-sufficient (and even that exception bears a slight pause):

> Wretched indeed! but far more wretched yet
> Is he who makes his meal on others wit:
> 'Tis chang'd no doubt from what it was before,
> His rank digestion makes it wit no more:
> Sense, past thro' him, no longer is the same,
> For food digested takes another name.
>
> (29–34)

While these differences in versification enable Pope's comic urbanity, they do not fully explain the different effect. The scatological simile remains: plagiarism is like stealing another's food and then defecating in public. By putting the last couplet in more polite diction Pope plays at being more fastidious:

unlike Donne, he will not use the word "excrement," substituting for it the euphemistic phrase "another name." But this fastidiousness is of course only apparent and fleeting. The audience must now supply the unspoken "name," and it is the rare reader who will not fill in the blank with a term cruder than Donne's.

Once regularity has become the norm, small departures from it may become important. In the passage by Donne above, five of the six lines are enjambed; occurring frequently, run-on lines contribute to a general impression of exasperation but do not call much attention to themselves individually. But in Pope's poems, where enjambment is the exception, the absence of a decisive line break can bear more weight. Here is a couplet from another of Donne's poems, Satire IV, as Pope modernized it. The lines describe a character suspicious-looking enough to be considered a clerical spy during an outbreak of anti-Catholicism:

> One whom the mob, when next we find or make
> A Popish plot, shall for a Jesuit take.
> (*Fourth Satire of Dr. Donne*, 34–5)

Normal speech patterns follow syntax and keep verb and direct object together (we find or make a plot), but the line break, especially given Pope's practice, suggests a pause. In the tension between sentence structure and lineation we are in fact likely to hesitate, performing the lines something like so:

> One whom the mob, when next we find–or *make*–
> A Popish plot . . .

Pope's lines strongly suggest that the original "plot" of 1678 was a fabrication, constructed rather than discovered, and that such fabrications will recur when fear "next" spreads. As part of the feared minority, Pope needs to propound all of this indirectly. It may not be too much to say that here he uses small details of versification to convey a large-scale view of history.

Changes in the relation of poet to audience between Donne's day and Pope's help explain their stylistic differences. Not printed until after his death, Donne's satires were written for manuscript circulation among a small and homogeneous audience. Donne probably knew most of his first readers, fellow Londoners and law students in their twenties. In contrast, by the time Pope remodeled Donne, he was writing for publication, like most of his contemporaries, and for an audience primarily of strangers. While the audience for even the best-known poet of the early eighteenth century was not as broad as that for prose, Pope's readership was considerably less culturally elite than Donne's. "True ease in writing" of the sort Pope commended in

*An Essay on Criticism* becomes more important, therefore. Its immediate function is to put a mixed audience at ease by creating an impression of conversational sociability and transparent meaning. Once those values have been established, more subtle and demanding maneuvers may be carried out.

But like any great poet, Pope requires interpretation of his readers, and it is important not to let preconceptions of his "regularity" or "ease" get in the way of thoughtful reading. Pope's well-known assertion that "A *little Learning* is a dang'rous Thing" (*Essay on Criticism*, 215) often applies to the reading of his own poetry by those who come to it expecting predictability. There is "creative reading," Emerson said, "as well as creative writing," and Pope elicits it, beginning at the most basic level of performance. Take the following four lines from *The Rape of the Lock*, for example, in which Pope is describing the effects of make-up on Belinda. As she looks in the mirror, cosmetic artistry

> Repairs her Smiles, awakens ev'ry Grace,
> And calls forth all the Wonders of her Face;
> Sees by Degrees a purer Blush arise,
> And keener Lightnings quicken in her Eyes.
>
> (I, 141–4)

Asked to read these lines aloud, a student who knows that Pope wrote in iambic pentameter and did so more regularly than, say Shakespeare or Milton, may produce a mechanical reading in which every second syllable is dutifully accented (in bold type below) and the rhymes especially so, getting a sort of "super-stress" (bold and underlined):

> Re**pairs** her **Smiles**, a**wak**ens **ev'**ry **Grace**,
> And **calls** forth **all** the **Won**ders **of** her **Face**;
> **Sees** by De**grees** a **pu**rer **Blush** a**rise**,
> And **keen**er **Light**nings **quick**en **in** her **Eyes**.

Yet a more interpretive reading, in which voice and sense are allowed to trump metrical rigidity, might produce something quite different. A good way to begin such interpretation is to ask ourselves what one or two words or syllables in a line might need special emphasis to get the most sense and vitality from it. In other words, what might happen if we put the "super-stresses" somewhere other than on the rhymes. Here is one possibility:

> Re**pairs** her **Smiles**, a**wak**ens ev'ry **Grace**,
> And **calls forth** all the **Won**ders of her **Face**;
> **Sees** by Degrees a **pu**rer **Blush** arise,
> And **keen**er Lightnings **quick**en in her **Eyes**.

If we emphasize the carefully chosen verbs in the first line we hear Pope saying that in Belinda's case cosmetics do not cover up a lack of beauty (a common idea in traditional satires portraying women) but instead elicit or liberate what is already latent. This idea develops more fully with the phrase *calls forth* in the second line. These verbs lead into the third line's brilliant paradox of a *purer Blush*. The phrase might first strike us as sarcastic (surely a natural blush would be purer than a powdered one), but it also seems to be true, as many critics have argued. A cosmetic blush might be "purer" because more uniform and less mottled, say, than a sudden natural one. On further reflection, it might also be "purer" because it is not the symptom of sexual desire or self-consciousness. All of these possibilities bring the word to the front of the stage. Emphasizing the *keener* lightnings in the last line continues the idea that Belinda was stunning even before the process began. The surprising verb *quicken* – which means to come to life perceptibly, as when a fetus is first felt to stir – doubly echoes the "k" sound of *keener* and reinforces a double sense of change. There is transformation, on the one hand, and, on the other, the revelation of a beauty somehow present all along.

Deciding how to perform a line, if only for our own ears, will require decisions about meaning and psychological emphasis. As with other kinds of interpretation, the possibilities are usually indefinite but not infinite; that is, we cannot predict in advance just how many interpretations will emerge as credible, but we will be able to recognize some as unsupportable. When Eloisa, torn between spiritual and erotic longing, envies the simple innocence of the nuns around her who have known nothing but the convent she imagines an "Eternal sun-shine of the spotless mind!" Plausible readings might put heaviest stress on blamelessness –

Eternal **sun**-shine of the **spot**less **mind**

– or on spiritual brightness despite the darkness of the cloister:

Eternal **sun-shine** of the spotless **mind**.

But one reading that clearly would not work is the metrically regular one:

Eternal sun-shine **of** the spotless **mind**.

Performed this way the line makes no sense and does indeed sound a lot "like the trotting of a horse."

If thoughtful performance lets us hear something better than a trot, what responses are necessary to avoid Jack Crabb's second complaint, feeling "like that fellow had the last word on everything"? The closed couplet can lend itself, of course, to the feeling of finality, especially when crafted and polished by Pope into epigram. Utterances such as

> True Wit is Nature to advantage dressed,
> What oft was thought but ne'er so well expressed.
> (*Essay on Criticism*, 297–8)

or

> All Nature is but Art, unknown to thee;
> All chance, direction, which thou canst not see.
> (*Essay on Man*, I, 289–90)

or

> Years following years, steal something every day,
> At last they steal us from ourselves away.
> (*Ep*, II.II, 72)

seem too self-contained to invite dialogue or argument – or anything but surrender. But, in fact, as one gets more experienced at reading Pope, such lines begin to seem less like isolated "quotations" than parts of larger structures – verse paragraphs and poems – which do invite active engagement and response. We turn to an example of the Popean paragraph in a moment.

A more immediate reason Pope's lines often seem so "final" is that he rarely rested until he felt they could not be improved. Pope revised more than most authors, and he never (I think) revised without intensifying. The most famous instance of Pope's powers of revision is *The Rape of the Lock*, a poem that Pope first published in 1712 in two cantos, without the sylphs (the tiny spirits who attend Belinda), and then expanded, in 1714 and 1717, to the poem we read today. In addition to this wholesale change, Pope also revised the poem at the micro level, for purely stylistic reasons. Here are Pope's lines setting the time of day for the poem's action as they appeared in 1712:

> *Sol* thro' white Curtains did his Beams display,
> And op'd those Eyes which brighter shine than they;
> *Shock* just had giv'n himself the rowzing Shake,
> And Nymphs prepar'd their *Chocolate* to take;
> Thrice the wrought Slipper knock'd against the Ground,
> And striking Watches the tenth Hour resound.
> (I, 13–18)

Here is how Pope revised them two years later:

*Sol* thro' white Curtains shot a tim'rous Ray,
And op'd those Eyes that must eclipse the Day;
Now Lapdogs give themselves the rowzing Shake,
And sleepless Lovers, just at Twelve, awake:
Thrice rung the Bell, the Slipper knock'd the Ground,
And the press'd Watch return'd a silver Sound.

(I. 13–18)

Pope always seeks concision, and the first thing one might notice is that he gets rid of unnecessary words, of the sort he elsewhere called "expletives" (*Essay on Criticism*, 346): "**did** . . . display," "**to** take." Pope's later injunction to "show no mercy to an empty line" is, like Keats's urging Shelley to "load every rift with ore," a call to poetic intensity.[5] In this instance, the playful Petrarchan formula that Belinda's eyes are brighter than the sun (a compliment reiterated in countless Renaissance love poems) intensifies into the astronomical metaphor of "eclipse," suggesting an event portentous enough to make even the sun "tim'rous." Lovers at noon replace Nymphs ready at ten for their hot chocolate. The mystery of exactly how "*sleepless* Lovers" can now "awake" is resolved by hearing the phrase as making fun of an amatory cliché (lovers are not *supposed* to sleep or eat) in what will soon be revealed as theater of clichéd operations. Finally, the watch that in 1712 had merely struck the hour returns, in 1714, a rich synesthetic "silver sound" that prepares the way for the poem's world of miniature splendor.

Robert Frost, who famously preferred regular forms to free verse, remarked during one of his poetry readings that he nonetheless liked to "take the rhyme as if it isn't even there." There is a stage in our reading of Pope's poetry when we do well to take the couplet as if it isn't even there, that is, to read for the verse paragraph. Some of the most vivid examples of Pope's artistry in constructing such paragraphs are the character sketches that animate his great satires, and the best way to understand quickly the importance of this larger unit of composition is to reread the portraits of Atticus and Sporus in the *Epistle to Arbuthnot*, of the Man of Ross in the *Epistle to Bathurst*, or of Flavia, Cloe, and Atossa in the *Epistle to a Lady*, asking whether any of the couplets comprising these sketches could be rearranged without loss.

Not only in the character sketches, which often have a narrative logic as they follow a character's "progress," can we see and hear the importance of sequence, accumulation, and climax, but in many of Pope's more purely expository passages as well. The opening sixteen lines of the first epistle of *An Essay on Man* and the opening eighteen lines of the second ("Know then thyself . . .") are famous examples. But let us look now at a twenty-line paragraph from the third epistle (lines 7–26) which is, appropriately, about interconnectedness. Like many other parts of *An Essay on Man*, these lines enjoin the reader to *look*. For both personal performance and critical analysis it helps to read the paragraph as rising in intensity through three stages. The numbers on the left have been added for this purpose:

> 1. Look round our World; behold the chain of Love
>    Combining all below, and all above.
>    See, plastic Nature working to this end,
>    The single atoms each to other tend,                    10
>    Attract, attracted to, the next in place
>    Form'd and impell'd its neighbour to embrace.
> 2. See Matter next, with various life endu'd,
>    Press to one centre still, the gen'ral Good.
>    See dying vegetables life sustain,                       15
>    See life dissolving vegetate again:
>    All forms that perish other forms supply,
>    (By turns we catch the vital breath, and die)
>    Like bubbles on the sea of Matter born,
>    They rise, they break, and to that sea return.    20
> 3. Nothing is foreign: Parts relate to whole;
>    One all-extending. all-preserving Soul
>    Connects each being, greatest with the least;
>    Made Beast in aid of Man, and Man of Beast;
>    All serv'd, all serving! nothing stands alone;
>    The chain holds on, and where it ends, unknown.

It becomes apparent in the first "movement" that the directives to *look* and *see* are really a directive to *imagine*. Since we cannot literally see atoms we are to imagine them endlessly attracting and attracted to each other. It is this act of imagination that enables Pope to turn the traditional metaphor of a Chain of Being into the more dynamic "chain of Love." Supposedly inert matter seems nearly alive here in its restless motion. Strong emphasis falls in this section to the verbs, especially the present participles "combining" and "working," and most of all to the adjective "plastic" (creative, shaping), which stresses Nature's formative energy.

Matter nearly alive is not the same as life, however, and the second section turns to *living* matter. Here, too, we are in the realm of imagination, despite the vocabulary of empirical observation. The grand processes of life, death, and renewal are not visible to ordinary observation, but Pope's instruction to see "dying vegetables life sustain" and "life dissolving vegetate again" suggests a sort of eighteenth-century time-lapse photography. The verbs again demand emphasis and do a large share of the work. Pope attempts to bring to mind what we would now call ecological process, something we still have trouble "picturing" broadly enough, even with our satellite cameras and other sophisticated instruments of observation. The striking phrase "sea of Matter" is too vast in scope to be a concrete image, but it is an invitation to the largest wide-angle perspective we might manage, spatially and temporally. As various life-forms are imagined as so many bubbles emerging from and returning to the sea of matter the phrase "life *dissolving*" from two lines earlier suddenly acquires its full force.

The third part of this paragraph opens with the declaration that "Nothing is foreign," a mere assertion unless one sees and hears it as a summation of the cosmic survey immediately before. The half-line is best preceded and followed by a deep breath: it represents a realization and a thoughtful movement to an even greater level of generalization. The statement that nothing is foreign is static in itself (X is Y); but it quickly modulates into a series of active verbs. God (earlier identified as the "Soul" of nature) is "all-extending," "all-preserving," and He "connects" all creatures; animals and humans are in turn "all-serv'd" and "all-serving," much as the atoms at the start of this paragraph "attract" and are "attracted to" each other. If these words are given their due emphasis and the couplets allowed to gather energy, then the paragraph itself becomes a model of how "Parts relate to whole." If we open our ears to the accumulated music of the passage, Pope's conclusion that "Nothing stands alone" and that the Chain of Love is beyond final imagining ("where it ends, unknown") rests less on sight than on something approaching mystical vision. Such a view of human experience is not of course contained *in* couplets, but it may be conveyed *through* them.

## NOTES

1. Thomas Berger, *Little Big Man* (New York: Fawcett, 1963), p. 133.
2. Richard Blackmore, *The Creation: A Philosophical Poem in Seven Books* (London: 1712), vol. I, pp. 480–1; Pope, *An Essay on Man*, I, 233–4.
3. "The Question of Poetic Form," reprinted in Donald Hall, ed., *Claims for Poetry* (Ann Arbor: University of Michigan Press, 1982), pp. 50–61 (p. 59).
4. "Poetic Diction," *A Hopkins Reader*, ed. John Pick (Oxford: Oxford University Press, 1953), p. 80.
5. *Ep.* II.ii, 175; Keats, letter to P. B. Shelley, 16 August 1820, in *Selected Letters of John Keats*, ed. G. F. Scott (Cambridge, MA: Harvard University Press, 2002), p. 464.

# 4

CYNTHIA WALL

## Poetic spaces

> Shut, shut the door, good *John!* fatigu'd I said,
> Tye up the knocker, say I'm sick, I'm dead . . .
> (*Epistle to Arbuthnot* 1–2)

Like an epic, Pope's autobiographical poem *Epistle to Arbuthnot* (1735) plunges *in medias res*, "into the midst of things"– or we might say, into the midst of *spaces*. Pope, the successful poet, is besieged by aspiring authors, with "Papers in each hand," who "rave, recite and madden round the land. | What Walls can guard me, or what Shades can hide? | They pierce my Thickets, thro' my Grot they glide" (5–8). So the poem acts pre-emptively, opening itself by closing the door, to create a sustained refuge of 419 lines where the poet can figure out how he got here in the first place. This is one of the most dramatic spatial gestures of Pope's poetry; this chapter will open the door on others less spectacularly visible.

Pope is one of the most visual of poets. He had learned painting from his friend Charles Jervas, and in "Epistle to Mr. Jervas" he hopes his poems will have the same colour, clarity, elasticity, and precision: "Oh lasting as those colours may they shine, | Free as thy stroke, yet faultless as thy line!" (63–4). But as Lawrence Lipking notes: "The vast majority of modern readers are blind to eighteenth-century poetry. We do not see poems well; we do not make the pictures in our minds that the poets direct and excite us to make."[1] Part of understanding Pope's poetry is understanding how to *see* things, because in the eighteenth century description was used very differently. Many early prosodic techniques went out of fashion with the Romantic poets and never quite came back in, so we've lost the power to appreciate their subtleties. As an Oxford professor, A. Clutton-Brock, said witheringly in 1911, eighteenth-century poets, employing "wrong standards of judgement . . . fell into the habit of using general rather than particular terms in their descriptions," but that tack led them into "vagueness and pomposity."[2] Revisiting Pope's various spatial strategies will help recover ways in which the visualness of poetry opened up more richly and specifically for Pope's contemporaries.

Pope's sense of the visual emerges in the *settings* of poems, of course, but also in their poetic structures and the way they occupy the page. *The Rape of the Lock* saturates the clear-edged world of everyday spaces and objects with invisible forms and incarnated thoughts; within the strict form of the heroic couplet the verbs are wriggling and the images escaping. In his translation of *The Iliad*, Pope explains the differences between descriptive practices in different ages, and fills in the classical catalogue with topographical epithets that would satisfy an eighteenth-century reader. He also supplies an index that maps punctuation onto the territory of poetic effect. *Eloisa to Abelard* employs the couplet structure and off-rhymes to generate an unremitting pattern of confinement and rebellion that resists final reconciliation. And *The Dunciad Variorum*, besides rewriting familiar epic spaces, also poises the carved poetic world above an overflowing prose sewer of notes, playing *with* as well as *within* the spaces of the page.

## The life and times of poetic diction

Thomas Quayle's *Poetic Diction: A Study of Eighteenth-Century Verse* (1924) sorts out the various categories that most irritated critics in the long wake of the Preface to *Lyrical Ballads* (1802), in which Wordsworth deplores "the gaudiness and inane phraseology of many modern writers" and wants to substitute "the very language of men."[3] "Poetic diction" had become "stock," including words with stereotyped character used over and over, or with a cumulative irrelevance of meaning, such as "shining sword," "mossy banks," "lucid orb." New adjectives were invented by adding the suffix "y" to nouns ("beamy," "bloomy," "moony," "roofy," "sluicy"). Epithets collected present participles, as in "rising ground" or "pleasing grove." Periphrasis – a roundabout way of expressing something without naming it – produced "bearded product" for corn, "loquacious race" for frogs, "scaly flocks" for fish, and "leafy nation" for trees. Compound epithets abounded: comet-eyes, tongue-valiant, sin-polluted, slimy-born, sick-feather'd. And abstract ideas and material objects were personified into speaking figures: ecstatic Wonder, wan Despair, Valour armed. Wordsworth often pointedly *excepted* Pope from his criticisms, but his criticisms ended up swallowing the whole of the eighteenth century, including Pope. By the end of the nineteenth century Matthew Arnold would damn with faint praise: "We are to regard Dryden as the puissant and glorious founder, Pope as the splendid high priest, of our age of prose and reason, of our excellent and indispensable eighteenth century" – the classics of *prose* rather than poetry.[4]

Their poems just didn't seem be Wordsworth's "spontaneous overflow of powerful feelings" (Preface to *Lyrical Ballads*, p. 393).

And of course they weren't spontaneous overflowings, strictly speaking. Pope crafted and recrafted his poetry: "After writing a poem one should correct it all over with one single view at a time. Thus for language, if an elegy: 'these lines are very good, but are not they of too heroical a strain?', and so vice versa" (*Anecdotes*, I, p. 171). And so vice versa: once is not enough. As Samuel Johnson recorded, "[Pope] examined lines and words with minute and punctilious observation, and retouched every part with indefatigable diligence."[5] That is not to say Pope was not passionate about poetry (or for that matter that Wordsworth didn't equally craft and recraft). "Why did I write?" he asks in *Epistle to Arbuthnot*; "As yet a Child, nor yet a Fool to Fame, | I lisp'd in Numbers, for the Numbers came" (125, 127–8). And as for spontaneous overflow: "The things that I have written fastest have always pleased most" (*Anecdotes*, I, p. 45). But he cared so much about his poems that "he kept his pieces very long in his hands, while he considered and reconsidered them" (Johnson, *LOP*, III, p. 221). Pope believed the best poems represented "*Nature Methodiz'd*" (*Essay on Criticism*, 89), restrained by rules but simultaneously ordaining them. Carefully seeing the spaces of Pope's poems – the ones they describe and the ones they embody – shows that every punctuation mark, every verb, every rhyme, every couplet, every paragraph, has its own carefully chosen place.

That cast of doomed dictional characters outlined by Quayle had a very different life and presence in the early eighteenth century, and Pope mastered the power of every one. "Stock" diction necessarily had a pre-cliché origin somewhere, either in Homer or Virgil (which thus sanctified it for repetition) or invented by Milton, Dryden, or Pope (and repeated endlessly by everyone else). Pope had acerbic things to say about the "sure *Returns* of still *expected Rhymes*":

> Where-e'er you find *the cooling Western Breeze*,
> In the next Line, it *whispers thro' the Trees*;
> If *Chrystal Streams with pleasing Murmurs creep*,
> The Reader's threaten'd (not in vain) with *Sleep*.
> (*Essay on Criticism*, 349–53)

Creating adjectives out of nouns and using present participles in epithets can create kinetic energy in a poem, tightening the line between image and motion: we see the ground in the very *act* of rising. Periphrasis can expand boundaries and suggest connections, creating larger worlds for smaller things. And personification renders the abstract present, palpable, a living thing inhabiting the visual world. Pope invests his poetic spaces with fluid motion and encapsulated detail that for an early eighteenth-century reader would open up layers of contrast, contradiction, possibility.

## The internal and the invisible: *The Rape of the Lock* (1714)

*The Rape of the Lock* reproduces the social spaces of early-eighteenth century England with crisp contemporary detail. Belinda's bed, the theater, the River Thames, and Hampton Court, as well as combs, card tables, coffee urns, and scissors, are just some of the familiar spaces and the objects that occupy them. Their physical presence and appearance is particularized, the boundaries and edges are concrete. But suffusing this "real" world are others more beautiful, more permeable, and more obscure: the interior spaces of thought, dream, and wish, and the invisible world of the sylphs and gnomes. Throughout, the themes that occupy those social and psychological spaces are reproduced in the structures of the heroic couplets themselves.

The poem specializes in articulating or implying the relationship between its vast quantities of objects and their location in space. Canto 1 begins in Belinda's bed: "*Sol* thro' white Curtains shot a tim'rous Ray" (1, 13). (The engraving in the 1714 edition shows that the white curtains are bed curtains, not window curtains: see Figure 1). The personified male Sun penetrates into the most private of spaces, as the poet penetrates the most private of dreams. The details of the bed-space are particularized: a downy pillow, a watch, a slipper, a bell. But Belinda and her lap dog, Shock, are not the only occupiers of the bed. Ariel, Belinda's guardian sylph, whispers in her dreaming ear. His visual presence – "more glitt'ring than a *Birth-night Beau*" – affects her slumbering sensuality, slipping innuendoes of body language into the *sotto voce* confines of parentheses: "(That ev'n in Slumber caus'd her Cheek to glow)" (1, 23–4). His speech repeats the pattern of everydayness surrounded and transformed by the strange: the familiar areas of theater box and the horse and carriage ring at Hyde Park are invisibly overlaid with another world of "unnumber'd Spirits . . . ever on the Wing" (1, 42, 43).

Belinda's mind is a strange transformative place of its own. Figured as Everywoman in Ariel's description, inside the "moving Toyshop of her Heart" we see "Wigs with Wigs, with Sword-knots Sword-knots strive, | Beaus banish Beaus, and Coaches Coaches drive" (1, 101–2). People become things that fight their mirror image for turf within a single line. The acts of attempted displacement are roomily accommodated by the structures of poetic placement.

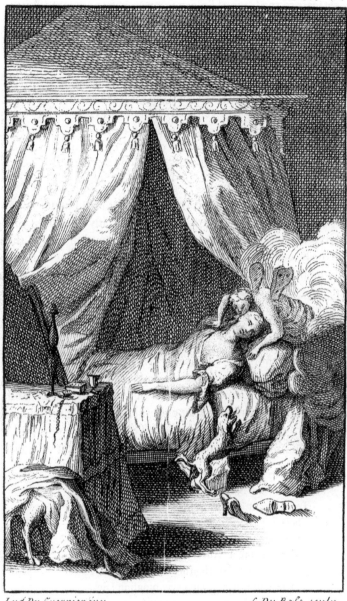

Figure 1. "Sol thro' white Curtains shot a tim'rous Ray." Frontispiece to Canto I, *The Rape of the Lock* (1714), courtesy of Special Collections, University of Virginia Library.

Things become people in the dark psychological spaces of Canto IV, where Belinda retreats to the Cave of Spleen to nurse her anger at the Baron cutting off her lock:

> Unnumber'd Throngs on ev'ry side are seen
> Of Bodies chang'd to various Forms by *Spleen*.
> Here living *Teapots* stand, one Arm held out,
> One bent; the Handle this, and that the Spout:
> A Pipkin there like *Homer*'s *Tripod* walks;
> Here sighs a Jar, and there a Goose-pye talks;
> Men prove with Child, as pow'rful Fancy works,
> And Maids turn'd Bottels, call aloud for Corks.
>
> (IV, 47–54)

The Cave is a place of "constant *Vapours*," "Strange Phantoms" in mists, the dimly seen shapes of "Spectres" and the ghastly emptiness of "gaping Tombs" (IV, 39–44). Dark emotions and forbidden desires find themselves simultaneously incarnated and insubstantialized. The Cave visualizes one of the dominant tensions in the poem: between the visible and the hidden, the fragment and the whole, what is contained and what escapes. Clean-cut vials contain "fainting Fears, | Soft Sorrows, melting Griefs, and flowing Tears" (IV, 85–6). "Paper-Durance" and "tort'ring Irons" and "Fillets," like couplets with words, bind, wreathe, and strain the hair (IV, 99–101), yet the lock in the end is "shot thro' liquid Air" (V, 127).

Poetic structures fix space; poetic contents continually escape, waft, drift off, evaporate, melt. Beyond the world of cosmetics, cards, and coffee, beyond familiar outlines and familiar patterns, lies something more delicately colored and softly edged. The description of the sylphs *flutters*, both visually and grammatically, dissolving the usual boundaries of time and space:

> Some to the Sun their Insect-Wings unfold,
> Waft on the Breeze, or sink in Clouds of Gold.
> Transparent Forms, too fine for mortal Sight,
> Their fluid Bodies half dissolv'd in Light.
> Loose to the Wind their airy Garments flew,
> Thin glitt'ring Textures of the filmy Dew;
> Dipt in the richest Tincture of the Skies,
> Where Light disports in ever-mingling Dies,
> While ev'ry Beam new transient Colours flings,
> Colours that change whene'er they wave their Wings.
>
> (II, 59–68)

The description, the actions, the verbs themselves create images that seem to slide beyond the exigencies of the couplet structure itself. The heroic couplet is by definition a strict form, the pair of rhymed pentameter lines governing all of Pope's poetry. To most post-Romantic poets and readers, the form has seemed too strict, too confining, too rigid. Yet in Pope's hands what moves within is full of light, color, motion, traveling beyond each line's end. As Ian Gordon says, "Pope establishes . . . transience . . . through the momentariness encapsulated in the use of present participles. Things are constantly 'trembling,' 'floating,' 'waving,' 'fluttering,' 'shining,' 'sparkling,' 'mingling,' 'melting,' and, above all, 'glittering'."[6] The present participles capture a temporal transience, yes, but they also (along with other vivid verbs) turn structural boundaries porous, continuing action visibly through space. The sylphs, "Transparent Forms" (there and not-there), waft and sink, dissolve and change – the visual and conceptual counterpoint to the combs and jewels, watches and slippers, vials and bodkins, of the fixed lines of furniture and rooms.

## Topography and typography: *The Iliad* (1715–1720)

"Every historical period," as Maynard Mack notes, "reformulates the great poetry of the past partly by its own conceptions of that greatness and that past as well as by its own views of what constitutes poetry and the art of translation" (*Life*, p. 348). Pope was well aware of this. In his translation of Homer's *Iliad*, he remarks on the fact that Virgil's catalogue of the ships is shorter than Homer's, and accounts for the difference historically and culturally:

> *Homer* might have a design to settle the geography of his country, there being no description of *Greece* before his days; which was not the case with *Virgil*. *Homer*'s concern was to compliment *Greece* at a time when it was divided into many distinct states, each of which might expect a place in his catalogue: But when all *Italy* was swallow'd up in the sole dominion of *Rome*, *Virgil* had only *Rome* to celebrate. *Homer* had a numerous army, and was to describe an important war with great and various events; whereas *Virgil*'s sphere was much more confined.[7]

Every age seems to feel a poetic obligation to "[invest] static spatial objects with vitality by transfusing into them its own rhythmic, temporal succession."[8] Just as Homer and Virgil tailored their catalogues to their contemporary audiences, so Pope created his own poetic lists of ships along eighteenth-century lines.

Pope "opened the prospect a little" on the classical tradition of ekphrasis "by the addition of a few epithets or short hints of description to some of the places mention'd; tho' seldom exceeding the compass of half a verse (the space to which my author himself generally confines these pictures in miniature)" ("Observations," p. 131). He creates what J. Daniel Kinney calls a "scenic cohesion" that contrasts sharply with the inventory inclusiveness of nature descriptions in pre-eighteenth century texts.[9] "Grassy *Pteleon*," for example, is "decked with chearful greens" (II, 849); Antron has "watry dens and cavern'd ground" (II, 852); Ithomè is "rough with rocks" (II, 887); Oloösson has "chalky cliffs" (II, 899). This because "a meer heap of proper names, tho' but for a few lines together, could afford little entertainment to an *English* reader, who probably could not be appriz'd either of the necessity or beauty of this part of the poem" ("Observations," p. 131). Pope wants to fill in the spaces of the classical catalogue with vivid little capsules that will rehydrate in the reader's mind into a fully visualized field.

Pope appended a number of indexes to his *Iliad*, to the persons (and gods), places, descriptions, speeches, similes, and ancient arts and sciences. The index to "Versification" (which is glossed, "*Expressing in the sound the thing describ'd*") supplies a map of how the spacing of words, phrases, and punctuation on the page will create an aural corollary – how textual space can conjure up experiential space:

> Made *abrupt* (and without conjunctions) in expressing haste, 7.282. 15.402.
> *Short*, in earnest and vehement entreaties, 21.420–23.506.
> Full of breaks, where disappointment is imag'd. 18.101, 144 – 22.378.
> – where rage and fury is express'd, 18.137.
> – where grief is scarce able to go on, 18.101. 22.616, 650.
> Broken and disorder'd in describing a stormy sea, 13.1005
>
> ("Poetical Index," p. 1179)

The "broken and disorder'd" line that calls up the stormy sea comes at the end of a swelling triplet on waves: "Wide-rolling, foaming high, and tumbling to the shore" (XIII, 1005). In Book XXII, when Andromache learns of Hector's death, she cries, "Would that I had never been! – O thou, the ghost | Of my dead husband! miserably lost! | Thou to the dismal realms for ever gone! | And I abandon'd, desolate, alone!" (XXII, 616–19). Not only are her lines broken by dashes, they are speared with exclamation points that turn words into wails. Pope's very punctuation is an exercise in spatial determination.

### *Eloisa to Abelard* (1717) and the spaces between rhymes

*Eloisa to Abelard* is itself a long lament based on the tragedy of the twelfth-century French lovers, Peter Abelard and his student Héloïse. Abelard was castrated at the order of Héloïse's angry uncle, and he became a monk; Héloïse became a nun; their correspondence became famous. Pope's version of the story is from Eloisa's point of view, a sustained internal struggle between her duty to put God first and her passion for Abelard – between "grace and nature, virtue and passion," as Pope's headnote to the poem frames the equation. The poem is famous for its visual representation of enclosed, dark, gothic space. Its poetic structures *enact* Eloisa's struggle: the couplets spin the same tensions round and round; the rhymes only seem to offer aural and visual balance, containment, resolution.

Pope figures this internal struggle in dim, chill, close spaces: "deep solitudes and awful cells," "grots and caverns," "dusky caves," and "intermingled graves" (1, 20, 163, 164). The inside of the convent is defined by "these lone walls (their day's eternal bound)," "moss-grown domes," and "spiry turrets." Its "awful arches make a noon-day night, | And the dim windows shed a solemn light" (141–4). The physical structure is a dark confinement; the sense of oppression extends beyond its walls:

> But o'er the twilight groves, and dusky caves,
> Long-sounding isles, and intermingled graves,
> Black Melancholy sits, and round her throws
> A death-like silence, and a dread repose:
> Her gloomy presence saddens all the scene,
> Shades ev'ry flow'r, and darkens ev'ry green,
> Deepens the murmur of the falling floods,
> And breathes a browner horror on the woods.
>
> (163–70)

Pope personifies melancholy into something almost haunting the landscape. Her one moment of action is to stifle sound and motion; colour drains away. Inside is mirrored by outside; there is no escape: "for ever, ever must I stay" (171).

Back and forth Eloisa goes. Each poetical paragraph is a tormented account of what she should be doing but cannot. If one line of a couplet follows duty, the next counters with desire: "Now turn'd to heav'n, I weep my past offence, | Now think of thee, and curse my innocence" (187–8). And even single lines – and acts – devoted to God are penetrated by Abelard: "I waste the Matin lamp in sighs for thee, | Thy image steals between my God and me, | Thy voice I seem in ev'ry hymn to hear, | With ev'ry bead I drop too soft a tear" (267–70). The measured regularity of the couplet structure does not *order* the anguish, but endlessly recycles it.

At first glance, the rhyme patterns seem simply to continue this eternal cycle of containment. The aural expectation set up by one rhyme is confirmed with the clang of the second, Eloisa's anguish bounding against walls of inevitable sound: stores/floors, bound/crown'd, wears/tears, caves/graves, burn/urn, keep/weep, go/woe, ordain/pain, destroy/joy. But the pattern is even more bitterly twisted. The three key conceptual words refuse a "perfect" rhyme: love, God, and join.

"Love" is used as an end-rhyme nine times in the poem. (In *Elegy to the Memory of an Unfortunate Lady* [1717], also a poem about "[loving] too well," the word never ends a line.) But none of its pairs is a "true" rhyme: move/love, remove/Love, prove/love, move/love, remove/love, remove/love, disapproves/loves, prove/love, mov'd/lov'd (67–8, 79–80, 87–8, 153–4, 193–4, 231–2, 259–60, 335–6, 351–2). We know that English pronunciation of some vowels has shifted over centuries ("tea" and "obey" are famous examples of formerly perfect rhymes). But Edward Bysshe, in his Preface to *The Art of English Poetry* (1702), explains that "Words [ending] in OVE have three different Sounds; as *Love, Prove, Rove*; and though they are all plac'd [in his "Dictionary of Rhymes"] under their own Termination, yet they do not in strictness rhyme to one another. Therefore to distinguish them from each other, a little space is left between the different Rhymes" (v). Dove, Glove, Shove, and Love rhyme, but there is "a little space" between "love" and the -ove words that are "near" or "off" rhymes: Move, Prove, Approve, Remove (*Art of English Poetry*, p. 31). Eloisa's "love" cannot seem to find its perfect mate, its snug home in the end of the couplet; it must ever move and remove – though never *to* anywhere.

"God" offers no home either. "God" and "abode" appear only twice, and only with each other (127–8, 287–8). Bysshe has them very decidedly in different places: "OD" and "ODE." The twin terms of Eloisa's anguish – love and God – cannot be reconciled. The verb of reconciliation proves that: "join" appears with "thine" (41–2) and then in one more try, with "mine" (359–60). But it is not to be. Bysshe doesn't have a category for OIN, but "joint" appears under OINT and "thine" and "mine" under INE. Eloisa is severed from Abelard, severed from God; the things that matter cannot be joined together.

The one hope for peace that Eloisa can imagine, the one way for her pain and the poem to close, lies in death, where "one kind grave" might "unite each hapless name" (343), and "some future Bard" will *join* his griefs with "mine." That future bard *seems* to grant this last wish in a footnote that places Eloisa where she wants to be: "Abelard *and* Eloisa *were interr'd in the same grave*." But not quite: "*or in monuments adjoining*." This is not a poem about closure.

## Sewer space: *The Dunciad Variorum* (1729)

One of the ways in which poetry is distinct from prose is the way it occupies a page.[10] Poetry takes up a lot of room, with large empty spaces surrounding self-limited lines. It's *expensive* in terms of production. Poetry is luxurious; poetry is lofty. Steven Shankman explains his editorial choice of formatting Pope's notes to the *Iliad* as endnotes rather than footnotes: "To place Pope's notes at the bottom of the page, as was done in the later editions published by the Lintots as well as in the deeply learned and indispensable Twickenham Edition, is to diminish the Longinian sense of spacious and uncluttered elevation that Pope saw in Homer and tried to simulate in English. It distracts the attention from the whole to parts, which Pope decries throughout his poetry" (*Iliad*, XVII). Maynard Mack describes John Ogilby's *Iliad* (which Pope read as a boy and loved): "His elegant column of verse (eight to twenty lines on a page) is surrounded like a tiny peninsula by a vast weedy sea of commentary rising against it from three sides" (*Life*, p. 45). But in *The Dunciad Variorum* that is *exactly* what Pope now wants to do: to clutter up textual space with a "vast weedy sea of commentary," to create visual chaos, to poise clean, sculpted lines of poetry above a seething sewer of septic voices.

The notes *overwhelm* the space of the page. In the first printing of the *Variorum* only two poetic lines manage to float above the underworld of commentary (Figure 2):

> Books and the Man I sing, the first who brings
> The Smithfield Muses to the Ear of Kings.

Indeed. For then the "Smithfield Muses" – all the critics who had been attacking Pope and otherwise lowering literary standards – launch in vociferously from below. Lewis Theobald ("Tibbald," the King of the Dunces here, so honoured because of his line-by-line criticisms of Pope's 1726 edition of Shakespeare) makes the first appearance, taking issue with the title itself: "Ought it not rather to be spelled *Dunceiad*, as the Etymology evidently demands? *Dunce* with an *e*, therefore *Dunceiad* with an *e*" – just as in his corrective "Shakespeare" to the then-traditional "Shakspear." Theobald is "personified" here (or perhaps we should say "objectified") into The Pedant. Line 104 of Book I introduces one of Pope's most hostile critics, John Dennis: "And all the Mighty Mad in Dennis rage." Then comes a note that swallows several pages whole, recapitulating all of Dennis's attacks on Pope's works and person, for the most part verbatim: "[Pope] is as stupid and as venomous [sic] as a hunchbacked Toad" (from *Reflections on the Essay on Criticism*). Dennis throughout the sewer-world of notes foams in impotent fury, along

THE

# DUNCIAD.

### Book the First.

BOOKS and the man I fing, the firft who brings
The Smithfield Mufes to the ear of kings.

*REMARKS* on Book the First.

\* The *Dunciad, fic* M. S. It may be well difputed whether this be a right Reading ? Ought it not rather to be fpelled *Dunceiad,* as the Etymology evidently demands ? *Dunce* with an *e,* therefore *Dunceiad* with an *e.* That accurate and punctual Man of Letters, the Reftorer of *Shakefpeare,* conftantly obferves the prefervation of this very Letter *e,* in fpelling the Name of his beloved Author, and not like his common carelefs Editors, with the omiffion of one, nay fometimes of two *ee*'s [as *Shak'fpear*] which is utterly unpardonable. Nor is the neglect of a *fingle Letter* fo trivial as to fome it may appear ; the alteration whereof in a learned language is an *Atchivement that brings honour* to the Critick who advances it ; and Dr. *B.* will be remembered to pofterity for his performances of *this fort,* as long as the world fhall have any efteem for the Remains of *Menander* and *Philemon.*

THEOBALD.

I have a juft value for the Letter E, and the fame affection for the Name of this Poem, as the forecited Critick for that of his Author ; yet cannot it induce me to agree with thofe who would add yet another *e* to it, and call it the *Dunceiade ;* which being a *French* and foreign Termination, is no way proper to a word entirely *Englifh,* and vernacular. One *E* therefore in this cafe is right, and two *E*'s wrong ; yet, upon the whole, I fhall follow the Manufcript, and print it without any *E* at all ; mov'd thereto by Authority, at all times with Criticks equal if not fuperior to Reafon. In which method of proceeding, I can never

F                                                enough

Figure 2. "Books and the Man I sing." *The Dunciad Variorum* (1729), Book the First, courtesy of Special Collections, University of Virginia Library.

with all the other critics. It's a noisy, dirty, scabrous world down below the poetry.

And within the poetry. Pope addresses the issue of sewers directly in his note to Book II, line 71: "Obscene with filth the Miscreant lies bewray'd". In this Book, which features the "epic games," the scurrilous bookseller Curll is racing another bookseller (Bernard Lintot, who had published Pope's *Works* in 1717), but loses when he falls into "a lake, | Which Curl's Corinna chanc'd that morn to make, | (Such was her wont, at early dawn to drop | Her evening cates before his neighbour's shop)" (*Dunciad,* II, 65–8). The note defends the incident, which "may seem too low and base for the dignity of an Epic Poem." It is "but a copy of *Homer* and *Virgil*," but this poet, says the underground Critic, has "(in compliance to modern nicety) . . . remarkably enrich'd and colour'd his language as well as rais'd the versification" here. The poet was clearly troubled at having to stoop so low, "but that he hoped 'twas excusable, since levell'd at such as understand no delicate satire: Thus the politest men are sometimes obliged to *swear*, when they happen to have to do with Porters and Oyster-wenches." The teeming subspace of intertextuality gives a proper home to those who cannot understand "delicate satire." The kennels of the page, where the dunces' spite bacterializes into a nastiness that seems to overrun the original poem, in fact poetically – and historically – contains it. It wasn't until the twentieth century that Theobald's Shakespearean editing received its critical due as "modern" scholarly recovery. Dennis and Curll have yet to resurface with clean faces.

Space restrictions in this volume do not leave room to talk about the paragraphical structuring of the tour in Pope's most explicit architectural criticism in the *Epistle to Burlington*, nor to examine the careful, clever perspectives of *An Essay on Man*, nor to walk with Pope through his gallery of paintings in *Epistle to a Lady*, nor duly to consider the spatial ramifications of his epigrams. But I hope this essay makes clear the extent to which Pope attended to the contours of poetic space – in description, word choice, rhyme, line, couplet, paragraph, and the page itself. I will close with Pope's *Epitaph. On Himself* (1741):

> Under this Marble, or under this Sill,
> Or under this Turf, or e'en what they will;
> Whatever an Heir, or a Friend in his stead,
> Or any good Creature shall lay o'er my Head;
> Lies He who ne'er car'd, and still cares not a Pin,
> What they said, or may say of the Mortal within.
> But who living and dying, serene still and free,
> Trusts in God, that as well as he was, he shall be.
>
> (*TE*, VI, p. 386)

Unlike Eloisa, the poet *of* as well as *under* this marble or sill or turf has an escape clause: the last couplet rhymes "be" with "free." The "Muse" who "mid'st the Stars inscribe[s] *Belinda*'s Name" (*Rape of the Lock*, V, 150), the "future Bard" who "best can paint 'em" (*Eloisa to Abelard*, 359, 366), the poet who fixes all his squirming enemies in textual amber, is in charge of his own worlds. Pope's poetic spaces give poetry the last word.

## NOTES

1. Lawrence Lipking, "Quick Poetic Eyes: Another Look at Literary Pictorialism," in *Articulate Images: The Sister Arts from Hogarth to Tennyson*, ed. Richard Wendorf (Minneapolis: University of Minnesota Press, 1983), p. 5.
2. A. Clutton-Brock, "Description in Poetry," in *Essays and Studies by Members of the English Association*, ed. H. C. Beeching 3 vols. (Oxford: Clarendon Press, 1911), II, p. 96.
3. Thomas Quayle, *Poetic Diction: A Study of Eighteenth-Century Verse* (London: Methuen, 1924); William Wordsworth, *Preface* to *Lyrical Ballads* (1802), in William Wordsworth and Samuel Taylor Coleridge, *Lyrical Ballads and Related Writings*, ed. William Richey and Daniel Robinson (Boston: Houghton Mifflin Company, 2002), p. 392.
4. Matthew Arnold, "The Study of Poetry" (1888), in *Poetry and Criticism of Matthew Arnold*, ed. A. Dwight Culler (Boston: Houghton Mifflin, 1961), pp. 321–2.
5. Johnson, *LOP*, III, p. 221.
6. I. R. F. Gordon, *A Preface to Pope*, 2nd edn. (London: Longman, 1993), p. 165.
7. Alexander Pope, "Observations on the Second Book," in *The Iliad of Homer Translated by Alexander Pope*, ed. Steven Shankman (London: Penguin, 1996), pp. 129–30.
8. Ruth Helen Webb and Philip Weller, "Descriptive Poetry," in *The New Princeton Encyclopedia of Poetry and Poetics*, ed. Alex Preminger and T. V. F. Brogan (Princeton: Princeton University Press, 1993), p. 284.
9. J. Daniel Kinney, collegial email, 13 January 2000.
10. J. Paul Hunter has discussed the sense of privileged space that poetry enjoys on a page in a plenary talk of the South Central Society for Eighteenth-Century Studies in New Orleans, February 1996, and will shortly publish the work.

# 5

STEVEN SHANKMAN

# Pope's Homer and his poetic career

We should not underestimate the effect on Pope's original poetry of the poet's translating virtually all of Homer.[1] Pope had been thinking about the problems involved in translating Homer since at least his early twenties. Writing in 1708 to his friend Ralph Bridges, he mentions Homer's seemingly paradoxical combination of copious diction and noble simplicity. "The Episode of Sarpedon," translated from *Iliad* XII and XVI, was published the following year. Four years later he proposed to translate the entire poem, which Lintot began to publish in 1715, when the first volume of the projected complete translation, containing Books I–IV, appeared. The final volume of the first edition was published in 1720. The *Odyssey* translation began appearing in 1725 and was completed the following year. This represents some sixteen years of a young poet's life – from the ages of twenty-one through thirty-seven – spent with Homer, as Pope repeatedly turned over the Greek lines in his head, struggled with how to translate them into readable and elegant English, and lived with the Homeric commentators and the Homeric characters.

## An Essay on Criticism

Is it any wonder, then, that Pope's first truly extraordinary poem, *An Essay on Criticism* (first published in 1711), is a paean to Homer? "First follow Nature," Pope urges in this poem, "and your Judgment frame | By her just Standard, which is still the same" (68–9).[2] If you want to find out what Nature is, the poet advises, "Be *Homer's* Works your *Study* and *Delight*, | Read them by Day, and meditate by Night" (124–5), for "*Nature* and *Homer*" are "the *same*" (135). Through his experience reading and translating Homer, Pope learned the salutary lesson that the best literary criticism emerges empirically from the perusal of actual literary works; that literary criticism in the West began specifically as an attempt to make explicit the principles of literary theory that were contained implicitly in the Homeric poems. From Homer he learned, in short, that "Those Rules of old *discover'd*, not *devis'd*, | Are *Nature* still, but *Nature Methodiz'd*" (88–9).³ In his *Poetics* Aristotle himself, Pope writes, was "*Led* by the Light of the *Maeonian Star*" (648), i.e. by Homer.

## The Rape of the Lock

That other great early success of Pope, *The Rape of the Lock*, would probably never have been written had Pope not been reading Homer by day and meditating upon him by night. The copiousness of diction he remarked upon to Ralph Bridges could here, in a mock-heroic context, be indulged in without fear of losing perspicuity. Pope composed the poem during some of his most active years with Homer, the first version (consisting of two cantos) appearing in 1712 and the final five-canto version in 1717, published in the same year as appeared the third volume of the ultimately six-volume complete translation. As William Frost has pointed out, Pope echoes his own *Iliad* translation in *The Rape of the Lock*.⁴ The poet invites us to read his poem through a Homeric prism, especially in Canto v where in a note Pope asks his readers to consult Sarpedon's speech to Glaucus in *The Iliad* if they wish to understand the full import of Clarissa's speech that the poet added "to open more clearly the Moral of the Poem." The ethical import of *The Rape of the Lock*, then, is tied by Pope explicitly to the heroic code enunciated by Sarpedon in *The Iliad*. Both he and Glaucus, Sarpedon tells Glaucus, must show themselves worthy of the high regard in which their societies hold them by gaining glory in battle or by allowing others to gain glory by slaying them. *Rape of the Lock*, v, 25–34 is a parody of *Iliad*, xii, 387–96 in Pope's own translation.

Sarpedon urges Glaucus to enter battle in order to show himself worthy of his high standing in society; Clarissa urges Belinda to refrain from battle for the very same reason. Sarpedon is receptive to the advice offered him, Clarissa is not. But Belinda compared to Sarpedon? At first this seems a most incongruous comparison, and of course we should expect this very kind of incongruity in a mock-heroic poem. And yet there is a sense in which there is a parallel between the cadences of Homer's attitude towards the brilliant world of Mycenae and Pope's toward Belinda's milieu. Critics have often remarked on how, despite his satiric intentions, Pope appears to be entranced by Belinda's glittering world. We have here none of the bitter satiric reductiveness of a Jonathan Swift. We should recall, in this context, the similarities between the two-fold purpose of Homer's epic poem and of Pope's mock epic. Homer recreates the glorious Mycenean world (some 500 years after the fact) in order to establish, through memory, a link between it and the remnants of it, now dispersed from the Greek mainland to the islands along the Anatolian coast. But *The Iliad* is no uncritical encomium. Homer also needed to analyze what went wrong, to criticize the intemperance of the Mycenean leaders. That dual achievement of glorifying through poetry and yet at the same time analyzing the sources of psychic and social disorder finds expression in *The Rape of the Lock* as well. It is this doubleness of purpose that makes the poem shine in a particularly Iliadic way: it is both admiring and critical.

Both poems, moreover, specifically explore the ways in which it is the pride of those admired by society that is responsible for social disorder. What begins the quarrel in *The Iliad* is the seizing by Agamemnon of Achilles's "prize", γέρας, that is Briseïs. What is responsible for the quarrel in the *Rape of the Lock* is the Baron's seizing "th'inestimable Prize" (compare "The prize, the beauteous prize" in Pope's *Iliad*, I, 149 with "this Prize, th' inestimable Prize" of *The Rape of the Lock*, IV, 113). In both poems it is in part the seizing of the prize that the poets criticize, but their main concern is to show how the offended party responds to the original violation. Both Achilles and Belinda, in their reactions, become as guilty as the offending party and in the end do more to threaten the stability of the social order than did the original offenders. Both poems show a fascination – but a critical one – with the vanity of their protagonists.

### *Eloisa to Abelard* and *The Elegy to the Memory of an Unfortunate Lady*

Both *Eloisa to Abelard* and the *Elegy to the Memory of an Unfortunate Lady* were published in 1717, a year that falls in the midst of Pope's publishing of the six volumes of *The Iliad* between 1715 and 1720. The passionate nature of "the unfortunate lady" and of Eloisa recalls Pope's passionate Achilles.

George Chapman – Pope's daunting Renaissance predecessor in the field of Homeric translation – tried consistently to rationalize Achilles' wrath and to turn Achilles into an ideal Renaissance hero who, from the opening moment of the poem, is largely in control of his emotions. Achilles is no ideal hero in Book IX, however, when he commits a fatal mistake by not re-entering the battle at once in order to save his fellow Greeks from destruction. Odysseus, Phoenix, and Ajax arrive as an embassy to Achilles's tent and try to persuade him to return, but to no avail. Achilles is coming slowly around to reason, but he is not yet there. He is still obsessed with his passionate hatred of Agamemnon, even after Odysseus, on Agamemnon's behalf, makes a more than generous offer to compensate Achilles for the loss of his prize. In Chapman's version, Achilles explains to Ajax at length that, in order to teach Agamemnon a lesson about the art of kingship, he has consciously chosen to "loose the reines" (617) of his anger.[5] Pope's Achilles is far less restrained:

> Well hast thou spoke; but at the tyrant's name,
> My rage rekindles, and my soul's on flame.
>
> (759–60)

In his *Observations* on this passage, Pope leaves the moralizing Renaissance epic tradition far behind:

> We have here the true picture of an angry man, and nothing can be better imagin'd to heighten *Achilles's* wrath; he owns that reason would induce him to a reconciliation, but his anger is too great to listen to reason. He speaks with respect to them, but upon mentioning *Agamemnon*, he flies into rage: Anger is nothing more like madness, than that madmen will talk sensibly enough upon any indifferent matter; but upon the mention of the subject that caused their disorder, they fly out into their usual extravagance.

Or as Pope puts the matter unforgettably in commenting upon Achilles' anger at Agamemnon in an earlier passage in this book:

> His rage, awaken'd by that injury, is like a fire blown by a wind that sinks and rises by fits, but keeps continually burning, and blazes but the more for those intermissions.[6]

Pope, like many European artists and thinkers of the late seventeenth and early eighteenth centuries, was deeply interested in what Descartes referred to as "The Passions of the Soul."[7] His sympathetic and accurate depiction of Achilles' uncontrollable anger is one of the things that sets his translation apart from Chapman's.[8] And it is this same interest in the passions that characterizes *Eloisa to Abelard* and the *Elegy to the Memory of an Unfortunate Lady*. The unfortunate lady is to her guardian as Achilles is to Agamemnon. Like Achilles, she chooses to "greatly think" and "bravely die" (10). She heroically chooses to follow her own desires – which, in her case, results in suicide – rather than be subjected to the continued authoritarian rule of her guardian. She has the ambition of a hero, the "glorious fault" (14) of an Achilles.

Pope's Eloisa is similarly free of Chapmanesque moralizing. *Eloisa to Abelard* does not teach a moral lesson. Like Ovid's *Heroides*, it uses the form of a letter to dramatize the heroine's feelings. Eloisa does not become an example to be avoided of sexual love prevailing over divine love, of *cupiditas* over *caritas*, as one might expect if this were a certain kind of work written in the Middle Ages. Eloisa is rather presented sympathetically as someone who is in an impossible situation. Pope explores her dilemma rather than moralizes about it. Pope will develop his view of the emotions into his theory of the ruling passion, which he explicates in the second epistle of *An Essay on Man* (published in 1734) and alludes to in both the first (first published also in 1734) and third (first published in 1733) of the *Moral Essays*. Might not Pope's early and long exposure to what he described as Achilles' "prevailing Passion" of "Anger" (see his note on *The Iliad*, XX, p. 489ff.), an obsessive anger that at last relents in *Iliad* XXIV only under the most extraordinary circumstances of divine intervention, have encouraged him to develop his theory of the prevailing or ruling passion?

### The First Satire of the Second Book of Horace (To Mr. Fortescue)

The final volume of Pope's unofficially collaborative version of *The Odyssey* appeared in 1726. Seven years later Pope published the first of his Horatian imitations, *The First Satire of the Second Book of Horace*, later subtitled *To Mr. Fortescue*. While Pope's Homer has had its detractors, no one has doubted the stylistic brilliance of Pope's imitations of Horace. Even Coleridge, just before castigating Pope's Homer for its "pseudo-poetic diction," reminds his readers in the *Biographia Literaria* that Pope's "*original* compositions, particularly . . . his satires and moral essays," are distinguished by an "almost faultless position in the choice of words."[9] As Pope observes in the postscript to his *Odyssey* (*TE*, X, pp. 382–97; see especially 389), what drove him to distraction when translating *The Odyssey* was the challenge of rendering – with the dignity required by Augustan epic style – the more domestic and everyday and hence less elevated portions of that work which, as observed by Longinus (the author of a great critical treatise on ancient literature), lacks the consistently elevated intensity of *The Iliad*. What a relief, in comparison with the rigorous demands of translating Homeric epic, it must have been for Pope when he began to turn the witty, conversational style of Horace's poems into English. At the inception of his efforts as a Homeric translator, he viewed his climb to the top of Mount Homer as a nightmare. He appears to have enjoyed versifying Horace. It was a natural fit.

For all its greatness as a translation, Pope in his *Iliad* sometimes appears to be straining. Not so in the Horatian imitations. *To Mr. Fortescue* begins:

> P. There are (I scarce can think it, but am told)
>   There are to whom my Satire seems too bold,
>   Scarce to wise *Peter* complaisant enough,
>   And something said of *Chartres* much too rough.
>   The Lines are weak, another's pleas'd to say,

Lord *Fanny* spins a thousand such a Day.
Tim'rous by Nature, of the Rich in awe,
I come to Council learned in the Law.
You'll give me, like a Friend both sage and free,
Advice; and (as you use) without a Fee.
    *F.* I'd write no more.
                          *P.* Not write? but then I *think*,
And for my Soul I cannot sleep a wink.
I nod in Company, I wake at Night,
Fools rush into my Head, and so I write.
    *F.* You could not do a worse thing for your Life.
Why, if the Nights seem tedious – take a Wife;
Or rather truly, if your point be Rest,
Lettuce and Cowslip Wine; *Probatum est.*
But talk with *Celsus, Celsus* will advise
Hartshorn, or something that shall close your Eyes.
Or if you needs must write, write CÆSAR's Praise:
You'll gain at least a *Knighthood*, or the *Bays.*
                                  (1–22)

Here is the tone of witty conversation captured with a polish that is unparalleled in English poetry. Note, for example, the ease of the enjambment ("*Celsus* will advise | Hartshorn"). The plain style of Sir Thomas Wyatt's epistles – the earliest examples of the conversational Horatian plain style in English verse – is clumsy in comparison, and Ben Jonson's couplets, though often possessing the transparency of the plain style at its best, at times lack Horatian wit. Pope has it all.

This is Horace, but it is Horace with a particularly Juvenalian – or, perhaps we should say, for reasons that will be made clear in a moment, *Achillean* bite. In the original Latin, Horace appears to be genuinely puzzled that some readers consider his satire too heated:

Sunt quibus in satura videar nimis acer et ultra
legem tendere opus.[10]
                    (1–2)

[There are those to whom I perhaps might seem excessively fierce and to push my work beyond what is lawful.]

The feigned modesty of the subjunctive *videar* ("I perhaps might seem") Pope works up and develops into a more aggressive sarcasm by means of his interpolated phrase "I scarce can think it, but am told" and by then going on to mention by name – none of this is in Horace – the scoundrels (the usurer and cheat Peter Walter and the rapist Francis Charteris) whose moral sensibilities will be shocked by his allegedly "too bold" truth-telling satire. The line "Tim'rous by Nature, of the Rich in awe" must be taken as thoroughly ironic, for this satirist does not fear the rich and the powerful and will depict himself throughout the poem as a warrior for truth. Like Achilles, he is hardly "Tim'rous by Nature".

In the lines that follow Pope shows that as a writer he is perhaps even more convincing – as we might be led to believe from reading the *Peri Bathous* (published in 1728) – when he attempts to parody epic bombast than when he tries to sustain serious epic elevation:

> P. What? like Sir *Richard*, rumbling, rough and fierce,
>    With ARMS, and GEORGE, and BRUNSWICK crowd the Verse?
>    Rend with tremendous Sound your ears asunder,
>    With Gun, Drum, Trumpet, Blunderbuss & Thunder?
>    Or nobly wild, with *Budgell*'s Fire and Force,
>    Paint Angels trembling round his *falling Horse*?
>
> (23–8)

Such is Pope's brilliant rendition of the typically Horatian refusal to write in a particular genre (usually epic) whereby, in the refusal, the poet demonstrates that he can indeed write in the rejected genre, though he chooses not to. It may well have been in part as the result of Pope's long and often frustrating struggles with trying to bring across Homer's epic elevation into readable, lively verse that the English poet turned with such relish to the more kindred stylistic spirit of the Horace of the *Sermones*. This is a Horace, however, whose voice is tense with Achillean anger. The lines quoted above, for example, are marked by Achillean outrage rather than modest Horatian self-deprecation. To Trebatius's advice that the poet should compose an encomium to Caesar rather than engage in the potentially libelous effort of writing satire, Horace humbly responds, "I wish I could, good father, but I lack the strength" (*Cupidum, pater optime, vires/deficiunt*). Pope omits the gentle and intimate vocative *pater optime* and instead replies with the incensed "What? like Sir *Richard* [the now long-forgotten epic poet Sir Richard Blackmore], rumbling, rough and fierce, | With ARMS, and GEORGE, and BRUNSWICK crowd the Verse?"

I mentioned how Pope, more empathetically than previous translators working in the moralistic tradition of Renaissance epic, responded to the fire in Achilles' character. Achilles was in many ways an anti-establishment figure, a fiery and valiant hero who goes it alone and pits himself against the power structure dominated by Agamemnon. As Howard Weinbrot reminds us, Horace was a friend of the ruling elite of Augustan Rome, and his truth-telling role as satirist was therefore compromised, from Pope's point of view.[11] Pope, in the days when he was composing his Horatian imitations, was no friend of the ruling elite. He felt profoundly unappreciated by and despised both Georges ("Still Dunce the second reigns like Dunce the first," the poet remarks in Book 1, line 6 of the 1742 *Dunciad*) as well as Walpole, men who, the poet was convinced, were hostile to true worth. Like Achilles with regard to a similarly unappreciating political superior (Agamemnon), Pope despised that rulership.

Pope in fact writes much of his greatest poetry from an anti-establishment stance, from a position of self-righteous Achillean defiance of authority. Pope saw himself, in his role as Horatian satirist, as an Achillean warrior, "armed for *Virtue* when I point the Pen" (105), his aim to "Brand the bold Front of shameless, guilty Men, | Dash the proud Gamester in his gilded Car [i.e. chariot]" (106–7). At one point in the poem Pope in fact represents himself, by clear implication, as Achilles, the greatest Greek warrior:

> Satire's my Weapon, but I'm too discreet
> To run a Muck, and tilt at all I meet;
> I only wear it in a Land of Hectors,
> Thieves, Supercargoes, Sharpers, and Directors.
> (69–72)

Pope wears his satiric weapon only in a land of Hectors, i.e. bullies. And if his enemies are Hectors, then Pope is Achilles.

Achilles may indeed be viewed as the original progenitor of the truth-telling satirist who is the speaker of the Horatian *sermo*. Horace's anti-rhetorical plain style is derived from the plain style of Plato's Socrates. And one of Socrates' heroes was Achilles, specifically the Achilles who, in *Iliad* XVIII, chooses to avenge Patroclus' death and re-enter the battle, even though he knows that this action will result in his death. In the *Apology* (28), Socrates points to Achilles' choice as a paradigm for his own refusal, in response to the coercion of the Athenian government, to abandon the philosophical life. The portrait Pope paints of himself as Achillean warrior for truth thus makes explicit the Achillean pedigree of the Horatian satirist. Pope's truth-telling did not fall on deaf ears. As Maynard Mack informs us in his monumental biography, after the publication of some particularly hard-hitting satiric verses, Pope felt it was necessary for him to carry a pistol for self-defense when he ventured forth into public (*Life*, pp. 487–8). The image of Pope as physically endangered Achillean warrior for truth was evidently more than a literary trope.

## The Dunciad

We must, in concluding this survey of the influence of Pope's encounter with Homer upon his original poetry, consider the case of *The Dunciad*. The poem was published in its first version in 1728, just two years after the final volumes of *The Odyssey* translation. In the postscript to his *Odyssey*, as I have mentioned, Pope expresses his frustration over the seemingly irresolvable difficulties he faced in trying to render the more lowly or domestic elements in Homer's epic with the requisite Augustan dignity. In *The Dunciad* Pope was able to make full use of his eye for sharply rendered (and sometimes uninhibitedly vulgar) particulars that would have been deemed too "low" for an Augustan version of Homeric epic, and he can place these particulars within a framework that allows him to make the kind of generalized major statement about the reasons for the decline of a civilization that is worthy of Homer's *Iliad*. *The Dunciad* is clearly more indebted for its structure to *The Aeneid* than to *The Iliad*, for it narrates the movement of civilization – though in an ironic, inverted form – from east to west, as Rome, in Virgil's conception, was founded by the Trojans who survived the catastrophic Trojan war and then made the journey westward to Italy. Despite its indebtedness to *The Aeneid* for its structure, *The Dunciad* possesses Iliadic fire rather than Virgilian pathos. Pope's grand mock-epic is characterized, moreover, by the kind of rugged excellence and disdain for careful mediocrity that Pope's admired Longinus associates with the Homer of *The Iliad*.

In *The Iliad*, Homer recreates the glorious Mycenean world of the distant past in order to establish, through memory, a link between that heroic world and the remnants of it, now dispersed from the Greek mainland to the islands along what is now the coast of Turkey. But *The Iliad* is no uncritical encomium. Homer celebrated the then-distant heroic Mycenean age, it is true, but, as I mentioned earlier, he as importantly took it as his task to analyze what went disastrously wrong in that age. It is perhaps the case that epic ceased to be a truly viable genre as soon as it abandoned its critical slant in favour of the encomiastic/nationalist mode established by Virgil's *Aeneid*, when this poem is read as propaganda, as "a party piece," as Pope believed it to be.[12] Like *The Iliad* (and unlike Pope's reading of *The Aeneid*), *The Dunciad* is a cultural critique and it remains vital, even if much of it – because of the myriad allusions to contemporary figures and events – is obscure. Moreover, for years constrained by the demands of Augustan decorum when translating Homer, Pope, when composing *The Dunciad*, must have felt enormously liberated by the chance to deploy epic devices with imaginative abandon in the service of a cause in which he deeply believed.

Had Pope not translated *The Iliad* and been rebuffed by the arrogant Bentley – the famously bellicose Cambridge classical scholar who discovered the Homeric digamma and who was also an editor of *Paradise Lost* – we would never have had the great passage on Aristarchus, the "mighty Scholiast, whose unweary'd pains | Made Horace dull, and humbled Milton's strains" (Dunciad, IV, 210–11) and the discoverer of the Homeric digamma in the fourth book of *The Dunciad* (1743). It was not just the personal slight ("It is a pretty poem, Mr. Pope," Bentley said in the famous remark about Pope's *Iliad*, "but you must not call it *Homer*")[13] that angered Pope, although we surely should not underestimate how central was the preoccupation with settling scores to the wickedly clever poet of *The Dunciad*. But having spent much of his life translating Homer and having become more and more convinced that Homer had something to say about the human condition that was eternally valuable, Pope came to have less and less tolerance for what he took to be the historicizing pedantry of the Moderns as represented (in Pope's view) by Bentley, who dismissed Homer as a quaint historical curiosity who pandered to his unsophisticated audience. In terms of the eighteenth-century debate between the Ancients and Moderns, Bentley's historicism placed him, for Pope, in the camp of the Moderns. The Ancients, in contrast, believed that Homer transcended his own era.

Anthony Collins, an eighteenth-century deist, articulates the position of the Ancients in regard to Homer in his *A Discourse of Free-Thinking Occasioned by the Rise and Growth of a Sect call'd Free–Thinkers* (1713). Collins's contention that Homer displayed a "Universal Knowledge of things" and that the poem was designed "for Eternity, to please and instruct Mankind"[14] was, by Bentley, refuted thus:

> Take my word for it, poor Homer, in those circumstances and early times, had never such aspiring thoughts. He wrote a sequel of Songs and Rhapsodies, to be sung by himself for small earnings and good cheer, at Festivals and other days of Merriment; the *Iliad* he made for the Men, the *Odysseis* for the other sex.[15]

It was in part his experience of translating the poetry of Homer that convinced Pope that Bentley had to be deeply wrong in a way that typified what he felt was ailing a contemporary civilization in which men "See all in *Self*, and but for self . . . [are] born" (*Dunciad*, IV, 480) and in which "The critic Eye, that microscope of Wit, | Sees hairs and pores, examines bit by bit" (IV, 233–4), but who fail to see "How parts relate to parts, or they to whole, | The body's harmony, the beaming soul" (IV, 235–6).

To Bentley's reductively historicizing view of Homer, Pope opposes his own belief in *The Dunciad* that the Homeric poems are of continuing relevance. And the English poet makes his point as he bids farewell to Bentley/Aristarchus in *The Dunciad*. "Walker! Our hat", Aristarchus imperiously orders Dr Richard Walker, the Vice-Master of Trinity College, Cambridge, where Bentley was Master, and now a Dunce serving as hat-bearer to Aristarchus in Pope's poem. The last in the poem's procession of narrow, philologically inclined pedants promising their devotion to the Goddess of Dulness, Aristarchus now superciliously departs and yields the floor to the spoiled and corrupt young fops who have just returned from the Grand Tour of classical sites in Italy. On that "Classic ground" (IV, 321), classical learning, robbed of its great moral value by the narrow-mindedness of pedants like Aristarchus, has been replaced by a vulgar, ostentatious, and shallow consumerist tourism. As Aristarchus departs, the poet writes:

> – Nor more he deign'd to say
> But stern as Ajax' spectre, strode away.
> (IV, 273–4).

These lines contain allusions to two of Pope's favorite ancient authors, Homer and Longinus. Longinus (*On the Sublime*, IX, 3), makes the provocative observation that sublimity can at times be more effectively achieved by silence than by words, such as we find, the great critic remarks, in the eleventh book of *The Odyssey*.

As the identical rhyme words reveal, these lines from *The Dunciad* are modeled on some lines in Pope's translation (or perhaps we should say William Broome's; this was one of the books translated by Broome, though *The Odyssey* translation was published under Pope's name). They occur in *Odyssey* XI, where Odysseus in the underworld remarks upon what Pope in his notes refers to as the "sow'r, stubborn, untractable [sic]" character of Ajax, who is "upon all occasions given to taciturnity" (*TE*, XI, p. 418):

> While yet I speak, the shade disdains to stay,
> In silence turns, and sullen stalks away.
> (*Odyssey*, 691–2)

Odysseus, in Homer's underworld, encounters Ajax. Ajax had competed unsuccessfully for Achilles' arms, which Thetis – who judged Odysseus to have been the most valiant of the Greeks because of his having secured her son Achilles' body after he had been slain in battle – awarded to Odysseus. Ajax, once he was judged inferior to Odysseus, took his own life. Still incensed that Achilles' armour had been given to Odysseus rather than to to himself, Ajax, now a shade in Hades, remains indignant and refuses to speak to Odysseus in the famously moving scene in *Odyssey* XI, 543–67. The sour, stubborn, intractable taciturnity of Homer's Ajax, it turns out, is no mere historical curiosity. The character of Ajax does indeed have continuing relevance in understanding the modern world, specifically in retaining the paradigmatic power to serve as a foil for Bentley's less noble but equally "sow'r, stubborn, untractable," and taciturn presence. The Ancient Pope has thereby cunningly defeated the Modern Bentley, for the spirit of Homer is alive and well and still speaks powerfully to those who possess generous literary minds. Homer is indeed dead, is a mere historical curiosity for those who – to their spiritual peril – condemn themselves to vices, such as a sour and unrelenting taciturnity, by failing to see what Homer has so powerfully represented in his moving, indeed sublime, poetry.[16]

The story behind Aristarchus' sullenness in *The Dunciad* is that Bentley was supposed to have rudely walked out during a dinner at Trinity College when he was asked, by a foreign visitor who had been hospitably invited to dine at the college, some scholarly questions that Bentley preferred not to answer. Offended by the foreign scholar's persistence, Bentley reportedly called out to his Vice-Master, "Walker, my hat!" and in a surly, Ajax-like manner, left the room. As the editor of the Twickenham edition informs us, "Bentley generally wore, while sitting in his study, a hat with an enormous brim, as a shade to protect his eyes" (*TE*, V, p. 362). The grand silence (μέγα. . . . σιωπή [*On the Sublime*, IX, 3]) of the essentially noble – albeit taciturn – Ajax is one thing, according to the poet of *The Dunciad*. The condescending and inhospitable snub by the pedant Aristarchus is of an entirely different order. As Longinus comments, "it is impossible that those whose thoughts and habits all their lives long are petty (μικρά) and servile should produce anything wonderful (θαυμαστόν), worthy of immortal life."[17] Bentley had snubbed the scholar who was a foreign dinner-guest at Trinity College, Cambridge. Aristarchus acts condescendingly towards the "lac'd Governor from France," a foreigner who has just returned from taking his pupils on the Grand Tour of Europe, which includes classical sites in Italy. Part of the irony here is that, for Pope, pedants like Bentley have no reason to be condescending towards the morally vapid pupils that these pedants' own brand of narrow, specialized classical scholarship has produced.

In *The Iliad*, which Pope formatively translated in his early career, Homer sings of Achilles' wrath. It is Pope's wrath that animates his final poem, the often ruggedly (if comically) sublime *Dunciad in Four Books* of 1743, a year before the poet's death. Pope's poetic career, from beginning to end, was shaped by his experience of Homeric verse.

## NOTES

1. On the subject of the influence of translating Homer on Pope's original poetry, see the perceptive and learned section, written by Maynard Mack, on "Pope's Homer: Its Relation to His Life and Work," in *TE*, VII, pp. ccxxi–ccxlix.

2. Cited from *TE*, as will be all references to Pope's poetry, apart from *The Iliad* translation, which will be cited from *The Iliad of Homer, Translated by Alexander Pope*, ed. Steven Shankman (London: Penguin, 1996).

3. See Steven Shankman, "Led by the Light of the Maeonian Star," *Classical Antiquity* II.1 (1983), pp. 108–16; and *In Search of the Classic: Reconsidering the Greco-Roman Tradition, Homer to Valéry and Beyond* (University Park: Pennsylvania State University Press, 1994), pp. 63–76.

4. "*The Rape of the Lock* and Pope's Homer," *Modern Language Quarterly* 8 (1947): pp. 342–54.

5. *Chapman's Homer: The Iliad*, ed. Allardyce Nicoll (Princeton: Princeton University Press, 1956), p. 197.

6. Pope's observations on *Iliad*, IX, 406ff.

7. Descartes' influential *Traité des passions de l'âme* was published in 1649.

8. See Chapter 1 ("The Passionate Design: Books I and IX") of Steven Shankman, *Pope's Iliad: Homer in the Age of Passion* (Princeton: Princeton University Press, 1983).

9. *Biographia Literaria*, eds. James Engell and W. Jackson Bate, 2 vols. (Princeton: Princeton University Press, 1983), vol. I., p. 39.

10. *Satires, Epistles, and Ars Poetica*, Loeb Classical Library (Cambridge, MA.: Harvard University Press, 1926), p. 126.

11. See *Augustus Caesar in "Augustan" England: The Decline of a Classical Norm* (Princeton: Princeton University Press, 1978); and *Alexander Pope and Formal Verse Satire* (Princeton: Princeton University Press, 1982).

12. Pope to Spence, July-August (?) 1739: "The *Aeneid* was evidently a party piece, as much as *Absalom and Achitophel*. Virgil [was] as slavish a writer as any of the gazetteers. I have formerly said that Virgil wrote one honest line" (*Anecdotes*, I, pp. 229–30).

13. Johnson, *LOP*, III, p. 213.

14. Anthony Collins, *A Discourse of Free-Thinking Occasioned by the Rise and Growth of a Sect call'd Free-Thinkers* (London, 1713), p. 9.

15. Bentley, *Remarks upon a late Discourse of Free-thinking* (London, 1713), p. 18.

16. The sullen disdain of Ajax must be inferred from the general sense of the passage rather than from an exact rendering of the Greek. Note that Pope's translation of the passage from *The Odyssey* flaunts the very disdain for literalness that word-catching pedants like Bentley deplored. Odysseus, in the Greek, simply says (XI, 563): "Ὣς ἐφάμην· ὁ δέ μ' οὐδὲν ἀμείβετο" ("Thus I spoke; he said nothing to me in response"). *The Odyssey of Homer*, ed. W. B. Stanford, 2 vols. (London: Macmillan, 1965), vol. II, p. 185.

17. *Longinus: On the Sublime*, trans. W. H. Fyfe, rev. Donald Russell, in *Aristotle: Poetics, Longinus: On the Sublime, Demetrius: On Style*, (Cambridge, MA: Harvard University Press [Loeb Classical Library], 1995), pp. 184–5.

# 6

HOWARD D. WEINBROT

# Pope and the classics

The question of Pope's relationship to the Greek and Roman classics once was thought clear: he was deeply indebted to them, generally reflected their values, and often imitated them to show modern inadequacy. He was variously called "neoclassical" and "Augustan" in order to suggest that indebtedness. He exemplified and moved within a world of polished, polite poetry and civilized discourse among other civilized neoclassical Augustans. To be "Augustan" was a sign of approbation.

Much of this vision was seen through spectacles regularly prescribed from about the later nineteenth to the later twentieth century. One distinguished American scholar argues that the "true Augustans" saw in "Horace's [65 BC–8 BC] poetry a concentrated image of a life and civilization to which they more or less consciously aspired." A subsequent distinguished British scholar adds that Pope's imitations recommend "the Augustan ideal in its civilized splendour."[1] More recently, Pope has begun to be seen surely as indebted to admired classical sources, but also skeptical regarding many of their values and selective in what he chose to respect.[2] So far from being politely "Augustan," he often was intentionally rude, crude, vulgar, and angry. For example, in what was called "This filthy Simile, this beastly Line" he characterized court politicians as Westphalian hogs feeding off one another's excrement (TE, IV, p. 323; Epilogue to the Satires [1738], II, 181). He also portrayed corrupt exhibitionist London booksellers engaged in a public urinating contest, in which a well-endowed syphilitic victor carries off a female writer of pornography as his prize so that they can produce infectious books (TE, V, pp. 303–4). In many cases, Pope and his contemporaries berated Augustus Caesar (63 BC–AD 14) and denigrated his supportive poets. The clichés no longer work as a reasonable version of eighteenth-century literary history.

This does not mean that Pope's relationship to the classics is any easier to establish, or that it is simple and clear in the opposite direction from the once

76

received version. Pope often disapproved of content while approving and adapting style and devices. As late as 1735 he could say that in his *Imitations of Horace* he thought that "*An Answer from* Horace *was both more full, and of more Dignity, than any I cou'd have made in my own person*" (*TE*, IV, p. 3). Nonetheless, there is an approximate shape to this complex history. It begins with admiration, imitation, and translation of the ancients, especially Homer, while recognizing their moral limits and need to be adapted to the modern world. Along the way, Pope recognizes the competing strengths of British literature and the political weakness of the great Roman Augustans who celebrated a tyrant. Pope modulates his Horatian voice in favor of the voice of the outsider, the Silver Age early second-century satirist Juvenal, someone demonstrably more useful for the opposition, religiously victimized Catholic, physically distorted British poet. He concludes his career with a mingling of Virgilian (70 BC–19 BC) and Miltonic devices in his final poem, *The Dunciad in Four Books* (1743), in which the Miltonic vastly outweighs the Virgilian in moral seriousness. I begin near the beginning.

## From affiliation to defection

"All that is left us is to recommend our productions by the imitation of the Ancients: and it will be found true, that in every age, the highest character for sense and learning has been obtain'd by those who have been most indebted to them." So Pope claims in the Preface to *The Works of Mr. Alexander Pope* ([1717]: *TE*, I, p. 7). Such a response was predictable for a young poet audaciously collecting his works in a handsome folio appropriate for the major authors with whom he hoped to be associated. That volume included classically based poems like the *Pastorals* (1709), *An Essay on Criticism* (1711), *Windsor-Forest* (1713), and the final version of *The Rape of the Lock* that added Clarissa's normative pacific speech as an improved version of Sarpedon's martial speech to Glaucus in Book XII of *The Iliad*. By implication, like Pope's worthy predecessors, he too deserved "the highest character for sense and learning." The *Works* also served to advertise and support Pope's ongoing publication of his great version of *The Iliad* (1715–20). The extensive notes to that translation embody both sensitive practical criticism and a handsome synthesis of response to Homer from Plato to Pope's own contemporaries. Here indeed seemed a golden compendium of poetry, criticism, and scholarship in a brilliantly budding career anchored in adaptation and emulation of the classical ancients. That gold soon would tarnish.

In about 1738 Pope writes his own epitaph "For One who would not be buried in Westminster Abbey." He there rejects two major ancients as either sources of benevolent imitation or as arguments on authority.

HEROES and KINGS! your distance keep:
In peace let one poor Poet sleep,
Who never flatter'd Folks like you:
Let Horace blush, and Virgil too.

(*TE*, VI, p. 376)

What has happened in the twenty-odd years to evoke so stern a reconsideration? Why should Pope exchange the young man's ostentatious affiliation for the older man's ostentatious distancing? Why should he single out Horace and Virgil among the Roman classics? The tentative answers to these questions suggest varied reconsiderations within Pope's varied contexts.

Moral reconsideration is perhaps the most obvious part of the Greek portions of the question. Pope of course acknowledged and praised Homer's transcendent achievement. He "had the greatest Invention of any Writer whatever." Since invention is the foundation of poetry, Homer also "has ever been acknowledg'd the greatest of Poets," Pope says in the Preface to *The Iliad* ([1715]: *TE*, VII, p. 3). He also acknowledged that whatever the presumed noble simplicity of Homer's age and its fertilizing myths, it was morally inferior to the Christian world and Christian virtues. Pope's generally approving notes to *The Iliad* nonetheless observe that in spite of some excess, commentators from Plato to Houdar de la Motte rightly objected to Homer's theology and culture. Pope disapproves of Homer's crude language, pagan gods, and their delight in slaughter and sensuality so well exemplified in the Greek warriors. Sometimes Pope softens the "mean and vulgar Words" in his original (*TE*, VIII, p. 64n, quoting Boileau on Longinus). He regards Thetis' advice that Achilles relieve his grief for the death of his friend Patroclus by taking Briseis to bed as an outrage to "Decency" and in "Expression . . . almost obscene" (*TE*, VIII, p. 543n). At other points he needs to apologize for, rationalize, or historicize Greek brutality, as when Achilles wishes all his Greek allies dead so that he and Patroclus alone could slay all the Trojans (*TE*, VIII, p. 241n). Pope often indeed finds Greek morality immoral. Agamemnon easily convinces Menelaus to kill the wounded Prince Adrastus because the times were "uncivilized" and "Mankind was not united by the Bonds of a rational Society" (*TE*, VII, p. 326n). The heroes' regular insults to the dead and dying are "barbarous" (*TE*, VIII, p. 475n); Achilles' murder of twelve Trojan prisoners to honour Patroclus' death was sanctioned by vulgar Greek religion (*TE*, VIII, p. 423n); Achilles' wretched treatment of the dead Hector deservedly has been condemned by ancients and moderns (*TE*, VIII, p. 476n).

Pope sums up some of these objections in his Preface and its disagreement with the avid Homerophile and pre-eminent classicist Madame Anne

Lefèvre Dacier to whom Pope is gratefully indebted in his notes. Defects like the gross representation of the gods and the vicious manners of the heroes "proceed wholly from the Nature" of Homer's Times (*TE*, VII, p. 13), and its theology so inferior to revealed scripture's God who is "all Perfection, Justice, and Beneficence" (*TE*, VII, p. 402n). Pope cannot agree with his French colleague's "strange Partiality to Antiquity" in which the more the modern world deviates from the ancient the worse it is. He asks about the Greeks: "Who can be so prejudiced in their Favour as to magnify the Felicity of those Ages, when a Spirit of Revenge and Cruelty, join'd with the practice of Rapine and Robbery, reign'd thro' the World, when no Mercy was shown but for the sake of Lucre, when the greatest Princes were put to the Sword, and their Wives and Daughters made Slaves and Concubines?" (*TE*, VII, p. 14). Such sensible remarks contributed to Pope's gradual reconsideration of the role of the ancient classical world as a source of positive imitation and consequent praise.

The years of Pope's precocious poetic advances also were part of the famous Anglo-French, if not pan-European, battle between the Ancients and the Moderns.[3] Swift's *Tale of a Tub* and *Battle of the Books* (1704) were among the chief British responses. Madame Dacier's prose translation and annotation of *The Iliad* (1711) and her *Des causes de la corruption du goust* (1714) were among the chief French responses. By translating, annotating, and generally praising Homer, Pope aligned himself with the Ancients, but alignment scarcely denoted congruence. One cannot read either Swift or Madame Dacier without being aware of the Ancients' basic assumption: mankind was in regular mental, spiritual, and physical decline from its classical peak. Pope also feared, and in the final *Dunciad* portrayed, the dreadful fragility of culture. Unlike the Ancients, he nonetheless recognized the liberating and enriching value of commerce and modern progress and rejuvenation.

In *An Essay on Criticism*, for example, he characterizes and rejects literary Calvinism. Some esteem only the Ancients or the Moderns, thus making "*Wit*, like *Faith*" applicable "To *one small Sect*, and All are *damn'd beside*" (396–7; *TE*, I, p. 285):

> Meanly they seek the Blessing to confine,
> And force *that Sun* but on a *Part* to Shine;
> Which not alone the *Southern Wit* sublimes,
> But ripens Spirits in cold *Northern Climes*;
> Which from the first has shone on *Ages past*,
> Enlights the *present*, and shall warm the *last*.
> (398–402; *TE*, I, p. 286)

Similarly, in *Windsor-Forest* Pope combines the biblical expansion of the human soul through trade, from Isaiah, Chapter 60, with Virgil's *Georgics* of Roman pacific stability. "Sacred *Peace!*" (355; *TE*, I, p. 185) evokes the glories of a pax Britannica after successful completion of the terrible War of the Spanish Succession. Then "Unbounded *Thames* shall flow for all Mankind" (398; *TE*, I, p. 191), the exchange of national commerce indicates the exchange of war for peace, British freedom both morally unifies the world and establishes national government for proper and secure nations. Discord, Pride, Terror, Care, Ambition, Vengeance, Envy, Persecution, Faction, Rebellion, and other Furies all are sent to Hell: "Oh stretch thy Reign, fair *Peace*! From Shore to Shore, | Till Conquest cease, and Slav'ry be no more" (406–22; *TE*, I, p. 192). This, alas temporary, optimistic vision was inconsistent with the Ancients' regular assumption of progressive decay. In these respects Pope clearly was a defector to the Moderns and their reservations regarding classical virtues. Pope further made these reservations clear regarding Rome in "*Messiah* A Sacred Eclogue, In Imitation of Virgil's Pollio" (1717) – the fourth *Georgic* as improved by the Old Testament Isaiah as seen through a Christian perspective. The adaptation was written, Pope says, "with this particular view, that the reader by comparing the several thoughts might see how far the images and descriptions of the Prophet are superior to those of the Poet" (*TE*, I, p. 111).

Pope's defection was aided by his reading in the best of British literature as well as the Bible. He admired Milton's *Paradise Lost* and observed how in comparable scenes "*Milton* has far surpass'd both the *Greek* and *Roman*" epic poets (*TE*, IX, p. 419n). He also extends poetic to moral superiority. In a note to *The Iliad* Pope harshly discusses one of Homer's licentious sexual episodes between Jupiter and Juno: "That which seems in *Homer* an impious Fiction, becomes a moral Lesson in Milton" (*TE*, IX, p. 182n). He makes such alterations as are "agreeable to a Christian Poet" (*TE*, VII, p. 400n). By 1725 Pope also had published his edition of Shakespeare's works. In spite of their demonstrable flaws, the dramas taught Pope that Shakespeare's "Excellencies" have "justly and universally elevated [him] above all other Dramatic Writers." Pope apparently agrees with and quotes Ben Jonson's praise: English Shakespeare transcends Sophocles, Euripides, and Aeschylus (*Prose*, II, p. 19). He also transcends Homer himself, who was indebted to Egyptian learning, whereas Shakespeare as an original drew directly "from the fountains of Nature . . . The Poetry of *Shakespear* was Inspiration indeed: he is not so much an Imitator, as an Instrument, of Nature; and 'tis not so just to say that he speaks from her, as that she speaks thro' him" (*Prose*, II, p. 13).

We have then, what might be called moral, conceptual, theological, and national reasons for Pope to modify his youthful judgment regarding "all that is left us is to recommend our productions by the imitation of the Ancients." There was another perhaps even more important reason for Pope's later denigration of the chief Augustan poets – namely, the political tar that had smeared the often imitated, always taught, and, as poets, almost always admired Virgil and Horace.

## Augustan politics

Eighteenth-century Whigs and Tories shared a dominant assumption: Britain's limited constitutional monarchy maintained freedom by its jealous balance among the Crown, Lords, and Commons. So long as each branch of government adhered to its proper role, Britons would enjoy liberty impossible for less enlightened arbitrary governments like those of France or Spain. Ancient Rome provided the major historical contrast and affirmation. As eighteenth-century readers knew from the first book both of Tacitus' *Annals* and *History*, among numerous other sources, destructively seminal civil wars initiated by Julius Caesar culminated in Augustus Caesar's triumphs – over Mark Antony's resistance, over Cleopatra's Egypt, and most ominously over Rome's own senate. That once free republican body soon became a pawn of the Augustan principate which destroyed earlier liberty and initiated the gradual decline of the Roman empire. The generation of great post-civil war poets was inherited from the declining republic and was not properly Augustan. As Thomas Blackwell the younger said in his overheated *Memoirs of the Court of Augustus* (Edinburgh, 1753–63), Virgil, Horace, and others "learned the Language of *Liberty*, and took the masterly Tincture, which that Goddess inspires both in phrase and Sentiment. This gave them that Freedom of Thought and Strength of Stile, which is only to be acquired under *Her* Influence . . . The *Roman* Composition began to degenerate even under Augustus" (III, pp. 467–8). The true Augustan thus is the verbally impure and sexually licentious Ovid, who better reflected the decline of letters that would begin more dramatically under Augustus' wretched successor Tiberius.

Indeed, one of the commonplaces of Roman history was that Augustus intentionally chose Tiberius, knowing that he would be a bad caesar and a tyrant, but would make Augustus look the better by contrast. From Tacitus forward, however, Augustus himself is viewed as the person most responsible for the collapse of the Roman empire and Roman letters. Thomas Gordon's politicized discourses on Tacitus precede his translation (1728) and make plain that under Augustus "Truth was treason" and no one "would venture to speak it." Conyers Middleton's *Life of . . . Cicero* (1741) later adds that after Augustus' complicity in the murder of Cicero "and the ruin of the

HOWARD D. WEINBROT

Republic," Roman oratory would only make "panegyrics, and servile compliments to . . . Tyrants," certainly including Augustus himself.[4] The highly Tacitean Edward Gibbon puts it this way in his first published work, the *Essai sur l'étude de la littérature* (1761): Augustus was a bloody tyrant, suspected of cowardice, and when he came to the throne he made Romans forget that they ever had been free. Chapter 3 of Gibbon's *Decline and Fall of the Roman Empire* (1776) argues that Augustus usurped power, annihilated the hitherto balanced constitution, and ruined Rome. As he says at the beginning of Chapter 8, "from the reign of Augustus to the time of Alexander Severus, the enemies of Rome were in her bosom; the tyrants, and the soldiers."[5]

As others pointed out, Rome's ample bosom included those like Virgil and Horace who were so willing to praise the tyrant and his political agenda. Such views were part of Pope's intellectual ancestry and posterity. What would Pope and his contemporaries committed to British "liberty" make of those who supported tyranny, censorship, the absorption of the arts into government propaganda, and the suppression of opposition? Such responses fell into three sometimes overlapping responses.

One response was to grant that Augustus was an enslaving tyrant, but that since the republic was lost Virgil and Horace concluded that, as Dryden said, national self-interest required reconciling the people to their new master and thereby "to confirm their obedience to him; and by that obedience to make them happy." A second less quietist response was to grant that Virgil and Horace were republicans at heart who knew that they were defeated and that brutal Augustus needed reform. They thus drew idealized pictures of what he should be in hopes that life would imitate art. In 1714 Samuel Cobb observed that Virgil did not believe in arbitrary government, and poetically advised Augustus "how to behave himself in his New Monarchy, so as to gain the Affections of his Subjects."[6] A third response was more consistent with the highly charged partisan history and literature of the earlier eighteenth century and one in which Pope and many of his contemporaries believed, namely that in so handsomely painting Augustus, Horace, and Virgil distorted truth, history, and the proper relationship of the throne to letters – which should support loyal opposition and not absorb it by threats, patronage, and flattery.

Even elements of the Whig court party and the smaller opposition Tory party shared that vision. It was, though, especially congenial to the "Patriot" opposition to Sir Robert Walpole, whom Pope also satirized and whom he regarded as the Hanoverians' agent of darkness. To flatter the court and throne, he contended, is to flatter wickedness. Pope was demonstrably influenced by this view. In the summer of 1739 he told Joseph Spence that Virgil was a "slavish" political writer whose *Aeneid* did not have one honest line.[7]

82

The author of *Plain Truth, or Downright Dunstable* (1740) sums up much of the moral outrage regarding such politically incorrect poetry. He recognizes that Horace and Virgil are self-interested *"flattering, soothing, Tools"* (p. 13) who were "Fit to *praise Tyrants*, and *gull Fools*" (pp. 15–16). They are so dangerous to the personal and political state that banishment is the best alternative. *"Away with 'em*, I can scarce bear 'em," he proclaims in the highest of high dudgeon:

> In monstrous times, *such Weeds* thrive best,
> They *ornament a Tyrant's Nest.*
> They serve to *lull and blunt the Pain,*
> Of *vilest Crime*, still hide such Stain,
> In Luxury, they thrive amain,
> Of *Tyranny bear up the Train.* (p. 17)

There was a significant variation on this theme, one to which Pope also responded by means of characterizing his own version of a redefined Horace.

The Walpole administration used its *Daily Gazetteer* to counter tirades in opposition newspapers like *The Craftsman.* On 9 December 1739 the *Gazetteer* makes plain that its Horace supported the government and its schemes for censorship of political excess, as well as its religion, laws, and other men of letters. Pope, in contrast, merely writes seditious and ridiculous *"Billingsgate"* very different from "the Verses of that *fine, courtly Satyrist."* In the same year and again thereafter, Thomas Newcomb joins the administration writers on this theme and invents a poem written by Horace from the underworld, in which he scolds Pope the "Pert meddling Bard" for praising traitors, maligning Walpole and George II, and being resolutely un-Horatian. The spectral Horace laments that it would destroy his fame "Cou'd it be wrote upon thy Grave, | That P – and H O R A C E thought alike."[8]

However crude, these were among the more modest attacks on Pope for being unlike the Horace he pretended to use as an argument on authority. As we have seen, in a sense they were correct, for Pope redefines Horace into an opposition, Juvenalian, satirist of vice and national corruption. Indeed, he makes plain that the Walpole administration has so captured Horace that he no longer is suitable for satire at all. In the first *Dialogue* of the *Epilogue to the Satires* (1738) Pope creates an administration spokesman who characterizes its Horace as radically unlike his Popean-Juvenalian counterpart. Walpole's Horace "was delicate, was nice," and "lash'd no sort of *Vice*" (11–12; *TE*, IV, p. 298). He would gloss over serious criminality in court, town, church, and international relations, ingratiate himself with the crown and protect – screen – the Prime Minister from investigation of his illicit deeds:

His sly, polite, insinuating stile
Could please at Court, and make AUGUSTUS smile:
An artful Manager, that crept between
His Friend and Shame, and was a kind of *Screen*.

(19–22; *TE*, IV, p. 298)

It is clear why Pope's own epitaph divorces himself from the shameful Horace and Virgil: each had been labeled the complicit agent of tyranny.

The further Pope moved into the 1730s, the harsher his satires became. Several of these were imitations of Horace, adaptations of specific satires or epistles made relevant to Pope's own circumstances and times. He would print the English on the right side of the page and the Latin on the left. He could leave certain areas blank on either side to suggest meaningful absence; he could print lines to which he drew attention in special typeface; he could show that unlike the "real" Horace he was in opposition and not in alliance with his Crown. On the one hand, that was a shame, since as Pope said early in the harmonious and optimistic *Windsor-Forest*, "Peace and Plenty tell, a STUART reigns" (42; *TE*, I, p. 152), and he felt more comfortable with that dynasty than with the German Hanoverians supported by Walpole and his Whigs. Pope nonetheless had no choice but to offer an alternative Horace. He would adapt his dialog form, modulation of voice, poetic address to powerful aristocrats, and rural seat that becomes an emblem of national peace. He would also raise his voice, converse with aristocrats out of power, not those in power, and make plain that he was hostile to the present throne's policies.

These last traits are uncongenial to perceived Horatian satire. In 1693 John Dryden had harshly described Horace as "a temporizing poet, a well-mannered Court slave, and a man who is . . . ever decent, because he is naturally servile." In 1763 Edward Gibbon also characterized Horace, Virgil, and their contemporaries as singers "of the ruin of their country, and the triumph of its oppressors . . . Juvenal alone never prostitutes his muse" and always arraigns "the folly and tyranny of those masters of the world and their deputies."[9] That Juvenalianism is the tone and the message Pope also, though not uniformly, uses in his nominal imitations of Horace. That also is why both personal enemies and writers for the Walpole administration often savaged him as being a ridiculous parody of Horace, who was an ally not an enemy of his monarch and whose sympathetic poetry they themselves would embody.

Pope's self-image and value for opposition politics required a redefinition of satire and of epic. He achieves the first by means of Juvenal, and in the dialog form often Persius (AD 34–62), who created an opponent incapable of recognizing truth or reason. Pope raises the stakes, decibels, and satiric conventions – from folly to vice, from accommodation to opposition, from support to resistance of his Crown and culture. He already had begun that process of redefining the epic by lamenting the dishonest and slavish, though poetically stunning, *Aeneid*. He would finish that process just one year before his death.

## The Augustan *Dunciad*

We recall that Pope began his career with cultural cohesion. His own poetry was indebted to the classical poetry it adapted and in ways improved upon. His final great poem is *The Dunciad in Four Books*. *Windsor-Forest* was a British georgic with Ovidian metamorphoses and specifically local mythology and history. The final *Rape of the Lock* adapts epic devices to British domestic and rural aristocratic Catholic concerns; it is an heroic poem of daily life. The notes to *The Iliad* translation are masterpieces of critical synthesis, as hundreds of scholars and many nations illumine Homer by means of Pope's containing imagination and learning. By the early 1740s, however, Pope can be neither synthetic nor sympathetic in a world that endangers both his body and his spirit.

Under such circumstances, the classics' earlier functions are significantly diminished – as arguments on authority, as norms, as variously excellent models that must yield to yet better excellences, as receptacles for successful literary devices that later authors could borrow and comment upon. Instead, *The Dunciad in Four Books* combines Virgilian and Miltonic key modes of proceeding. Pope borrows Virgil's device of the transfer of power supported by the gods on behalf of the new founding of imperial Rome: the once defeated Trojans rise again, are divinely supported, and are fulfilled in the power of the ideal Caesar Augustus. Pope rejects that assumption, since he regarded *The Aeneid* as a great poem but a slavish political document.

He thus adds what had become a familiar device, the addition of a superior moral and literary statement that at once respects, complements, and diminishes the power of his classical source. Pope's epic Augustus now is George Augustus King of England, for Pope as destructive a political force as his namesake. Such modern Augustanism unleashes Dulness and offers a theory of causation. It reverses the Miltonic paradigm of creation, light, and ultimate design by a benevolent and loving God who is "all Perfection, Justice, and Beneficence." Pope's world now is one of uncreation and, at its conclusion, of universal darkness burying all as Georgian-Walpolean Dulness makes the moral and cultural rubble so different from the creation and ultimate forgiveness at the heart of *Paradise Lost*.

Devices from *The Aeneid* suggest that secular government and order are being destroyed by (George) Augustan power. However important that surely is, the evocation of Milton makes plain that far more important government and order are being destroyed – those by the God of creation whose light, energy, and seminal love are being chucked down a moral and intellectual sewer. Samuel Johnson's "Life of Milton" (1779) from his *Lives of the Poets* (1779–81) illumines a relevant implication of Pope's juxtaposition of Milton and Virgil. Milton's "subject is the fate of worlds [and] . . . rebellion against the Supreme King . . . Before the greatness displayed in Milton's poem all other greatness shrinks away."[10] Pope thus ends his poetic career with another absorption of the classic writers whom he adapts and surpasses with the help of national art, religion, politics, and his own splendid and splendidly eclectic genius.

## Synthesis

What then can we say about "Pope and the Classics"? The most obvious answer is that Pope knew classical literature intimately, admired it enormously, was guided by it in many ways, and often sought to adapt its conventions for his own use. He was especially admiring in his earlier years, when he also became financially independent thanks to the success of his Homer translations. The world, however, was more complex than young Alexander Pope had appreciated, and he often was savaged for what he rightly thought were his poetic and critical virtues. As the Walpole administration and the Hanoverian monarchy established themselves, he found himself aligned with what he considered the morally and politically virtuous opposition to the powerful Prime Minister Sir Robert Walpole. Pope's chief allies and intellectual colleagues were Jonathan Swift, Henry St John, Lord Bolingbroke, and other opposition aristocrats. In the process, Pope learned to compartmentalize and to continue his affection for Greek and Roman literary achievement. In each case, however, he distinguished between often morally or politically unacceptable content, and generally brilliant literary talent that had given pleasure for thousands of years. In the process as well, he would redefine some of those poets and their conventions for his own use. We note in Pope's epitaph, for example, that he tells only Horace and Virgil to blush. Pope reluctantly moved to the Juvenalian outrage appropriate for the satirist he had become, the poet now at odds with his declining culture, about which he can only protest rather than cure. Further in that process, he learned the achievement of his own national transcendent authors. Pope lacked the dramatic skills to adapt Shakespeare, but he recognized the strength of "nature" in his works and its power over Greek art. He also knew that Milton's *Paradise Lost* could serve his purposes in *The Dunciad*. Pope is a handsomely copious poet who learns a great deal through his career. One aspect of those lessons was that there was far more for a modern poet to do than to recommend himself by the imitation of the ancients, several of whom he had come to believe were politically or morally unworthy, and no better than the national models then revered in Britain and becoming better known on the Continent.

Sometime between 1706 and 1710 Pope gave several lines of poetry to William Wycherley. He called "Dulness, the safe Opiate of the Mind, | The last kind Refuge weary Wit can find." Such Dulness "Is satisfy'd, secure, and innocent: | No Pains it takes, and no Offence it gives" (1–2; *TE*, I, p. 5). Pope's own practice regarding the classics reverses that witless pattern. He takes risks, never tires in adapting, rejecting, or praising where appropriate; he never is satisfied, secure or innocent; and he takes great pains and does not fear giving offence – certainly including to those who had taken blushing Horace into their political grasp. For Pope "The Feast of Reason and the Flow of Soul" (*Sat*, II, i 127; *TE*, IV, p. 17) included judgments on the past, present, and himself. In some cases those judgments included revision of earlier views and modes of proceeding.

## NOTES

1. Reuben A. Brower, *Alexander Pope: The Poetry of Allusion* (Oxford: Clarendon Press, 1959), p. 176; Howard Erskine-Hill, *The Augustan Idea in English Literature* (London: Edward Arnold, 1983), p. 325.
2. For the most important discussions of this subject, see Further Reading, pp. 237–246 below.
3. Many of the French sources of the controversy have been usefully reprinted in *la Querelle des anciens et des modernes* XVIIe–XVII *siècles*, ed. Anne-Marie Lecoq (Paris: Gallimard, 2001). For Madame Dacier's unfortunate argument with Pope, see Howard D. Weinbrot, "'What Must the World Think of Me?' Pope, Madame Dacier, and Homer – The Anatomy of a Quarrel," in *Eighteenth-Century Contexts: Historical Inquiries in Honor of Phillip Harth*, eds. Howard D. Weinbrot, Peter J. Schakel, and Stephen E. Karian (Madison: University of Wisconsin Press, 2001), pp. 183–206.
4. Thomas Gordon, *The Works of Tacitus*, 2 vols. (London, 1728), I, 150; Conyers Middleton, *History of the Life of Marcus Tullius Cicero*, 3 vols. (London: Printed for W. Innys, 1741), II, pp. 449–50, 534–5.
5. Edward Gibbon, *Essai sur l'étude de la littérature*: "Tyran sanguinaire, soupçonné de lâcheté le plus grand des crimes dans un chef de parti, il parvient au trône, et fait oublier aux républicains qu'ils eussent jamais été libre": in *Miscellaneous Works of Edward Gibbon, Esq.*, ed. John Lord Sheffield, 5 vols, (London: J. Murray 1814), IV, pp. 89–90; Edward Gibbon, *The History of the Decline and Fall of the Roman Empire*, ed. David Womersley, 3 vols. (London: The Penguin Press, 1994), I, p. 213.

6. John Dryden, "Discourse on Epick Poetry" (Preface to Virgil), in *John Dryden: Of Dramatic Poesy and other Critical Essays*, ed. George Watson, 2 vols. (New York: Dutton, 1962), II, p. 239; Samuel Cobb, *Clavis Virgiliana: or New Observations on Poetry, Especially the Epic* (London: Printed for E. Curll, 1714), p. 8.

7. *Anecdotes*, I, pp. 229–30. Pope there also regards Virgil's first georgic and its flattery of Augustus as gross and "mean," but nobly expressed.

8. Newcomb's poem appears in *The Daily Gazetteer* for 16 June 1739, and in Newcomb's *A Miscellaneous Collection of Original Poems* (London, 1740), pp. 52–6. This was among the many attacks upon Pope's inadequate Horatianism.

9. John Dryden, "Discourse on the Original and Progress of Satire," Preface to Juvenal, in *Of Dramatic Poesy and Other Critical Essays*, II, p. 131; Edward Gibbon, "Extraits de mon Journal," in *Miscellaneous Works*, II, 103–4.

10. Johnson, *LOP*, I, p. 172.

# 7

DAVID FAIRER

# Pope and the Elizabethans

In narratives of English literary history Pope has tended to be seen as a figure of discontinuity rather than one who finds his natural place in the native tradition. By the end of the eighteenth century, Milton was the acknowledged heir to the poetic inheritance of the age of Shakespeare and Spenser, while Pope represented the triumph of neoclassical refinement after an earlier "barbarity." In many ways this took Pope at his own valuation: he accepted the prevailing view that the achievement of the Elizabethans was marred by incorrectness, faulty versification and lapses of taste, and that only with Waller, Dryden, and Addison had the English language reached perfection.[1] There certainly could be no return to styles of the past or to an obsolete English. The very title of Pope's *The Fourth Satire of Dr. John Donne, Dean of St. Paul's, Versifyed* assumes that Donne's poem cannot claim to be "verse" at all. Unlike the ancient writers or those of the Restoration, Elizabethan poets were not his stylistic models, and we look in vain for any acknowledgment, public or private, of the scale of his indebtedness to them.

But a stylistic influence (Waller, say) might be worn more lightly than one that fills the imagination. In his youth Pope read Elizabethan poets, along with much else, during his "great reading period" before the age of twenty-one (*Anecdotes*, I, p. 20). He read *The Faerie Queene* at "about twelve" and throughout his life he loved Spenser, for all his obsoleteness of language; later as a translator of Homer he recognised in George Chapman's old version, in spite of its stylistic "Fustian," "a daring fiery Spirit that animates his Translation" (*Anecdotes*, I, p. 182; *Prose*, I, pp. 250–1). *Animation* in its various meanings is a characteristic feature of Pope's writings at those moments when he is drawing on Elizabethan materials. He could also never conceal an underlying disappointment that the Restoration of 1660 had made poetry too "easy," in every sense of the word. He scorned "the Mob of Gentlemen who wrote with Ease" and who fluttered round a corrupt court (*Ep*, II.i, 108). For all its rust and roughness, Elizabethan poetry took shape within a Renaissance world in which writers wrestled with ideas and valued principles. Readers of Erasmus and Montaigne felt themselves part of a European-wide culture rather than a court coterie. Verses were much more than "the affair of idle men who write in their closets, and of idle men who read there" (*Prose*, I, p. 290). It is evident that many Renaissance ideas were more than congenial to Pope: they spoke to him at a deep level about things essential to human nature. He valued humanist argument with its skeptical wit and its respect for individual experience and intelligent conscience. But it is clear from his poetry that he also relished another side of Renaissance culture, the rich symbolic language that the Elizabethan world in particular offered him. It fed an art in which truth was embedded in symbol, and where poetic meaning shared an iconography with politics and philosophy. There was still a common allegorical language. "Idea" had not yet shrunk to items in a Cartesian a priori logic, and could be celebrated by sonneteers. A field of inherited symbolic reference was available to poetry, through which layers of allusion and suggestion might be worked.

An example of how complex this layering could be is *Windsor-Forest* (1713). It is a highly topical poem, but its political theme (supporting the Tory Peace of Utrecht) is structured by a historical topography that was first used to celebrate the England of Elizabeth the First. Pope draws directly from Britain's foundational national history, William Camden's *Britannia* (1586), and his early reading of this (probably in Gibson's expanded 1695 edition) influenced the structure and imagery of his most patriotic poem. Like Camden, Pope constructs national history through local topography. In *Britannia* individual small-scale histories and ecologies find themselves mapped onto a united and resourceful "Britannia," and the account of each shire is organized by its main river, which is traced along its course, taking in tributaries as it goes. This thematic idea left its imprint on the river-imagery of *Windsor-Forest*, in which Pope's native stream of the Loddon, along with other tributaries, swells the national river and pays its "tribute." It is an Elizabethan patriotic iconography that Pope knew well, one that includes Spenser's extended description of the marriage of Thames and Medway (*The Faerie Queene* [1596], IV.xi,29), Michael Drayton's poetic mapping of the nation in his topographical epic *Poly-Olbion* (1612–22), and Camden's own poem, quoted in *Britannia*, on the symbolic marriage of the Thame and the Isis.[2]

Behind Pope's graceful compliments to Queen Anne in *Windsor-Forest* are several hinted allusions to Elizabeth I, a figure with whom Anne wished to be associated and whose motto, *Semper eadem* ("always the same"), she adopted.[3] But the typology becomes strained when Pope evokes Diana the huntress, goddess of chastity, and for a moment he sounds like an Elizabethan poet celebrating his Virgin Queen:

> Nor envy *Windsor*! Since thy Shades have seen
> As bright a Goddess, and as chast a Queen;
> Whose Care, like hers, protects the Sylvan Reign,
> The Earth's fair Light, and Empress of the Main.
>
> (161–4)

Anne's fondness for hunting seems hardly enough to qualify her for the Diana role, given her seventeen children; and from a passage like this the reader can sense how in later years Pope will find satiric potential in this Elizabethan allegorical mode. On his return to the Thames in *The Dunciad* the tributary has changed, and the Loddon has been replaced by Fleet Ditch, who "with disemboguing streams | Rolls the large tribute of dead dogs to Thames" (II, 271–2). *The Dunciad* similarly functions as a sump for receiving grotesque versions of many of the symbolic images that Pope had earlier drawn from the Elizabethans.

Of all the Elizabethan writers it was the poet of *The Faerie Queene* whom Pope absorbed most deeply.[4] As he remarked to John Hughes, who had sent him his newly published edition of Spenser's *Works* in six volumes (1715): "Spenser has ever been a favourite poet to me; he is like a mistress whose faults we see, but love her with 'em all."[5] Pope's self-conscious fondness here (in the earlier sense of "excessive attachment") represents a Spenserian ambivalence of head and heart, a divided response that underlies many of the vivid allegorical scenes in Pope's poetry; it informs his creative engagement with excess and indulgence, his sense of how celebration and satire might become entangled, and imagination bring delight and danger.[6] Such dualities are a feature of Pope's visual exuberance as a poet, and the Spenserian moments in his work are often those in which poetic qualities are in tension with a satiric judgment, aesthetics with morality. As well as being an imaginative stimulus to his eighteenth-century readers, Spenser was also the great moral poet, who declares in the opening invocation to *The Faerie Queene*: "Fierce warres and faithful loves shall moralize my song," a phrase which reminds us that Pope's boast of himself in *Epistle to Arbuthnot*, "That not in Fancy's Maze he wander'd long, | But stoop'd to Truth, and moraliz'd his song" (340–1), is also a renewed commitment to Spenser.[7]

Pope, like his Elizabethan predecessor, was fascinated by the spaciousness of the human mind, its labyrinths, locked rooms and inviting doorways, where hope, fear, and desire are shaped into images. He is aware of these as sites of creativity as well as delusion. When, in the revised version of *The Dunciad*, the goddess Dulness tells the ecstatic Cibber, "what thou seek'st is in thee! Look, and find | Each Monster meets his likeness in thy mind" (*Dunciad*, III, 251–2), Pope is recalling many allegorical scenes in *The Faerie Queene* where the heroes are tested by their own human vulnerability, and their inner struggle is pictured as a confrontation with giants, monsters, enchanters and tempters. In the "Cave of Poverty and Poetry" (*Dunciad*, I, 33–84) and the "Cave of Spleen" in *The Rape of the Lock*, Pope creates spaces like Malbecco's cave or Phantastes' upper room in the House of Alma, chambers where imagination does its dubious work (*Faerie Queene*, III.x, 57–60, II.ix, 50–2); and in the great crowd scenes in *The Temple of Fame* (1715) and *The Dunciad* (1728–43) he explores the magnetism of ambition, pride, and desire such as Guyon encounters in the cave of Mammon or Britomart in the House of Busyrane (*Faerie Queene*, II.vii, III.xi-xii). In *The Temple of Fame* Pope's goddess holds her followers in thrall like Mammon's daughter tantalizing aspirants with the golden chain of ambition ("there, as in glistering glory she did sitt, | She held a great gold chaine ylinked well . . . | And all that preace did rownd about her swell | To catchen hold of that long chaine," II.vii, 46). In revisiting the scene in *The Dunciad* Pope darkens Spenser's satire on the Elizabethan court into a nightmare of Walpole's Britain, where the goddess Dulness assumes aspects both of the wicked enchanter Archimago and the false Duessa,[8] Spenser's dazzling female emblem of the ways "by which deceit doth maske in visour faire, | And cast her colours, died deepe in graine, | To seeme like truth" (*Faerie Queene*, I.vii, 1):

> She, tinsel'd o'er in robes of varying hues,
> With self-applause her wild creation views;
> Sees momentary monsters rise and fall,
> And with her own fools-colours gilds them all.
> (*Dunciad*, I, 81–4)

*The Dunciad* has frequently been discussed in its epic context, but other ironies come to the fore when it is seen in terms of allegorical romance. In Pope's satire Spenser's imagined Britain, the "land of Faery," is doomed because the hero himself is under the enchanter's spell, incapable of reading the many symbolic images of the poem: there is no diamond shield, as there is in Spenser's poem, to expose "all that was not such as seemd in sight" (*Faerie Queene*, I.vii, 35). Illusion is no longer an allegorical shadowing of Truth, but has supplanted it, so that Pope's monsters become crowd pleasers. Rather than striving to "seek for another Meaning under these wild Types and Shadows,"[9] his audience applauds them as special effects. The age of Dunce the Second has lost the code, and the moral bearings that go with it.

For Pope, influences from the Elizabethan period were not superficial ones. He did not play with images and ignore the system of ideas that gave them meaning. It is evident, for example, that especially in his earlier career, from 1714 to 1717, he was remarkably responsive to Renaissance conceptualizations of body and mind. Several of the best known poems of this period, *The Rape of the Lock, Eloisa to Abelard*, and *Elegy to the Memory of an Unfortunate Lady*, draw on humoral pathology and faculty psychology, and on the old concepts of psychomachia and metempsychosis, which were popular among Elizabethan writers. After half a century of the Royal Society and the new experimental science this may seem anachronistic, but Pope and his fellow Scriblerians were no scientific "moderns". At their centre was Dr John Arbuthnot, a physician whose theory of the human constitution rested on a physiology of the four bodily humors, which he offered to the public on the authority of the classical medical tradition of Hippocrates and Galen: see *An Essay Concerning the Nature of Aliments, and the Choice of Them, According to the different Constitutions of Human Bodies* (1731). The Scriblerian farce, *Three Hours after Marriage* (1717), on which Gay collaborated with Pope and Arbuthnot, is a Jonsonian comedy of humors partly modeled on *The Silent Woman* (1609), and it featured as its newly married couple a pair of actors who were famous for the equivalent roles of Morose and Epicœne in Jonson's play.[10] When Dr Fossile tells his wife that he has chosen her "for the natural Conformity of our Constitutions . . . thou art hot and moist in the Third Degree, and I myself cold and dry in the First" (*Three Hours after Marriage*, III, 313–15) it is Arbuthnot who is the butt of an affectionate joke. It seems that Pope was sympathetic to Arbuthnot's humoral theory, given the following detailed analysis of music's power to heal the human body: "as the musical notes move the air," Pope writes, "so the air moves the inward spirits, and the humours of the body, which are the seat of diseases; so that by this new motion they may be condensed, rarefied, dissipated or expell'd, according as they are agitated or influenc'd by the concussion of the musical notes."[11]

This intimate, troubled relationship between matter and spirit, drawn from Renaissance thinking, is a feature of *The Rape of the Lock* (1714). Pope's playful system of elemental spirits is a comic tour de force, but through the sylphs and gnomes he is also articulating an allegorical emotional conflict about girlhood and maturity, in which the melancholy humors prove victorious.[12] Belinda's splenetic "inward spirits" are Umbriel's concern, and it is these that invade the surface world of ritualized beauty over which the sylphs preside. Scholars have found a range of Renaissance analogs for the poem's mythology, drawn from the miniature "faery" poetry of Drayton's *Nymphidia*, Shakespeare's *A Midsummer Night's Dream*, Spenser's *Muiopotmos or the Fate of the Butterfly*, his *Faerie Queene*, and Ariosto's "Limbo of Vanity";[13] the idealization of Belinda's beauty has parallels in the

imagery of Elizabethan sonnets, and the poem repeatedly echoes Spenser's
lyrical bridal celebrations, *Prothalamion* and *Epithalamion*, the first of which
was written for the marriage of the Second Lord Petre, great-grandfather of
Pope's Baron.[14] Beneath these various reminiscences, however, at the core of
*The Rape of the Lock* is a conceptual structure that is indebted to Renaissance
notions about how thoughts and emotions work. Pope took this seriously
because, unlike the more recent organic theories of the brain (concerning
nerve fibres, "medulary matter", etc.),[15] it left open areas of choice and
moral responsibility. Renaissance faculty psychology, with its hierarchical
view of the mind, placed reason as a separate faculty presiding over issues
of truth, while imagination delighted in shows.[16] The Scriblerian satirists
mocked the emergent organic theories because they undermined the vital
responsibility of rational judgment – what Pope in *An Essay on Man* calls
"the God within the mind" (II, 204). Just as Jonson's obsessive "humour"
characters are swayed by their imaginations and emotions, so the objects
of Pope's satires tend to be people who allow desires and fancies to pursue
their own ends. When Pope writes to Lady Mary Wortley Montagu, "I fancy
myself, in my romantic thoughts & distant admiration of you, not unlike
the man [Dapper] in the Alchymist that has a passion for the Queen of the
Faeries," he is reflecting ruefully on his own capacity for Jonsonian self-
deception (*Corr*, I, p. 439). Judgment finally comes at the end of Jonson's
comedies, and in the 1717 text of *The Rape of the Lock* Belinda is given a
moment of choice between being fancifully governed by the dark humors of
her spleen or heeding the sensible judgment of Clarissa, who reminds her
that in the real world "Locks will turn to grey" (V, 26). In this physiological
aspect of *The Rape of the Lock* Pope is heir to a Miltonic-humanist tradition
deriving from the Renaissance (Adam instructs Eve in this theory, *Paradise
Lost*, V, 100–13).

Elizabethan neoplatonic thought was another strong influence on Pope's
pre-1717 poetry, and in the final stellification of Belinda's lock, celebrating
her beauty as eternal divine Idea, he plays lightly with a set of concepts
that meant a lot to him. In his own life Pope felt acutely the constrictions
of the body (his "Carcase," as he called it) and the potential freedom of
his soul,[17] and these tensions are played out in *Eloisa to Abelard* (1717).
But Eloisa's monologue also recalls the medieval psychomachia, or dueling
for possession of the soul. The idea remained popular on the Elizabethan
stage (in Marlowe's *Doctor Faustus*) and it shaped Shakespeare's Sonnet
144 ("Two loves I have"). In Pope's version Eloisa is enacting internally the
kind of psychomachia represented in Marlowe's play when the good and
evil angels compete for Faustus's soul: "Come", she tells Abelard, "if thou

dar'st, all charming as thou art! | Oppose thy self to heav'n; dispute my heart" (281–2):

> Snatch me, just mounting, from the blest abode,
> Assist the Fiends and tear me from my God!
> No, fly me, fly me! Far as Pole from Pole;
> Rise *Alps* between us! (287–90)

It is the poem's emotional climax, the equivalent of Faustus's terrified words in the final scene: "O, I'll leap up to my God! Who pulls me down? . . . | Mountains and hills, come, come and fall on me, | And hide me from the heavy wrath of God! | No, no!"[18]

Pope's classical model for *Eloisa to Abelard* is Ovid's *Heroides*, but he filters this source through the Renaissance heroic epistles of Michael Drayton and Samuel Daniel.[19] Ovid's heroines give vent to surging passions (usually in imagery of sea, wind, and sails), but such movement is not checked by a contrary idea of confinement. This Pope found in Elizabethan versions of the genre where neoplatonic elements of psychic enclosure parallel the soul's imprisonment in the body. Animation pulls against constriction. A passage like the following from Daniel's *A Letter sent from Octavia to her Husband Marcus Antonius* (1599) catches a sense of emotional suffocation very similar to Eloisa's:

> We, in this prison of our selves confin'd,
> Must here shut up with our owne passions live,
> Turn'd in upon us, and denied to find
> The vent of outward meanes that might relieve:
> That they alone must take up all our mind,
> And no room left us, but to think and grieve.
> (137–42)

Behind Daniel's imagery, as behind Pope's, is the neoplatonic concept of the "vent" through which the soul could glimpse its freedom beyond the mortal body. The idea is memorably caught by Pope in *Elegy to the Memory of an Unfortunate Lady* (1717): "Most souls, 'tis true, but peep out once an age, | Dull sullen pris'ners in the body's cage" (18–19). Here he draws on the imagery of the caged soul common in emblem books, like Francis Quarles's *Emblems* (1635), V, 10, where a girl is pictured cooped up in a birdcage ("My Soule is like a Bird; my Flesh, the Cage"). The image of the soul as a "sullen" prisoner was perhaps suggested to Pope by a passage in Donne's *Second Anniversary*: "no stubborn, sullen anchorite | . . . dwells so foully as our souls, in their first-built cells. | Think in how poor a prison thou dost lie".[20] Pope accepted the theory of metempsychosis, or the progress of the immortal soul through a series of bodies (including animal and vegetable). It was, said Spence, "a settled notion with him"; and Donne's extraordinary poem about a migrating soul, *Metempsychosis* (1601), was a favourite of his (see *Anecdotes*, I, pp. 188, 239). Part of the mystery of Pope's "unfortunate lady" is the way she hovers between soul and body, a "beck'ning ghost" and a "heap of dust," a woman he knows intimately but who has utterly eluded him. Pope's enigmatic elegy places her alongside women like Donne's Elizabeth Drury (the subject of his *Funeral Elegy* and the two *Anniversaries*), or Ben Jonson's Lady Jane Pawlet, celebrated as released souls who leave a mystery reverberating behind them. Pope's dramatic opening ("What beck'ning ghost . . .?") was probably suggested by the first lines of Jonson's elegy on Lady Pawlet: "What gentle Ghost, besprent with April dew, | Hayles me, so solemnly, to yonder Yew? | And beckning wooes me?"[21]

The restlessness of the human soul is a motif that gives a protean energy to Pope's writing, whether it is in the "escapes of soul" of his intimate correspondence,[22] in his sketch of Flavia in *Epistle to a Lady*, in Eloisa's struggle, or parodically in the *Peri Bathous* and the wayward energies of the dunces. It is a mark of humanity's incurable inability to rest content. We are buffeted about by passions and affections, and never able to possess our souls quietly. Such restlessness is evident throughout *An Essay on Man* (1733–4), a poem that is infused with Renaissance reworkings of classical thought. Behind Pope's proverbial line, "Hope springs eternal in the human breast," is an image of the soul longing to leave its prison: "The soul, uneasy and confin'd from home, | Rests and expatiates in a life to come" (I, 95–8). Life is not a myriad of independent organisms, but the sum of beings sharing a divine essence: "All are but parts of one stupendous whole, | Whose body, Nature is, and God the soul" (I, 267–8). Body is temporal, mortal, part of nature, but for a spell this uncomfortable transitory being is our lodging-place. In this context, the difficult issue of knowing oneself becomes the starting-point for moral action – which means understanding one's limitations as a tiny part of nature but also one's infinite potential as a piece of divinity. In such passages Pope is close to the neoplatonism of Sir John Davies, whose 1599 poem *Nosce Teipsum* ("know thyself") was republished in 1733 with an essay by Thomas Sheridan.

But *An Essay on Man* draws from a range of philosophical positions, and when Pope opens Book II with the exhortation, "Know then thyself," he reveals a markedly less reassuring vision. Now the stress is on the human species as a paradoxical "Chaos of Thought and Passion," erratic, vulnerable, and also ridiculous. This perspective seems indebted to the Stoic tradition deriving from Seneca and Epictetus, which advocated a rational mastery over

the passions. But it is soon evident that Pope is rejecting the *apatheia*, or cultivated indifference to passion, of classical stoicism ("In lazy Apathy let Stoics
boast | Their Virtue fix'd" [II, 101–2]),[23] and is moving to the Neo-Stoicism
of the Elizabethan Renaissance, which was more animated and combative
in its analysis of human nature. Its representative satiric voice is that of John
Marston, whose indignant response, "Preach not the Stoickes patience to
me" (*The Scourge of Villanie* [1598], II, 6) reminds us that Christianized
Neo-Stoicism was anxious to distance itself from imputations of spiritual
lethargy. Marston has not previously been linked to *An Essay on Man*, but
a reader of the *The Scourge of Villanie* may glimpse beneath its incessant
cynical railing a motif that runs through Pope's ethical epistles of the 1730s,
and into *The Dunciad* too: how easily individual fancy and opinion are preferred to truth. Marston deplores the way the human mind, instead of align-
ing with reason, abuses itself by preferring appearances and shows: "These
are no men, but Apparitions, | Ignes fatui, Glowormes, Fictions, | Meteors,
Ratts of Nilus, Fantasies" (*Scourge of Villanie*, VII, 13–15). For Marston, a
mind buoyed up with its own comfortable ideas needs to be brought back
to earth: "Opinion mounts this froth unto the skies | Whom judgment's
reason justly vilifies | . . . Juggling Opinion, thou enchanting witch! | Paint
not a rotten post with colours rich" (*Scourge of Villanie*, X, 43–4, 61–2).
In *An Essay on Man* Pope too is conscious of the self-pleasing colors of
imagination, when "Opinion gilds with varying rays | Those painted clouds
that beautify our days" (II, 283–4). There is nothing dispassionate about
Elizabethan Neo-Stoicism, rather there is a recognition that all mankind
is in this way caught up in its own subjective passions. As Pope says in
*Epistle to Cobham* (1731): "All Manners take a tincture from our own, | Or
come discolour'd thro' our Passions shown" (25–6).

The recognition that human beings can see only refractions of the truth,
that certainties and man-made systems are manifestations of pride, and that
to trust in reason or vision alone is to ignore the paradox of our nature,
links the later Pope particularly to the tradition of Renaissance skepticism –
before it became freethinking libertinism. Looking back across the seventeenth century with its new clashing certainties of religion, science, politics,
and philosophy, Pope felt more at home intellectually and emotionally with
the earlier humanist inheritance, with what Maynard Mack has called the
"Erasmian virtues of tolerance, moderation, civility, and wit, together with
a learning lightly worn" (*Life*, p. 81). The two Renaissance men closest to
Pope's heart were Erasmus and Montaigne, Catholic writers who understood human folly and pride, and steered their way through them, doubt-
ing yet principled, always true to themselves. Pope was "fond of Erasmus's
Principles in matters of religious opinion," and he considered writing his

biography (*Anecdotes*, I, p. 261). In *The Praise of Folly*, Erasmus's scenario of a world in thrall to a goddess of sublime self-belief who supplies all hopes and ambitions, we see a prototype for *The Dunciad* and its vision of universally misdirected energies. Montaigne's *Essays* were another voice of sanity, "the very best Book for Information of Manners, that has been writ," Pope noted inside his copy, "This Author says nothing but what every one feels att the Heart." As well as a French edition, he possessed Charles Cotton's 1685 translation.

The finest of Montaigne's essays, Pope thought, was "On the Inconstancy of our Actions" (*Anecdotes*, I, p. 142), and it was an idea that struck a chord with his own sense of the "quick whirls, and shifting eddies, of our minds" (*Epistle to Cobham*, 30). We are carried along, says Montaigne in Florio's 1603 translation, "as things that flote, now gliding gentlie, now hulling violently . . . We floate and waver between divers opinions: we will nothing freely, nothing absolutely, nothing constantly." To underscore his point Montaigne quotes from Horace's epistle to Maecenas some lines that Pope himself adopts when confessing his own inconsistencies to his friend Bolingbroke:

> . . . no Prelate's Lawn with Hair-shirt lin'd,
> Is half so incoherent as my Mind,
> When (each Opinion with the next at strife,
> One ebb and flow of follies all my Life)
> I plant, root up, I build, and then confound,
> Turn round to square, and square again to round.
>
> (*Ep*, I. i, 165–70)

Pope's Horace is someone at home in the Renaissance as much as Augustan Rome, and Pope hears his voice partly through the tones of writers like Montaigne and Ben Jonson. In taking Horace as his alter ego in the 1730s, Pope knew that "our English Horace" was a title Jonson had worn with pride,[24] and that in his struggle during the last years of Elizabeth to recommend Augustan ideals to a corrupt court, he had made Horace his cultural and moral spokesman. The play *Poetaster* (1601), set in the Rome of Augustus, presents Horace as a man of integrity and simple virtue who is contemptuous of malice, envy, and flattery. The emperor values his honest judgment: "Thanks, Horace, for thy free and wholesome sharpness | Which pleaseth Caesar more than servile fawns" (*Poetaster*, v.i, 94–5.) But at the end Augustus allows him publicly to administer an emetic to his infuriating detractor, Crispinus – a scene, I would suggest, that supplied Pope with a neat Jonsonian precedent for his own similar revenge on Edmund Curll in 1716 (he perhaps smiled at the thought that Crispinus means "curly").

When Pope in 1733 chose to imitate Horace's *Satire* II. i, the first of his series of imitations of Horace during the 1730s, he was offering as his calling card the same satiric dialogue Jonson had used to assert his Horatian identity at the end of Act III of *Poetaster*. This might be seen as his declaration of a collateral kinship with Jonson through their Roman ancestor. But the two poems are different: where Jonson's is a reasonably faithful translation, Pope's imitation moves some distance from the original: he bares more of his soul, he is more defiant and self-justifying, and he applies to himself the idealized satiric character that Horace celebrates in his predecessor, Lucilius. It is a bold and egotistical move. But if Pope's poem reaches well beyond the Jonson of 1601, it is only to identify himself more closely with the later Jonson, and particularly with his "Epistle answering to one that asked to be Sealed of the Tribe of Ben" (1623). In Pope's reworking of *Satire* II. i, three interlocking elements are set in place: the circling enemies (libelers, toadies, cheats), the stockade of intimate friends (the virtuous circle), and the poet's self (the inner core of integrity). It is just such a pattern we see in Jonson's later epistle, which is built around the nucleus of his own virtue: "Live to that point I will, for which I am man, | And dwell as in my Center, as I can" (59–60). In Pope's imitations of Horace this Jonsonian triple combination of "myself, my Foes, my Friends" (Pope's words in *Sat*, II.i, 58) forms a recurring pattern.

In his "versification" of Donne's satires also, Pope sought out a more embattled version of the Horatian identity enriched by its Elizabethan context.[25] In his fourth satire Donne develops the humorous street scene of Horace's *Satire* I.ix (his meeting with the garrulous talker) by relocating it to Elizabeth's court, and inverting the power relationship. Where Horace is trying to shake off a hanger-on who envies his status in the establishment, Donne is an uncomfortable outsider at the edge of the room, watching the courtly performances and finding himself in danger of being entangled in the political game. It is clear which situation suited Pope's case. Donne's animated descriptions give Horace a menacing edge (these are men of power): "He, like to a high stretcht lute string squeakt, 'O Sir, | 'Tis sweet to talke of Kings." Pope responds to this and makes it a gracefully poised performance:

> At this, entranc'd, he lifts his Hands and Eyes,
> Squeaks like a high-stretch'd Lutestring, and replies:
> "Oh 'tis the sweetest of all earthly things
> To gaze on Princes, and to talk of Kings!"
>
> (98–101)

This could be the "squeak" of Lord Hervey, or Sporus, in Pope's version of Jonson's "Court-worme": "In silke | 'Twas brought to court first wrapt, and white as milke; | Where, afterwards, it grew a butter-flye".[26] When the man's gossip takes a seditious turn, Pope catches Donne's sudden sense of unease and fear, and his need as an Elizabethan Catholic to be circumspect:

> I fear'd th'Infection slide from him to me,
> As in the Pox, some give it to get free;
> And quick to swallow me, methought I saw
> One of our Giant *Statutes* ope its Jaw!
>
> (170–3)

The last line, with its vivid image of anti-Catholic persecution, is Donne's. Although Pope smooths out what Dryden in his *Essay of Dramatic Poesy* called Donne's "rough cadence," he retains the striking wit and strength of thought. To make Donne too "easy" might have compromised his integrity – as Pope's Latin epigraph suggests: "We ask whether it was his genius or the harsh nature of his themes that prevented his verses from flowing more easily." These are Horace's words about Lucilius (*Satires*, I.x, 56–9), and they carry the further implication that Donne is the Lucilius to Pope's Horace.

A darker and more pessimistic vision is also part of Pope's Renaissance inheritance, and *The Dunciad*'s assault on contemporary culture draws on writers like Marston or the later Jonson who feared that a classically enlightened wisdom was being lost sight of in a world of ephemeral fashions and shows, fed by an over-active press and a public thirsty for sensation. In *The Dunciad* Pope revisits the urban topography of Jonson's *Famous Voyage* (1616), making Fleet Ditch once again a dirty cultural thoroughfare; but he raises the stakes by using it as a symbol of lost ideals, misdirected energies, and prurient obsessions. Pope's satire is also subtly indebted to *An Execration upon Vulcan* (1623), a poem in which Jonson indicts a popular taste that has lost its classical bearings. In response to the burning of his library, Jonson curses Vulcan, god of fire, for not directing his flames elsewhere at the mounting heaps of trashy romance and false wit ("fiftie tomes | Of Logogriphes, and curious Palindromes"). "These," Jonson concludes, ". . . Had made a meale for Vulcan to lick up" (83–4). This vivid image finds its place in *The Dunciad* when Dulness's prophet, Elkanah Settle, looks forward to her approaching triumph: "From shelves to shelves see greedy Vulcan roll, | And lick up all their Physic of the Soul" (III, 81–2). Jonson's all too real nightmare becomes Settle's gleeful vision of a bonfire of the classics.[27]

The pageantry of *The Dunciad* draws on the iconography of Renaissance classicism to create a pessimistic scenario of the loss of a unified culture informed by the principles of the ancients. The satire is Pope's equivalent of a disorderly antimasque, but with no final reassertion of order, no transformation to light and harmony. Jonson's *Masque of Queens* (1609) opens in hell, where the witches' dame leads the infernal dance ("Let us . . . blast the light; | Mix hell with heaven, and make Nature fight | Within herself; loose the whole hinge of things, | And cause the ends run back into their springs," and she calls on Chaos to "strike the world and nature dead."[28] At the end of the expanded *Dunciad* this very wish is granted: "Lo! Thy dread Empire, CHAOS! is restor'd" (IV, 653). Where Jonson transforms the hellish scene to a magnificent House of Fame, from which the voice of "Heroic Virtue" speaks to dispel the forces of darkness, for Pope there could be no return to his earlier cultural optimism. In this he is closer to Donne's despairing thought that "new philosophy calls all in doubt . . . | . . . 'Tis all in pieces, all coherence gone" ("An Anatomy of the World" [1611], 205–13).

Pope often reflects Jonsonian ideals, but unlike his predecessor he had no fondness for works of abstruse learning; indeed, *The Dunciad* footnotes sometimes imitate Jonson's scholarly annotation of his masques, pompous and chatty by turns, as they explicate the symbolic machinery for us: "The sable Thrones of Night and Chaos, here represented as advancing to extinguish the light of the Sciences . . ." (note to IV, 629). For Pope in the 1740s the scholarly world has joined the enemy, and night is closing in from every direction. Book IV of *The Dunciad* opens with the plea, "Yet, yet a moment, one dim Ray of Light | Indulge, dread Chaos, and eternal Night!", and the uncertain glimmer allows Pope to complete his poem before darkness swallows all. This would seem to be an allusion to the divine *synteresis*, the precarious remnant of God's divine light within the soul. It is Sir John Davies's "dying Sparkle, in this cloudie place" (*Nosce Teipsum* [1599], 66), the surviving spark of the divine to which Marston desperately pleads, before "Oblivion" takes over in the resonant lines of *The Scourge of Villanie* (1598): "Return, return, sacred Synderesis! | . . . Awake our lethargy, | Raise us from our brain-sick foolery!" (VIII, 211–14). Pope's satiric pageant stages itself as the last Renaissance spectacular, the final big show before the lights are turned out.

Pope was interested in English literary history, its "schools" and lines of influence, but he also had a ruthless satiric eye for claims of poetic paternity and inheritance. While he openly signalled his indebtedness to the classical tradition and publicised his ancient models, his links to the Elizabethans, if noted at all, were treated more casually. In a note to *Windsor-Forest* (65), Pope acknowledges "an old monkish writer, I forget who": this is the very un-monkish Camden. Many scattered allusions have previously been traced, but the impression remains a fragmentary one, as Earl Wasserman concluded:

DAVID FAIRER

"When a possible influence is discoverable, it appears in a borrowed line, a snippet of thought, an ingeniously turned figure of speech, a pattern for organization, but never does it mould the general cast of a poem."[29] But a more coherent picture is waiting to emerge. Beneath the verbal echoes of Elizabethan poetry is an identifiable body of Renaissance thought that helped to shape Pope's work, and a response to the imaginative and moral dimensions of these writers that was integral to his poetry.

## NOTES

1. Edmund Waller (1606–87), John Dryden (1631–1700), and Joseph Addison (1672–1719). In this essay the term "Elizabethan" covers those writers active in the later years of the Queen's reign, many of whom remained productive under James and Charles I.
2. Michael Drayton (1563–1631). See Pat Rogers, *The Symbolic Design of Windsor-Forest: Iconography, Pageant, and Prophecy in Pope's Early Work* (Newark: University of Delaware Press, 2004), pp. 113–37.
3. See Vincent Caretta, "Anne and Elizabeth: The Poet as Historian in *Windsor-Forest*," *Studies in English Literature 1500–1900* 21 (1981): pp. 425–37 (p. 436).
4. For a concise discussion of Pope's affinities with Spenser, see Howard Erskine-Hill's entry on "Pope" in *The Spenser Encyclopedia* (London: Routledge, 1990), pp. 555–6.
5. Pope to Hughes, 7 October 1715 (*Corr*, I, p. 316). Pope also owned Dryden's copy of Spenser's *Works* (1611 folio).
6. For a fuller discussion of eighteenth-century responses to *The Faerie Queene*, in which imagination and judgment challenged each other, see David Fairer, "*The Faerie Queene* and Eighteenth-Century Spenserianism," in *A Companion to Romance from Classical to Contemporary*, ed. Corinne Saunders (Oxford: Blackwell, 2004), pp. 197–215.
7. See Kathleen Williams, "The Moralized Song: Some Renaissance Themes in Pope," *ELH* 41 (1974): pp. 578–601.
8. In Book IV of *The Dunciad* Pope draws on the satiric allegory of Walpole as Archimago in Gilbert West's *A Canto of the Fairy Queen. Written by Spenser* (London, 1739). See Christine Gerrard, *The Patriot Opposition to Walpole* (Oxford: Clarendon Press, 1994), pp. 177–80.
9. "An Essay on Allegorical Poetry," in *The Works of Mr. Edmund Spenser*, ed. John Hughes, 6 vols. (London: Printed for Jacob Tonson, 1715), I, p. xxxvi.
10. Benjamin Johnson and Anne Oldfield. See R. G. Noyes, *Ben Jonson on the English Stage, 1660–1776* (New York: Benjamin Blom, 1966), pp. 188–9.
11. Pope, note to *Odyssey*, XIX, 536. Pope's analysis of musical affect is very close to that of Thomas Wright, *The Passions of the Minde in Generall* (London, 1604), p. 168. See David Lindley, *Shakespeare and Music* (London: Arden, 2006), pp. 28–30.
12. See David Fairer, *Pope's Imagination* (Manchester: Manchester University Press, 1984), pp. 53–81.

13. See C. H. Carter, "'Nymphidia,' 'The Rape of the Lock,' and 'The Culprit Fay,'" *Modern Language Notes* 21 (1906): pp. 216–19; John Preston, "'Th'Informing Soul': Creative Irony in *The Rape of the Lock*," *Durham University Journal* 53 (1966): pp. 125–30; Pat Rogers, "Faery Lore and *The Rape of the Lock*," *Review of English Studies* 25 (1974): pp. 25–38; and Robert McHenry, "Pope and Spenser," *N&Q* 228 (1983): pp. 33–4. Pope himself draws attention to the *Orlando Furioso* parallel in a note to v, 114ff.

14. See Arthur W. Hoffman, "Spenser and *The Rape of the Lock*," *Philological Quarterly* 49 (1970): pp. 530–46.

15. See Michael V. DePorte, *Nightmares and Hobbyhorses: Swift, Sterne, and Augustan Ideas of Madness* (San Marino: Huntington Library, 1974), pp. 6–12.

16. See Raymond Klibansky, Erwin Panofsky, and Fritz Saxl, *Saturn and Melancholy* (London: Nelson, 1964), pp. 68–9; Lawrence Babb, *The Elizabethan Malady: A Study of Melancholia in English Literature from 1580–1642* (East Lansing: Michigan State College Press, 1951), pp. 2–5; and Baxter Hathaway, *The Age of Criticism: The Late Renaissance in Italy* (Ithaca: Cornell University Press, 1962), p. 34.

17. "Were not my own Carcase (very little suited to my Soul) my worst Enemy, were it not for the *Body of this Death*, as St Paul calls it) I would not be seperated from you" (Pope to Bathurst, 10 May 1736, *Corr*, IV, p. 15). In February 1728 he told Swift "to expect my soul there with you by that time; but as for the jade of a body that is tack'd to it, I fear there will be no dragging it after" (*Corr*, II, p. 472).

18. Christopher Marlowe, *Doctor Faustus* ([?]1592), A-Text, v.ii, 77–86. Though it is uncertain whether Pope knew Marlowe's play, but he could have read this scene in the 1663 edition ("as it is now acted").

19. The popularity of Drayton's *Englands Heroicall Epistles* (1600) in the eighteenth century is discussed by Earl R. Wasserman, *Elizabethan Poetry in the Eighteenth Century* (Urbana: University of Illinois Press, 1947), pp. 73–4.

20. John Donne, *Of the Progress of the Soul. The Second Anniversary* (1612), 169–73. Another phrase in the poem, "Thou shalt not peep through lattices of eyes" (296), perhaps suggested Pope's "peep."

21. Ben Jonson, "An Elegie on the Lady Jane Pawlet," in *The Under-Wood* (London, 1640) LXXXIII, 1–3.

22. Writing to the Earl of Orrery, 27 August 1742, Pope speaks of "my frequent Dreams, & Escapes of Soul toward you" (*Corr*, IV, p. 413).

23. Stoic "apathy" is neatly summed up by Robert Burton in 1621: "a wise man, Seneca thinks, is not moved, because he knows there is no remedy for it" (*Anatomy of Melancholy* [1621], II.iii, 7).

24. On the implications of the title, see Howard Erskine-Hill, *The Augustan Idea in English Literature* (London: Edward Arnold, 1983), pp. 169–71.

25. On Pope's "versification" of Donne, see Ian Jack, "Pope and 'the Weighty Bullion of Dr. Donne's Satires,'" *PMLA* 66 (1951): pp. 1009–22.

26. Jonson, *Epigrammes* (1616), xv. See *Epistle to Arbuthnot*, 305–18.

27. *The Dunciad* burlesques the continuing tradition of spectacular London pageants, devised by Settle as "city poet," 1691–1708, and recalling the iconography of the Elizabethan and Jacobean city pageants. See Fairer, *Pope's Imagination*, pp. 141–3.

28. *Ben Jonson: The Complete Masques*, ed. Stephen Orgel (New Haven: Yale University Press, 1969), pp. 127, 132–3. The parallel is discussed by Laura Tosi, "La *Dunciad* e il *masque* elisabettiano: scene di metamorfosi e sovversione dell'autorità," *Merope* XI (2000): pp. 23–45 (p. 28).
29. Wasserman, *Elizabethan Poetry in the Eighteenth Century*, p. 77.

# 8

PAT ROGERS

# Pope in Arcadia: pastoral and its dissolution

During much of the nineteenth century, readers viewed Pope as an incorrigibly "social" poet, the laureate of tea cups and trivial gossip. For a critic of the Romantic age, William Lisle Bowles, he ranked no higher than "the painter of external circumstances in *artificial life*; as Cowper paints a morning walk, and Pope a game of cards!"[1] Today we see him as one who exposed the crass commercialism of the age, who anatomized political corruption by depicting figures of vice like the reptilian Sporus in the *Epistle to Arbuthnot*, and who gave us an early vision of a squalid Nighttown in *The Dunciad*. To the Victorians, the primarily urban focus of Pope's later works seemed an evasion of the poet's true duty, while to modern readers it appears a badge of his modernity. What neither position fully allows for is the depth of Pope's involvement in the natural world, a direct outcome of his boyhood and youth spent in the Berkshire countryside.

In this essay I shall try, first, to describe the literary and biographic elements which helped to form the "pastoral" basis of his early works. Only if we appreciate what was going on in the years he spent "in Fancy's Maze" can we understand the nature of his later achievement once he "stoop'd to Truth, and moraliz'd his song" (*TE*, IV, p. 120). The account Pope gave in his *Epistle to Arbuthnot* drips with irony:

> Soft were my Numbers, who could take offence,
> While pure Description held the place of Sense?
> Like gentle *Fanny*'s was my flow'ry Theme,
> A painted Mistress, or a purling Stream.
> (147–50; *TE*, IV, pp. 106–7)

The last line here parodies a verse by Addison, whom Pope attacks later in the *Epistle*. But the work in question, published when Pope had reached the age of sixteen, was one that Pope "used formerly to like . . . extremely" – many years later, he still regarded it as his favourite among Addison's poems (*Anecdotes*, I, p. 176). Besides, no "painted mistress" makes an appearance in the early works. Pope cannot have supposed for a moment that his first poetic efforts lacked sense, however much description they may include. Moreover, description remained a *serious* literary property in forms like pastoral.

In the second part of this essay I shall try to show how Pope's Arcadian world collapsed around him in his mid-twenties, as events dictated the move from his boyhood home. A seismic shift in national politics and the loss of his elders (his father and his most important mentor, Sir William Trumbull) occurred soon after he left Binfield for good. In a coda the essay touches briefly on *The Dunciad*, as this poem sets out the systematic trashing in later years of many values that Pope had imbibed in his rural retreat.

### Descending gods

The immense impact on Pope's sensibility of the family home at Binfield can hardly be overestimated. In the first place, his surroundings near the village in Windsor Forest, with Easthampstead Park (Trumbull's home) close by, supplied him with subject matter, imagery, and a word-hoard with the names of fields, groves, and streams in the neighbourhood. With very little exaggeration we could say that the region created as potent an imaginative matrix for his work as Cumbria did for Wordsworth, Wessex for Hardy, or Mississippi for Faulkner.

One reason we tend to resist this conclusion lies in the brute facts of modern geography. Hawkshead, Dorchester, and Oxford, Mississippi remain quite sequestered, because they are a long way from major centres of population. By contrast, Berkshire has become in large measure a bedroom community for London, with a satellite "new town" at Bracknell (in Pope's day, a small village just a couple of miles down the road from his home). Another "overspill" community for the capital has grown up at Basingstoke, then a small town in the edge of the forest and fed by the River Loddon, for Pope an image of pastoral peace – "The *Loddon* slow, with verdant Alders crown'd" (*TE*, I, p. 183). Motorways and railways crisscross the county, and its border stops only just short of Heathrow airport. The nearest town to Windsor is Slough, thought unlovely by most, if scarcely deserving of the fate John Betjeman envisaged, "Come friendly bombs and fall on Slough." Small wonder that we have trouble imagining the district as a place of mystic forces and rural bliss, ideal for the reveries of a solitary walker, and instilled with the memory of ancient pagan spirits haunting the woodland.

In the second place, Pope's allegiance to his adopted home derives to a large extent from his pieties as a son. We must think our way back to an era when young people were invited to write exercises on the theme of what children owe to their parents – today that formulation looks almost like a misprint, with the key nouns accidentally swapped. In later years, too, Pope showed equal devotion in the care of his aging mother. As for the poet's father, Alexander Pope senior had retired from his business in the City of London, moving out first to Hammersmith, still a rural location, and then to Binfield in the heart of Windsor Forest. Like his wife, he was getting on in years, and the young Alexander, with his half-sister already married, spent his boyhood largely surrounded by much older men and women. The family had been driven out of central London by the restrictive "ten mile act" of William and Mary, which created a no-go area for Catholic residents at the heart of London. Alexander *père* set up home at Whitehill House in 1700 and began to improve the property, which extended to less than fifteen acres. Here his son developed his lifelong passion for gardening, exercised "In Forest planted by a Father's hand" (*Sat*, ii.ii, 135). From all this we can detect a number of attributes characterizing the "paternal cell" which incubated so much of his early poetry: quiet, (relative) distance from the city, a kind of happy exile prompted by religious loyalty, beautiful natural surroundings, space to cultivate one's garden. It was here that the essential Pope came into being: here that he forged his *literary* identity – both as writer and, logically and temporally prior, as reader.

Late in life, Pope told Joseph Spence that in childhood he had managed to avoid most of the usual constraints of a formal education. Instead he spent his time in Binfield in a sort of creative idleness: "in a few years I had dipped into a great number of the English, French, Italian, Latin, and Greek poets. This I did without any design but that of pleasing myself, and got the languages by hunting after the stories in the several poets I read, rather than read the books to get the languages. I followed everywhere as my fancy led me, and was like a boy gathering flowers in the woods and the fields just as they fall in his way. I still look upon these five or six years as the happiest part of my life" (*Anecdotes*, I, p. 24). Similarly, the hermit philosopher in *Windsor-Forest* (235–57) gathers health-giving herbs from the forest and fields. This noble Cincinnatus may represent Trumbull, or alternatively Pope's own father, both of whom could be portrayed as virtuous exiles from a corrupt metropolitan power-base.

For the poet to turn this corner of the English Home Counties into classic ground, he obviously needed first a good grounding in the ancient authors. Unlike Robinson Crusoe, he committed no original sin in devoting himself to literature: "I left no Calling for this idle trade, | No Duty broke, no Father dis-obey'd" (*Epistle to Arbuthnot*, 19–30; *TE*, iv, p. 105). Indeed his father had been brought up strictly as a tradesman, although he was the son of an Anglican clergyman; and doubtless he felt considerable pride in witnessing the progress his sickly offspring made through self-education. Much of the boy's early enthusiasm went in the direction of epic, especially Homer, but he read far more widely. From the poetic fabulist Ovid, above all, he would have imbibed the notion of a Golden Age when men and women lived in an idyllic state, prior to the fall through silver and bronze to the degenerate Iron Age of modern times. He probably did not take this schema literally: the purpose of the trope lay less in berating actuality than in suggesting the possibility of a primitive ideal to which humanity can aspire during its better moments.

The most relevant application of this notion emerged in the theory and practice of pastoral poetry. Quite early in his life Pope would have become familiar with the ancient pastoral writers. At their head stood the Greek poet Theocritus, who specialized in contests of skill between two peasants: he employs a bucolic setting and a language deliberately mimicking rural dialect, but the verse technique remains highly polished. Later poets such as Moschus and Bion developed the Greek tradition by importing a strand of elegy. Their Roman counterpart was Virgil, whose *Eclogues* dramatized the complaints of lovers in the imaginary world of Arcadia, a lush and remote landscape. The form flourished again in the Italian Renaissance with the work of Torquato Tasso and Giovanni Battista Guarini: meanwhile, poets such as Spenser, Michael Drayton, Robert Herrick, and Andrew Marvell extended its compass in English. At the same time a large body of critical theory grew up around the form, coming to a head close to the time of Pope's birth with a dispute that involved the French critics René Rapin and Bernard de Fontenelle. In his early "Discourse on Pastoral Poetry," written about 1706 but unpublished until 1717, Pope tracks a skilful adjudicatory path between the views of these two men on the way in which modern authors might recreate the form. For its part, the "Discourse" clearly recognizes the artificiality of pastoral fiction. Thus Pope describes how the genre originated: "From hence a Poem was invented, and afterwards improv'd to a perfect image of that happy time; which, by giving us an esteem for the virtues of a former age, might recommend them to the present." Then again: "If we would copy nature, it may be useful to take this idea along with us, that pastoral is an image of what they call the Golden Age. So that we are not to describe our shepherds as shepherds at this day really are, but as they may be conceived then to have been, when the best of men followed the employment." At the same time, a hint of rationalization emerges when Pope comes to modern imitations of the ancient form: "But with respect to the present age, nothing more conduces to make these composures natural than when some Knowledge in rural affairs is discover'd" (*Prose*, I, pp. 297–9).

We can gauge the use Pope made of his studies if we turn to "Summer," the most accomplished of the four *Pastorals* he wrote as a teenager. Here it seems that even Paradise can harbour a snake in the grass:

> See what Delights in Sylvan Scenes appear!
> Descending Gods have found *Elysium* here.
> In Woods bright *Venus* with *Adonis* stray'd,
> And chast *Diana* haunts the Forest Shade.
> Come, lovely Nymph, and bless the silent Hours,
> When Swains from Sheering seek their nightly Bow'rs;
> When weary Reapers quit the sultry Field,
> And crown'd with Corn, their Thanks to *Ceres* yield.
> This harmless Grove no lurking Viper hides,
> But in my Breast the Serpent Love abides.
> Here Bees from Blossoms sip the rosie Dew,
> But your *Alexis* knows no Sweets but you.
> Oh deign to visit our forsaken Seats,
> The mossie Fountains, and the Green Retreats!
> (59–72; *TE*, I, pp. 76–7)

Yet the pains of love seem finally a small price to pay for the consolations of these green retreats, and somehow the dream of a magically transformed future outweighs any sullen realities of the present:

> But wou'd you sing, and rival *Orpheus'* Strain,
> The wondring Forests soon should dance again,
> The moving Mountains hear the pow'rful Call,
> And headlong Streams hang list'ning in their Fall!
> (81–4; *TE*, I, pp. 78–9)

This is a young man's vision of an antique fantasy, but one which escapes the inanities of pure primitivism thanks to the way it is rooted in concrete language, if not the Keatsian sensuous mode which readers like Bowles desired:

> A Shepherd's Boy (he seeks no better Name)
> Led forth his Flocks along the silver *Thame*,
> Where dancing Sun-beams on the Waters play'd,
> And verdant Alders form'd a quivering Shade.
> Soft as he mourn'd, the Streams forgot to flow,
> The Flocks around a dumb Compassion show:
> The *Naiads* wept in ev'ry Wat'ry Bow'r,
> And *Jove* consented in a silent Show'r.
> (1–8; *TE*, I, pp. 71–2)

Even the conventional terms of diction like "Bow'r" go beyond the generic, and they are not vague at all. In the phrasing of the last line, Pope displays a humour redolent of his master John Dryden, and sly wit close to that of the Roman poet Ovid, as mighty Jove "consents" to add his own weight of water in a sudden downpour that falls on the landscape.

## Paradise threatened

After the *Pastorals* (1709) comes the georgic *Windsor-Forest*, which the poet once again set in his own home territory. But by now the idyll has started to come under threat, and a more venomous snake than love is lurking in the undergrowth. The work opens with a famous evocation of the paradisal world:

> The Groves of *Eden*, vanish'd now so long,
> Live in Description, and look green in Song:
> *These*, were my Breast inspir'd with equal Flame,
> Like them in Beauty, should be like in Fame.
> Here Hills and Vales, the Woodland and the Plain,
> Here Earth and Water seem to strive again;
> Not *Chaos*-like, together crush'd and bruis'd,
> But as the World, harmoniously confus'd;
> Where Order in Variety we see,
> And where, tho' all things differ, all agree.
> Here waving Groves a checquer'd Scene display,
> And part admit, and part exclude the Day;
> As some coy Nymph her Lover's warm Address
> Nor quite indulges, nor can quite repress.

And, continuing a little further:

> There, interspersed in Lawns and opening Glades,
> Thin Trees arise that shun each others Shades.
> Here in full Light the russet Plains extend;
> There wrapt in Clouds the blueish Hills ascend:
> Ev'n the wild Heath displays her Purple Dies,
> And 'midst the Desart fruitful Fields arise,
> That crown'd with tufted Trees and springing Corn,
> Like verdant Isles the sable Waste adorn.
>
> (7–28; *TE*, I, pp. 148–50)

This is writing of extraordinary delicacy, with the stereotyped diction made, against its instincts, to express precise topographic details. But it takes a little more effort than before to transform the forest into Eden. Here the woodland lies in peril of violation, dramatized in the inset story of the nymph Lodona, a mythical personification of the river that ran close to Pope's home in Berkshire. After she has suffered pursuit and the threat of rape by the brutal satyr Pan, she returns to her original element:

> "Let me, O let me, to the Shades repair,
> "My native Shades, – there weep, and murmur there,"
> She said, and melting as in Tears she lay,
> In a soft, silver Stream dissolv'd away.
>
> (201–04; *TE*, I, p. 168)

So pastoral itself begins to dissolve as the harsher realities of the modern world encroach ever nearer to the heart of the forest. A sense of lost innocence had imbued the form ever since its origins in ancient Greece; but loss in *Windsor-Forest* is felt more urgently and more pervasively.

Elsewhere in the poem, the Arcadian theme surfaces again:

> Let old *Arcadia* boast her ample Plain,
> The immortal Huntress, and her Virgin Train;
> Nor envy, *Windsor*! since thy Shades have seen
> As bright a Goddess, and as chast a Queen;
> Whose Care, like hers, protects the Sylvan Reign,
> The Earth's fair Light, and Empress of the Main.
> Here too, 'tis sung, of old *Diana* stray'd,
> And *Cynthus'* Top forsook for *Windsor* Shade;
> Here was she seen o'er Airy Wastes to rove,
> Seek the clear Spring, or haunt the pathless Grove;
> Here arm'd with silver Bows, in early Dawn,
> Her buskin'd Virgins trac'd the Dewy Lawn.
>
> (159–70; *TE*, I, pp. 164–5)

In the *Pastorals* we had the fiction, playfully indulged, of gods descending to earth. This time the apposition of the Arcadian huntress, Diana, and the real monarch, Anne, clearly suggests that the queen was an avatar of the goddess of the hunt. It involves a more daring strategy, and of course a more risky one, because it implies a particular identification rather than a mere generic similarity. What would happen if the queen no longer ruled over the forest or held empire over the war-torn "Main"? And supposing "Peace and Plenty tell, a STUART reigns" (42), what might come about, should the emperor in waiting prove not to be a Stuart at all – rather, an imported Hanoverian who, by Jacobite calculations, ranked no higher than fifty-fifth in his claim to the throne?[2]

Such questions would have occurred to any thoughtful reader when *Windsor-Forest* made its appearance in 1713. And Pope had certainly

considered them, as the entire poem demonstrates. For reasons both personal and political, the potential – soon to be actual – death of the queen
brought issues of the royal succession *home* to Windsor, and hence to the
whole idea of pastoral.

## Et ille in Arcadia

The tag "Et ego in Arcadia (fui *or* vixi)," I too have known Arcadia, has
acquired its most resonant embodiment in the picture by Nicolas Poussin
(c.1638). Shepherds in Tempe, the sacred vale of Thessaly, unexpectedly discover an ancestral monument with the gnomic inscription. Most students of
art history interpret the phrase to mean, "even in Arcadia, bad things may
happen"; but in the light of a seminal article by Erwin Panofsky, the drift of
the iconography Poussin employed has been read as Death speaking: "I too
am found in Arcadia."[3] *Windsor-Forest* enacts the same message, with the
violence dramatized in the fate of Lodona.

In 1713 Pope found himself witnessing the break-up of the Tory administration led by his friends Oxford and Bolingbroke. As the long-drawn out
war finally came to an end, instead of peace and plenty came the dissolution
of the government amid growing fractiousness. Oxford was dismissed by the
queen just days before her own death on 1 August 1714. With the accession
of the new king, George I, everything changed for the Catholic population.
New laws soon required them to take an oath of loyalty – Pope apparently
refused to do this. After this they had to register their real estate and its
value. A hard choice lay before the Popes: either to sell out while they could,
or else hang on with the prospect of crippling double taxes. The family took
the first course, and prepared to abandon their treasured home in early 1716
for a new base outside London at Chiswick. During this period the poet's
letters constantly refer to the impending events. He tells his co-religionist
John Caryll in March, "I write this from Windsor Forest, which I am come
to take my last look and leave of. We here bid our papist-neighbours adieu"
(*Corr*, I, p. 336).

What made it even worse was that Pope's closest women friends, Teresa
and Martha Blount, also had to take their leave from the environs of the
forest. Their brother's marriage obliged them to leave their home at Mapledurham, an Elizabethan mansion which lay hidden among trees on the riverside. Now they faced a new life in London. Pope's imagination had turned the
young women into something like woodland nymphs. For the purposes of
their own make-believe world of private correspondence, they had adopted
fanciful names, appropriate to romance and pastoral, such as Zephalinda
and Parthenissa; and Pope had even used these forms in his exquisite

"Epistle to Miss Blount, on her leaving the Town, after the Coronation," dating probably from late 1714 (*TE*, VI, pp. 124–6). In real life the sisters were driven in the opposite direction from the heroine of this poem, and compelled to give up the country pleasures they (Martha especially) had enjoyed. Pope's friend John Gay went down to Berkshire at this time, and reported, "Binfield alas is sold, The Trees of Windsor-Forest shall no more listen to the tunefull reed of the swain, & no more Beeches shall be wounded with the names of Teresa & Patty. Teresa & Patty are forced to leave the Groves of Mapledurham . . . as Binfield is for ever sold."[4]

As Pope explained to Caryll, a relative of the Blount sisters and godfather of Martha, it had all been a traumatic experience: "Tho' the change of my scene of life, from Windsor Forest to the water-side at Chiswick, be one of the grand ra's of my days, and may be called a notable period in so inconsiderable a history" (*Corr*, I, p. 343). To the squire of Binfield, he was more explicit:

> I have not dined at home these 15 days, and perfectly regrett the quiet, indolence, silence, and sauntring, that made up my whole life in Windsor Forest. I shall therefore infallibly be better company and better pleased than ever you knew me, as soon as I can get under the shade of Priest-Wood, whose trees I have yet some Concern about. I hope, whatever license the freeborn Subjects of your Commons may take, there will yet be Groves enough left in those Forests to keep a Pastoral-writer in countenance. Whatever belongs to the Crown is indeed as much trespas'd upon at this time in the Court as in the Country. While you are lopping his timber, we are lopping his Prerogative.
>
> (*Corr*, I, p. 352)

Despite the joking tone, we should have no doubt of the serious issues at stake. "Quiet, indolence, silence, and sauntering" look like trivial or even culpable ways of passing the time. Pope means the *otium* of classical poets, such as Horace, Martial, and Ovid, a desirable space for reflection, not so much leisure as an inner peace or spiritual tranquillity. A year later, Pope enclosed in a letter to the Blount sisters a "Hymn Written in Windsor Forest":

> All hail! once pleasing, once inspiring Shade,
> Scene of my youthful Loves, and happier hours!
> Where the kind Muses met me as I stray'd,
> And gently pressd my hand, and said, Be Ours! –
> Take all thou e're shalt have, a constant Muse:
> At Court thou may'st be lik'd, but nothing gain;
> Stocks thou may'st buy & sell, but always lose;
> And love the brightest eyes, but love in vain!
>
> (*TE*, VI, p. 194)

Here Pope movingly reanimates a stock antithesis between court and country by infusing a keen personal sense of loss, drawing on the poet's formative years with his friends in the forest.

As a Protestant, Sir William Trumbull had no need to desert his estate at Easthampstead. But even he, Pope believed, may have felt the urge to hunker down when the Jacobite rebellion and political riots overtook the nation in 1715: "I cannot but applaud your resolution of continuing in what you call your Cave in the forest, this winter; and preferring the noise of breaking Ice to that of breaking Statesmen, the rage of Storms to that of Parties, and fury and ravage of Floods and Tempests, to the precipitancy of some, and the ruin of others, which I fear will be our daily prospect in London" (*Corr*, I, p. 324). A few months later the old man died, commemorated in an epitaph of studied moderation by his disciple. In Pope's eyes, Trumbull had seemed like "a venerable prophet, foretelling with lifted hands the miseries to come upon posterity, which he was just going to be removed from!" (*Corr*, I, p. 337). He acts here like the prophetic figure of Father Thames in *Windsor-Forest*, foretelling the future course of civilization – a river god drawn straight from the staffage of pastoral painting and poetry.

On 23 October 1717 Alexander Pope senior followed Trumbull to the grave. Now Pope had lost most of the tutelary figures who had inspired him in his youth: his immediate family consisted only of his aging mother and a half-sister with whom he had a slightly patchy relationship. Soon he would move to Twickenham, in an effort perhaps to recapture some of the boons of "retirement" which had come to him so easily in the forest, before events in the larger world had begun to impinge on life there. Some famous lines, quoted elsewhere in this volume (see p. 130), lamented the savage laws against Catholics, originally imposed by William III and then renewed by George I: "But knottier Points we knew not half so well, | Depriv'd us soon of our Paternal Cell." The effects went beyond political identity and civic rights, though they included these: "And certain Laws, by Suff'rers thought unjust, | Deny'd all Posts of Profit or of Trust" (*Ep*, II.ii, 58–61; *TE*, IV, p. 169). The new controls affected Pope's sense of his own vocation, realigning both the subjects he could write about and the way in which he would approach his material. Many factors went into the decision to "moralize his song." But at one level the swerve proceeded from a deep internal need, which might be called existential in character. It is not just that Pope outgrew childish fantasy as he matured. Rather, pastoral had become unavailable because his mind had always bound up its fundamental assumptions with the idealized world of the Stuart regime. As his imagination constructed events, the death of the queen meant that nature would droop, and the forest would fall prey to aggressive invaders – like Nimrod, William the Conqueror and, implicitly, William III in the plot of *Windsor-Forest*.

Behind the symbolic tale of Lodona in that poem lies an Ovidian myth related in *Metamorphoses*, Book VIII. Despite warnings from a wood nymph, a prince in Thessaly named Erysichthon violated a grove sacred to Deme-ter (in Roman mythology, Ceres), by cutting down an oak, possessing a "strength matured with centuries of growth." The dryads complained to Ceres, and at her command he was punished by Famine, who came from barren Scythia, a land without trees, to inflict on him an insatiable hunger. This episode haunts the text of Pope's poem: in a crucial passage he refers to the "Fact accurst" (321) of the execution of Charles I, the darkest deed of modern times according to Stuart myth. He probably recalled Ovid's description of Erysichthon, who took his axe and cleaved the trunk with his "impious stroke" in an act of sacrilege, as the blood pours forth from the "smitten neck" (*Metamorphoses*, VIII, 761–4). Again, Ceres signifies her assent to the dryads with a nod of her head that shakes the fields of ripening grain. Similarly in *Windsor-Forest* the Stuarts rescue the woodland from its earlier depredation and barrenness: "Here *Ceres*' Gifts in waving prospect stand, | And nodding tempt the joyful Reaper's Hand" (39–40; *TE*, I, p. 152). In Pope's application of the myth, a pastoral conceit tells us of the death of the pastoral vision.

## The Dunciad

In many ways Pope designed *The Dunciad* as an anti-Arcadian poem. Of course, it draws on many models: one of these, relevant to its negative use of classical forms, is the urban pastoral or town eclogue, pioneered by Swift in works such as his "Description of a City Shower" (1709) and further developed by Gay in his urban georgic, *Trivia* (1716). Here Swift parodies the ancient *descriptio*, a point-by-point representation of a scene, set out in almost diagrammatic form. But, as Claude Rawson has shown, these trans-muted versions have the effect less of deflating the original than of "leveling" it out.[5] Meanwhile Gay domesticizes and, literally, trivializes georgic as he applies it to the street life of modern London: but the device does not have a *critical* function, and indeed the poem seems to celebrate the squalor of the city more than to deplore it. By contrast, when Pope sets the conventions and style of classical forms up against the harsh reality of modern life, this has the effect of removing any aspirations to greatness which the capital might harbor. If mock-epic shows the contemporary world to be less than heroic than its predecessors, then mock-pastoral shows its noise and ugliness to be the emblem of its decadence. A failure in aesthetics becomes a failure in compassing the nature of civilized living.

The way in which *The Dunciad* subverts pastoral expectation shows up most clearly in Books II and III. However, reminiscences of Virgil's *Eclogues* permeate the entire text: at least sixteen, according to Pope's notes, with all but three of them occurring within the inner books. When the poem alludes to the branch of Styx into which Smedley dives, the echoes come thick and fast:

> First he relates, how sinking to the chin,
> Smit with his mien, the Mud-nymphs suck'd him in:
> How young Lutetia, softer than the down,
> Nigrina black, and Merdamante brown,
> Vy'd for his love in jetty bow'rs below;
> As Hylas fair was ravish'd long ago.

The setting lies near the Fleet Ditch, a malodorous channel silted up with rubbish, fed by half the sewers of London. Hints of a far-off classical world turn the ditch into a perverse recycling of the waters celebrated in myth:

> Then sung, how shown him by the nut-brown maids,
> A branch of Styx here rises from the Shades,
> That tinctur'd as it runs with Lethe's streams,
> And wafting vapours from the Land of Dreams,
> (As under seas Alphæus' secret sluice
> Bears Pisa's offerings to his Arethuse)
> Pours into Thames: Each city-bowl is full
> Of the mixt wave, and all who drink grow dull.
> How to the banks where bards departed doze,
> They led him soft; how all the bards arose,
> Taylor, sweet Swan of Thames, majestic bows,
> And Shadwell nods the poppy on his brows;
> While Milbourn there, deputed by the rest,
> Gave him the cassock, surcingle, and vest;
> And "Take (he said) these robes which once were mine,
> "Dulness is sacred in a sound Divine."
>                                   (II, 307–27: *TE*, V, pp. 139–41)

We see immediately how the nymphs, with their incongruously euphonious names, have escaped from stock pastoral contexts. The lines about the Arcadian river Alpheus and the spring Arethusa go back directly to the opening of Virgil's tenth *Eclogue*. But most of the passage replays a section of the sixth poem in the series, which tells the story of Hylas, a beautiful boy carried off by Hercules on the Argonaut expedition. At a stopping point the water nymphs in attendance at the fountain glimpse Hylas, and fall in love with him. Subsequently they draw him to his death in the spring. The later part of the excerpt closely parodies other verses from the same *Eclogue*, describing Linus, a shepherd-poet who taught Orpheus in the skills of music. Pope adds to the absurdity by applying the Spenserian title "sweet bird of Thames" to John Taylor, a journeyman author and Thames boatman from the early seventeenth century, whose ragged verses would inspire no great musician to set their halting rhythms.

Another debasing reference occurs when the poem introduces "two slipshod Muses," a cutting reference to Eliza Haywood and Susanna Centlivre. Haywood was a prolific writer and journalist specializing in novels of erotic adventure, while Centlivre wrote some of the most popular stage comedies of the age. The two women authors "traipse" along, "With tresses staring from poetic dreams, | And never wash'd, but in Castalia's streams" (III, 143–4; *TE*, v, p. 162). To bathe in Castalia's stream meant to enter a spring on Mount Parnassus, named after a nymph whom Apollo had pursued, and hence to imbibe poetic inspiration. Once more the allusion has the effect of bringing the sacred places of pastoral art into raw conjunction with decadent modern writing reliant, the poem suggests, on mere afflatus.

*The Dunciad*, we could surmise, testifies to the enduring hold which the lost paradise of Pope's early enthusiasms maintained over his imagination. Something of the pastoral dream lives on as a normative force in the poem, long after its potency had been shrunk by the hard knocks of public and private experience.

## NOTES

1. William Lisle Bowles, *The Invariable Principles of Poetry* (1819).
2. Actually, when Pope wrote, the claimant was George's mother, the Electress Sophia, so that there would have been a new "Empress" to oversee the nation. She died a few weeks before Anne, in June 1714.
3. See Erwin Panofsky, "Et in Arcadia Ego: Poussin and the Elegiac Tradition," in *Meaning in the Visual Arts* (Chicago: University of Chicago Press, 1955), pp. 295–320.
4. *The Letters of John Gay*, ed. C. F. Burgess (Oxford: Clarendon Press, 1966), p. 29.
5. C. J. Rawson, "The Nightmares of Strephon: Nymphs of the City in the Poems of Swift, Baudelaire, Eliot," in *English Literature in the Age of Disguise*, ed. Maximillian E. Novak (Berkeley: University of California Press, 1977), p. 59.

# 9

BRIAN YOUNG

# Pope and ideology

> What is now published, is only to be considered as a *general Map* of M A N,
> marking out no more than the *greater parts*, their *extent*, their *limits*, and their
> *connections*, but leaving the particular to be more fully delineated in the charts
> which are to follow.
>
> (*An Essay on Man*, "The Design" [*TE*, III.i, p. 8])

This essay will unpack the simple statements that Alexander Pope was born
to Catholic parents in 1688, and that he died in 1744, still a Catholic. His co-
religionists constituted a small percentage of the national population. They
formed a conspicuous block of society in only a few parts of the country,
notably Lancashire and Cheshire, although there was an important group
of recusant gentry in the Thames Valley, with whom Pope made lasting connections during his youth. Some humbler folk in the provinces retained an
allegiance to the old faith, but as yet there had been no large-scale immi-
gration from Catholic countries to major centers, so that the urban poor
were Protestant for the most part. Within months of Pope's birth, James II
was ousted from the throne, having lost popularity in considerable measure
because of his attempts to impose freedom of worship, that is official tolerance of Catholicism. The backlash which followed under William and Mary
saw the introduction of severe penal laws against the papist community.
Excluded from succession to the throne, Catholics had to take oaths of loyalty, on pain of losing most civic rights. At the same time they were precluded
from living within ten miles of the center of London, and from becoming
members of the legal profession. Out of fear that insurrection would break
out, they were likewise forbidden to keep arms, ammunition or, bizarrely,
a horse worth more than ten pounds. A particularly fierce law passed in
1700 incapacitated all Roman Catholics from inheriting or purchasing land,
unless they formally abjured their religion. If they refused, their property
was legally transferred for life to their next of kin in the Protestant faith.
They were even prohibited from sending their children abroad, to be educated in their own faith. Finally, the measure laid down that any Catholic
priests caught exercizing their vocation should be imprisoned for life, and it
set a reward of one hundred pounds for informing against priests who said
mass.

These draconian powers had a direct and personal impact on the Pope family. It was because of these laws that the poet's father left London shortly after the Revolution of 1688; and even their ultimate refuge involved a legal fiction, since they were not permitted to buy their house in the country. As time went on, the operation of the laws was relaxed under Queen Anne, and several of Pope's friends and neighbours continued to send their children, both boys and girls, to Continental Europe for a Catholic education. But the Hanoverian accession in 1714 led to a renewal of the old laws and the introduction of even more stringent measures.

The name of Pope joined with the word "ideology" might seem to be an anachronistic conjunction, but the opening sentence of this essay implies the deeply ideological parameters in which Pope lived both his diurnal and his imaginative life. In this essay I shall seek to demonstrate that few words so accurately describe Pope's political and religious positions as the word "ideology" in its original sense. The term is a direct product of the French Revolution. It was coined by revolutionary secularists to denote systems of belief, emphasizing in particular the supremacy of a sense-based science of man over those false systems of metaphysical belief which it decried as having been promulgated by priests to their own power-hungry ends. By demystifying the understanding of humankind and its life in society, promoters of the concept of an ideology aimed to free modern politics from its previous domination by religion and its handmaid, monarchy. The unmasking of religion as an institutionalized ideology drove humankind's social relations away from notions of the divine and the imperatives of Christian belief, clinically exposing it as a socially and politically-driven system of ideas. In its original sense, an ideology is the result of this distilling of the allegedly sacred into its purely social and political components.[1] In the eighteenth century, the politics of religion could quickly turn into the religion of politics, as was most apparent in the desacralization of monarchy in the period of the French Revolution. Most tellingly for our understanding of Pope's intellectual character, this development had been foreshadowed in England when a limited parliamentary Hanoverian monarchy had pulled the teeth from Stuart attempts at developing politically efficacious notions of divine right monarchy. The collapse of Jacobitism as a serious political challenge to the limited monarchy of Hanoverian England, a process enacted in the course of Pope's lifetime, was analogous to what would follow in the France of the late 1780s and early 1790s, during which time the concept of ideology was developed as the sacred space of monarchy gave way to the secular public space of republicanism.

Here I shall focus on the cultural politics of Pope's writings, to indicate how central his problematic relationship with religion is in understanding the ideology at work here. Pope was born a Catholic, but was strongly influenced by his friend Henry St John, Viscount Bolingbroke, whose posthumously published writings reveal him to have been a freethinking deist. Bolingbroke's critical perspectives on the nature and purpose of religion had a profound impact on Pope's thinking, and this led in turn to a good deal of philosophical reflection on natural religion in his poetry; his Catholicism gradually shaded into an almost classical freedom of thought on religious matters. Pope had originally known and admired Bolingbroke from the latter's years as a Tory minister, and he remained loyal to him when Bolingbroke was forced into exile by the new Whig regime as a result of his contacts with the exiled Stuart dynasty. On his subsequent return to England, Bolingbroke set up as a leading light of the "Patriot" opposition to Walpole, and Pope remained loyal to his idol's cause. Deism and "Patriotism" succeeded Catholicism and Jacobitism in guaranteeing opposition status to Pope and his writings, a position from which he was briefly saved towards the very end of his life through his subsequent association with William Warburton, a Whig cleric who subsequently shaped Pope's posthumous reputation. I shall explore these ideological dimensions in Pope's experience as they were reflected in his writings. Jacobitism and deism were dangerous elements in any man's thinking, and Pope shadowed his thinking with a free play of satire as a means of sanitizing such potentially compromising reflections. As will become apparent as we proceed, shadowing and doubling were to become important elements in Pope's writing.

The crucial issue here is what Pope's writings meant in the age in which they were written.[2] This requires a historicized reading of literary texts, in this instance chiefly *An Essay on Man* and *The Dunciad*, rather than a politicized reading of that history and those texts. Thus my purpose here differs from some approaches to Pope.[3] The primary elements in any reading of Pope and "ideology" are constituted by politics and religion, but more specifically by the peculiar relationship between the two that held sway in early- and mid-eighteenth century England. In politics this is particularly marked for Pope by the politics of opposition, whether voiced through the language of "Patriotism" or the counter-ideology of Jacobitism; in religion, the competing claims of Catholicism and deism can be seen as providing directly analogous theaters of ideas for Pope, appeal to either of which – let alone both – likewise involved a form of intellectual opposition to the then prevailing orthodoxies. As Laura Brown rightly observes regarding his unique place in a world of Whig panegyric, there was always an "implicit ambivalence in Pope's imperialist poems."[4] Indeed, there is an implicit ambivalence in much that Pope has to say about a broad range of political and religious issues.

## Outsiders and opposition

Pope was very profoundly a poet of opposition, and the depths of that opposition are only gradually becoming apparent. Far from being the laureate of Augustan England, Pope was a firm witness to the perceived shortcomings of the Whig alliance between Church and State. As a professed Catholic and at least an emotional Jacobite (to use Douglas Brooks-Davies's felicitous phrase),[5] Pope was very much an outsider in Whig-Anglican - still more so in Whig-Dissenting – England. Had his health allowed him to travel, Pope might have found himself more at home in the sometimes religiously skeptical, if professedly Catholic, Jacobite circles exiled in France and Rome. His outsider status in England necessarily made him something of an intellectual cosmopolitan, even if his satirical barbs might now occasionally look somewhat provincial, but it was often precisely what he correctly identified as the provincialism of his targets that he was especially keen to penetrate through satire.

Satire can, of course, often be a means of putting critics off the scent of one's own values. Two lines of The Dunciad (II, 367–8) can be read in exactly this way:

> Toland and Tindal, prompt at Priests to jeer,
> Yet silent bow'd to Christ's No kingdom here.
>
> (TE, v, pp. 144–5)

These lines berate two of the most prominent deists of the early 1700s, and do so by associating them with the Low Church bishop, Benjamin Hoadly (although Warburton sought to limit the collateral damage done to an Anglican dignitary in his exculpatory footnote). Why did Pope do this (remembering that at least one critic has found an echo of Toland in two lines in An Essay on Man)?[6] Catholic deism had made Pope extraneous to the established rhythm of the government of his age in a manner directly contrary to the notoriety experienced by his older contemporary, Matthew Tindal (1657–1733). This is a useful perspective in understanding Pope, since Tindal's religious journey was directly comparable with his own; Tindal's career also firmly embodies precisely those elements which the word "ideology" was designed to explain and, indeed, expose. The son of a clergyman, Tindal became a Roman Catholic during the reign of James II, adjudging this an astute thing to do (as, had things turned out differently, it might well have been). He worked for James's interest during the Monmouth Rebellion, but seems to have been talked out of Catholicism in conversations in London coffee houses, quickly becoming an enthusiastic proponent of the "Glorious Revolution" instead. In the wake of Williamite success, he reverted to the

Church of England, but quickly turned anti-clerical, and his freethinking – and bad morals – ultimately gained him the disapprobation of the Oxford Jacobite Thomas Hearne, who called Tindal a "Libertine," "that notorious Atheist," "that Rascal," denouncing him as a promoter of "vile, republican Rascals." In a poem entitled *The Apparition* (1710), Abel Evans, an Oxford ally of Pope, similarly decried Tindal, describing him as a dangerously immoral force:

> In vice and Error from his *Cradle* Nurs'd:
> He studies hard, and takes extreme Delight,
> In Whores, or Heresies to spend the Night.[7]

Tindal would consummate his freethinking by producing a dialog, *Christianity as Old as the Creation* (1731), in which he emptied out the dogmas of revealed religion into the territory of natural religion, a religion of reason which predated later, priest-driven, factional, warring religions. This tract gained him yet more notoriety, and legions of clerics assembled to denounce it in print.

Tindal's journey from Catholicism to deism can be read alongside Pope's altogether more circumspect equivalent of that journey, and Tindal's public reception demonstrates yet again why Pope may have wished to remain under the oddly protective cloak of his parents' religion, especially as he had moved into the ambit of the freethinking Bolingbroke precisely when Tindal was producing his anti-clerical writings. By denouncing revealed religion as the tool of priestcraft, Tindal the ex-Catholic convert was preparing the way for ideology as a secular critique of religion. Pope's journey from faith into poetic explorations of freethinking philosophy can be read in a similar way, but *An Essay on Man* was in an entirely different category from Tindal's exercises in haute vulgarisation, and Tindal's blunt and vulgar Whiggism was completely unlike Pope's principled politics of cultural opposition.

Pope, a cradle Catholic in a political culture predicated on anti-Catholicism, necessarily enjoyed an anomalous experience of religion and politics in early- and mid-eighteenth century England. It was this perspective that enabled him to distance himself from much of the religious debate that engulfed a lifetime deeply marked and shadowed by the politics of religion, both at its beginning (he was born in the year of the Glorious Revolution), and at its close (he died one year before the final abortive Jacobite rising of 1745). As noted earlier, the year of Pope's birth also witnessed James II's ill-starred attempts to re-Catholicize his kingdoms which were quickly to end in ignominious failure, and England and Ireland were instead to be immediately subjected to a Dutch invasion in which their former isolationism was abandoned in favour of commitment to more than a century of Franco-British warfare. Likewise, Pope died immediately prior to the savage suppression of Jacobitism in the wake of the 1745 rebellion, when "Butcher" Cumberland put down the forces of Charles Edward Stuart at Culloden in a way his subsequent nickname sufficiently conveys to posterity. The Whiggish history that grew up around these events would have provokingly challenged Pope's directly contrary experience of his times. Distanced as he was from the established faith, he experienced its part in the politics of England in much the way that French revolutionaries had observed the Catholicism into which he had been born. Just as with religion, so with political life generally: Pope the Catholic outsider forever shadowed Pope the "Tory" insider.

There is a politics of internal exile in Pope's poetry, nowhere more apparent than in poetry about actual exile, as is vividly apparent in one of the most affecting of his poems, the epitaph for the Jacobite Francis Atterbury. Pope removed the epitaph at the last minute from publication in 1735; the lines would remain unpublished until 1751. There is something particularly telling in a poem written by an English Catholic deist to commemorate an English clergyman, a former dean of Christ Church, Oxford and bishop of Rochester, who had died in political exile in France.[8] The poem ends in an appeal to religiously-inflected patriotism voiced by Atterbury himself:

> O more than Fortune, Friends, or Country lost!
> Is there on earth one Care, one Wish beside?
> Yes – *Save my Country, Heav'n,*
> — He said, and dy'd.
> (*TE*, VI, p. 344).

The England in which Atterbury had believed was decidedly not the England of the Hanoverian settlement. Pope, who was similarly disinclined to accept the rule of Walpole and his allies, was thus united with men of directly contrary religious persuasions in an emotional commitment to Jacobitism.[9] The politics of opposition often unite strange bedfellows, and this was especially true of the cultural politics of the English opposition in the first half of the eighteenth century. Jacobitism was more than mere political factionalism, and its meaning is best appreciated when it is considered as an ideology. Jacobitism led to internal as well as external exile, and the doubling nature of inner and outer exile accurately reflected the always shadowy character of political opposition.

## Warburton and Bolingbroke

Doubling was a necessary fact of both Pope's public and his private life; indeed, the fact that it is not always easy to distinguish the two is further testimony to the centrality of doubling in his experience. His forays into the world of ideology were likewise usually undertaken in the potent company of a guide completely at home in the established culture of an England in which Pope was a born stranger, albeit a licensed one. In politics, he observed the public world alongside the religiously suspect Viscount Bolingbroke; in religion, he sought respectability alongside the more outlandishly circumspect William Warburton. That Warburton was a staunch critic of Bolingbroke, and that in secret Pope was a steady critic of Warburton, further demonstrates how this process of doubling and shadowing always informed the poet's life, career, and, in no insignificant way, his writings. Pope's negotiation of this complex texture of associations reveals him as a born survivor, a supreme player of the ideological games that underpinned the political and religious life of England between the accession of Mary II and William III and the final Jacobite rout of 1745. Why Pope, whose religious character remains obscure, chose to remain a Roman Catholic when conversion to Anglicanism would have procured him an altogether easier and more comfortable political identity, is a genuine enigma. To seek to explain this on the grounds of *pietas* (namely that he did not wish to offend the religious sensibilities of his parents), is surely inadequate as an explanation in a career that was not above exploiting circumstance. In attempting to resolve the enigma, however, it has to be admitted that continuing to be a Catholic enabled Pope to play a unique role as a protected outsider looking in at a religious and political world direct entry to which was otherwise denied him.

Pope's use of satire in disguising his own commitments, a technique not unknown to Erasmians and freethinkers, makes it occasionally difficult to disentangle the religious elements of his thinking.[10] Despite the apparent transparency of his writings, there is often an oblique quality to his work, particularly when it alludes to ideology (itself a shadowy concept since it always wants to be seen as the natural state of affairs). Pope was especially shadowy when it came to discussion of religion, and it is plainly the case that he was greatly relieved when Warburton came along to provide his poetry with a respectable Anglican veneer, which would culminate in the notes he supplied to a posthumous edition of the poems in 1751. Pope was dependent on Bolingbroke early on in helping to shape his mind, and later he grew dependent on Warburton for apparently clarifying it before a potentially suspicious public. Shadowing and doubling played a part in these friendships.

The attempt to understand Pope's politics by referring to those of his mentor and protector Bolingbroke is a complicated enterprise in that the latter's own politics have elicited different interpretations. One view is that Bolingbroke's famous tract *The Idea of a Patriot King* appeals to a politics of nostalgia, deploying the age of Elizabeth as a golden age to which England might return if only the right politics, those of patriotism, are engaged actively by its monarch and his people. (It is worth reflecting, in the light of this, on Pope's own use of golden age motifs in his poetry). The second approach is to read Bolingbroke as an adept at the politics of opposition, who draws on the politics of patriotism to secure support for his own participation in a supposedly popular programme in politics that would guarantee him an entrepreneurial role in a newly virtuous kingdom. We also appreciate how the literary culture of opposition to Walpole flourished within the patriotic rhetoric of disinterested virtue, and also how it subsequently came apart when the necessarily compromising practice of politics claimed some of its former adherents. This Bolingbrokean-inflected patriotism would allow Pope to glory in the double-edged interpretation of Augustanism, namely that one could celebrate its achievements whilst denigrating its corruptions. Again, the language of patriotism allows for a doubling of precisely the kind that Pope relished, as he could both lambast the corruptions of his contemporaries and appeal to a patriotic counter to it. Ambivalence is the key to such an enterprise. Finally, we have learnt to trace the contours of Pope's complicated political filiations with Bolingbroke's philosophy of virtuous patriotism, and to identify the congruence between the apparent deism of *An Essay on Man* and the freethinking materialism later uncovered when Bolingbroke's philosophical writings were published after the deaths of both men.[11] Pope had to manage a balancing act between Erasmian Catholicism and deism, the more difficult because deism was particularly critical of Catholicism.

Deism presented itself as a religion of gentlemen, boosted in this self-confidence by the polite philosophy adumbrated by Lord Shaftesbury in his *Characteristicks* (1714), an influential series of reflections and dialogs on morality and esthetics. For its Christian opponents, such as William Law, whose mysticism was later to lead to accusations of enthusiasm being leveled against him, deism was *too* gentlemanly, lacking the commitment to charity necessary in any form of proper Christian commitment. The battle for the hearts and minds of the aristocracy and the gentry dominated much anti-deist writing in the first half of the eighteenth century, and John Wesley would take the battle into the realms of the poor and the unchurched. As is the case with many belief systems, deism has often been defined by its enemies, and a sometimes specious coherence has resulted. The many varieties of deism and freethinking have finally, however, begun to be examined in all their distinctiveness by historians of religion and philosophy, but it still remains possible to offer a plausible root meaning of deism: a belief in the congruity between nature appreciated as the work of a beneficent creator with a universal morality, again construed as evidence of divine beneficence in a supremely moral universe. Constructive deism instanced the fitness of the world of things, especially of nature, and also of moral agreement between human beings, as twin evidences of the existence of the God of nature.

Something of its naturalistic thinking is evident in Pope's "The Universal Prayer," with its suitable dedication: "Deo Opt. Max" (a form of benediction to God often used in memorial inscriptions). Even this dedicatory abbreviation is eloquent, instancing Pope's perceived unwillingness to spell out the nature of God directly, taking refuge instead in Latinate cultural practices that can be interpreted as an appeal both to the authority of classical Roman religion and to the necessarily private language of English Roman Catholicism. Shadowing and doubling are again apparent in his work in this dedication. Two of the poem's stanzas are closer to the classical world of universal religion than they are to the claims for universality made by the Roman Catholic Church. Stanza 9, at lines 33–6, evokes exactly the natural and moralistic apologetic common amongst deists both at the time the poem was first written, between 1703 and 1715, and when it was published, in 1738 (near the close of a religiously significant decade, as this was the most strongly anti-clerical period of the entire eighteenth century, during which Walpole's parliament was seeking to undo many of the privileges of the Church of England).[12]

> Save me alike from foolish Pride,
>   Or impious Discontent,
> At ought thy Wisdom has deny'd,
>   Or ought thy Goodness lent.

It was the duty of man to accept his fallibility when judging the world of creation, and he was always to infer that, were he not fallible, he would appreciate the fitness of things yet more strongly then he already did.

The identification of the Creator with nature is close to, but not identical with, the pantheism of the philosopher Benedict Spinoza. It is made explicit in the closing stanza, at lines 49–52:

> To Thee, whose Temple is all Space,
>   Whose Altar, Earth, Sea, Skies;
> One Chorus let all Being raise!
>   All Nature's Incence raise!
>     (*TE*, VI, p. 148)

These were words that would not have gained anything like universal acceptance amongst Pope's Christian contemporaries, as a Swiss critic of his *Essay on Man*, Jean-Pierre de Crousaz, was quick to point out.[13] Indeed, the very notion of a *universal* prayer would have troubled many, with its problematic assumption that all humankind could accept the religion whose devotions the prayer represented. Universality was a Christian desire rather than an apologetic reality; only deists believed that something that Shaftesbury called "the religion of all reasonable men" actually existed universally, let alone that its sentiments could be expressed, whether in prose or in poetry.

We can detect in *An Essay on Man* much of the style of thinking associated with Bolingbroke and the higher deism (that is, the more theologically sophisticated versions of freethinking, as opposed to the popular brands of anti-Christian propaganda). Along with this goes a lack of reference to revelation, and a reading of humanity's place in creation very different from the one found in Milton's sacred mythology. One view is that the poem "assembles, in a sort of brilliant disarray, the fractured systems of the age."[14] There may well be designed inconsistency at work in the *Essay*, there may also be a lack of philosophical finesse; what is *not* here is anything like a consistently or straightforwardly Christian exercise in apologetics. That the *Essay* was read by Crousaz as a deistic poem indicates that such an interpretation was at least available to Pope's readers; it took the intervention of Warburton to save the appearances in order for a Christian interpretation safely to emerge.

Warburton was not the safest of apologists for Pope to have acquired. His was a decidedly eccentric position in eighteenth-century religious life. Warburton was best known for defending Christianity in his *Divine Legation of Moses Demonstrated* (1738–41) largely by appeal to an enormous paradox, namely that Moses knew of a future life precisely because he had hidden the revealed doctrine from his followers, a paradox which Warburton elaborated at great length in a welter of curious digressions covering, *inter alia*, the very origins of written language, and confidently culminating in controversial interpretations of classical literature. The whole exercise, interestingly, was described as having been undertaken "on the principles of a religious Deist," precisely in order to undo deism on its own terms. He had also defended, in his *Alliance of Church and State*, exactly that prohibitive Whig establishment which deliberately discommoded Catholics such as Pope. In many ways, it was an act of desperation that drew Pope, through their mutual friend William Murray, later Lord Mansfield, into this unexpected and unpredictable apologetic alliance with Warburton. Was Pope aware that accusations of deism would continue to be made were he to go unchampioned by such a bullying critic (like Pope an autodidact)? If so, Catholic deism was plainly in need of rescue by a variety of decidedly unconventional Anglicanism that flattered itself as being orthodox.

It was against both Catholicism and deism that Warburton thunderously declaimed in his reply to Crousaz, *A Critical and Philosophical Commentary on Mr. Pope's Essay on Man* (1742):

> There are two sorts of Writers, I mean the BIGOT and the FREE-THINKER, that every honest Man in his Heart esteems no better than the Pests of Society; as they are manifestly the Bane of *Literature*, and *Religion*. And whoever effectively endeavours to serve either of These, is sure immediately to offend both of Those. For, the Advancement of Literature is as favourable to true Piety, as it is fatal to *Superstition*; and the Advancement of Religion is as propitious to real Knowledge as discrediting to *vain Science*.

*An Essay on Man* contains both Catholic theology and elements of freethinking: by saving it for orthodoxy, Warburton was probably knowingly undoing its philosophical core. Warburton's reading imposed coherence where A. D. Nuttall rightly sees rich disarray. Warburton insisted that its precision and forcefulness were "rarely to be met with, even in the most formal Treatises of Philosophy." His overly systematic reading of the poem turned it into just such a formal treatise, fatally undoing its vitality in the process. All the more paradoxical, then, that it ends with an appeal to Christian charity voiced in the unmistakable accents of anti-Catholic Anglicanism. Appealing to the example of the primitive Christians, was Warburton also alluding to what he had done for a Catholic poet?

> For their Faith being yet chaste from the Prostitutions of the Schools, and their Hierarchy yet uncorrupted by the Gifts of Constantine, the Church knew neither *Bigotry* nor *Ambition*, the two fatal Sources of uncharitable Zeal.[15]

Small wonder, then, that Pope, invoking the anti-clerical language of deism, should have referred to Warburton, in a letter to his co-religionist Martha Blount in August 1743, as "a sneaking Parson". Intriguingly, as late as April 1742, Pope had written to Warburton hoping to effect an introduction between his two friends: "I should not be sorry you saw so great a genius, tho he & you were never to meet again" (*Corr*, IV, pp. 464, 394). Warburton was laying a personal ghost as well as repelling a deistic threat when he censured some of Bolingbroke's posthumously produced philosophical writings in his combative *View of Lord Bolingbroke's Philosophy* (1754–5).

## Religion and rationalism

With or without Warburton's tutelage, Pope was not afraid to take on the cultural heroes of Whig England, and this was especially true of his treatment of Newton and his theological lieutenant, Samuel Clarke. There is a trace of condescension in Pope's famous remark regarding the angels in the second epistle of *An Essay on Man* (31–4):

Superior Beings, when of late they saw
A mortal Man unfold all Nature's law,
Admir'd such wisdom in an earthly shape,
And shew'd a NEWTON as we shew an Ape.
(*TE*, III.i, pp. 59–60)

Newton has widely been seen in recent writing as a star in the firmament of Whig cultural politics in the first half of the eighteenth century; to slight him, however incidentally, was a politically significant act. To slight Samuel Clarke was both a religious and a political act, and Clarke was subject to much abuse in the fourth book of *The Dunciad*, produced when Pope had cautiously moved from Bolingbroke to Warburton as his guide to the public world.

In Book IV Pope famously registers a denunciation of religious rationalism, in particular the errors attendant on dictating a priori grounds for belief in God (lines 469–86):

All-seeing in thy mists, we want no guide,
Mother of Arrogance, and Source of Pride!
We nobly take the high Priori Road,
And reason downward, till we doubt of God:
Make Nature still incroach upon his plan;
And shove him off as far as e'er we can:
Thrust some Mechanic Cause into his place;
Or bind in Matter, or diffuse in Space.
Or, at one bound o'er-leaping all his laws,
Make God Man's Image, Man the final Cause,
Find Virtue local, all Relation scorn,
See all in *Self*, and but for self be born:
Of nought so certain as our *Reason* still,
Of nought so doubtful as of *Soul* and *Will*.
Oh hide the God still more! And make us see
Such as Lucretius drew, a God like Thee:
Wrapt up in Self, a God without a Thought,
Regardless of our merit or default.
(*TE*, v, pp. 386–9)

This tirade is spoken by "a gloomy Clerk" (*Dunciad*, IV, 459), read in the notes to the Twickenham edition of Pope as a sly allusion to Samuel Clarke, who had argued in just such a manner for the existence of God in his Boyle lectures for 1704. Pope's challenge to a priori theology, elaborated in his notes by Warburton, is typical of that undertaken by a number of Anglican divines in the 1730s; it is also congruent with Bolingbroke's freethinking critique of Clarke's theological method.[16] The whole poem ends with a catalog of the dire consequences of such religious rationalism, one line of which presciently alludes to the very definition of "ideology" that was to be developed some fifty years later (*Dunciad*, IV, 646): "And *Metaphysic* calls for aid on *Sense*!"

Pope and Warburton had taken on the religious rationalism which they thought gave too much ground to critics of Christianity, but Pope did so by taking on a touchstone of Whiggish Anglicanism when berating Clarke and his immediate influence. Warburton had to work hard in his notes to contain this consequence, referring to "some better Reasoners" as falling into error alongside the readily decried Hobbes, Spinoza, and Descartes. The Whig religious establishment had been an object of rebuke to Pope, be it as a Catholic or as a deist, but supremely as a poet. As Abigail Williams has demonstrated in an important revaluation of his poetic contemporaries, Pope had also had to take on a Whig literary culture whose considerable contemporary strength has tended to be severely underestimated in modern, canonically-weighted estimates of the period.[17]

Skepticism and subversion are endemic to verse, and the expression of the fluidity of things, albeit sometimes held up by the excremental detritus of a society of dunces, is peculiarly well suited to the articulations provided by the free flow of Pope's verse. Pope knew that things fall apart, even the classics of verse, which he sought to refashion, and hence fleetingly preserve, through translation; it was, however, the power of verse that enabled things to be at least tolerable, and for their shortcomings to be analyzed in a medium infinitely greater than any single attempt to alleviate those things. Pope's own verses were formed in such a mood of civilized and civilizing, if quietly angry, skepticism.

Ideology could be reflected in verse, and simultaneously undercut by it. Something of this process can be seen in autobiographical lines from the *Imitations of Horace* in which Catholic dissent is subtly transformed into poetic freedom as Pope inherits his father's righteous sense of wrong (*Ep* II.ii, 52–67):

> Bred up at home, full early I begun
> To read in Greek, the Wrath of Peleus's Son.
> Besides, my Father taught me from a Lad,
> The better Art to know the good from bad:
> (And little sure imported to remove,
> To hunt for Truth in *Maudlin's* learned Grove.)
> But knottier Points we knew not half so well,
> Depriv'd us soon of our Paternal Cell;
> And certain Laws, by Suff'rers thought unjust,
> Deny'd all Posts of Profit or of Trust:
> Hopes after Hopes of pious Papists fail'd,

While mighty WILLIAM's thundring Arm prevail'd.
For Right Hereditary tax'd and fin'd,
He stuck to Poverty with Peace of Mind;
And me, the Muses help'd to undergo it;
Convict a Papist He, and I a Poet.

(*TE*, IV, pp. 167–9)

These lines have been read as a hereditary commitment to Jacobitism; they also reflect a secularizing drift from religion to poetry as a means of ideological resistance.

In conclusion, we may heed an important literary caveat that may strengthen my reading of Pope's contrast between "Papist" and "Poet", a contrast that can also be read as yet another shadowing and doubling in his writings. Here it is well to bear in mind Helen Vendler's warnings about the relationship between poetry and what she insists is inadequately equated with "ideas" by non-literary critics of poetry. Vendler offers a firmly estheticized reading of the *Essay on Man* and other works by Pope, insisting that "In poems, thinking is made visible not only to instruct but also to delight; it must enter somehow into the imaginative and linguistic fusion engaged in by the poem." Again, as she argues:

> "Ideas" undergo peculiar stresses when they are incorporated into powerful poetry, and poets writing what we call "philosophical" verse are well aware of the degree to which, once domesticated in the topologically flexible mode of poetry, "ideas" are bent into peculiar shapes.

Having offered a variety of persuasive close readings, Vendler concludes that Pope's linguistic play leads to his admission of "man's need for the guides of system but at the same time his demonstration of the instability and insufficiency of all systems, whether literary, legal, or ethical." Addressing the claim that Pope's is a "subversive" form of "thinking," she opens the door to the sort of historical and philosophical reading against which she signally warns as being reductive.[18] This essay has recognized that poetry is much more powerful than the interpretative nets thrown over it by contextualists, but it has also attempted to show that something valuable can always be gained by contextualizing classic texts – provided, of course, that other readings, not least esthetically alert ones, can be made alongside them.

## NOTES

I am grateful to Mishtooni Bose, Noël Sugimura, and Abigail Williams for their helpful comments and criticisms.

1. Mark Goldie, "Ideology," in *Political Innovation and Conceptual Change*, ed. Terence Ball (Cambridge: Cambridge University Press, 1989). For important

recent studies, including ideological readings of Pope, see Further Reading, pp. 237–246 below.

2. For some sense of the distinction implied here, see Quentin Skinner, "The Idea of a Cultural Lexicon" in *Visions of Politics*, 3 vols. (Cambridge: Cambridge University Press, 2002), vol. I, pp. 158–74.

3. For example Laura Brown's comment: "In the poles of Pope's poetic corpus . . . we can catch a glimpse of the process that constitutes ideology: the movement of history, the determining dynamic in which we can locate the meaning of Pope's poetry and make it our own." See Brown's *Alexander Pope* (Oxford: Blackwell, 1985), p. 158.

4. Brown, *Alexander Pope*, p. 27.

5. Douglas Brooks-Davies, *Pope's* Dunciad *and the Queen of Night: A Study in Emotional Jacobitism* (Manchester: Manchester University Press, 1985).

6. See the notes in the Twickenham edition to *An Essay on Man*, I, 267–8 (*TE*, III.i, p. 47); and to *The Dunciad*, II, 367–8 (*TE*, V, pp. 144–5).

7. B. W. Young, "Matthew Tindal," in *Oxford Dictionary of National Biography*, 60 vols. (Oxford: Oxford University Press, 2004), vol. LIV, pp. 814–17; C. E. Doble, D. W. Rannie and H. E. Salter, eds., *Remarks and Collections of Thomas Hearne*, 11 vols. (Oxford: Printed for the Oxford Historical Society at the Clarendon Press, 1885–1921), vol. II, pp. 332, 72; vol. III, pp. 255, 381, 439; Abel Evans, *The Apparition* (London, 1710), p. 6.

8. On Atterbury, see G. V. Bennett, *The Tory Crisis in Church and State: The Career of Francis Atterbury, Bishop of Rochester* (Oxford: Clarendon, 1975); Eveline Cruickshanks and Howard Erskine-Hill, *The Atterbury Plot* (Basingstoke: Palgrave, 2004).

9. Howard Erskine-Hill, "Alexander Pope: The Political Poet in his Time," *Eighteenth-Century Studies* 15 (1981–82): pp. 123–48; Howard Erskine-Hill, *The Poetry of Opposition and Revolution: Dryden to Wordsworth* (Oxford: Clarendon, 1996), pp. 57–109; Pat Rogers, *Pope and the Destiny of the Stuarts* (Oxford: Oxford University Press, 2005), pp. 114–25.

10. Fred Parker, *Scepticism and Literature: An Essay on Pope, Hume, Sterne, and Johnson* (Oxford: Oxford University Press, 2003), pp. 136, 130. Pope played with the theme in the *Imitations of Horace*, Sat, II.i, 63–8: "My Head and Heart thus flowing thro' my Quill, | Verse-man or Prose-man, term me which you will, | Papist or Protestant, or both between, | Like good *Erasmus* in an honest Mean, | In Moderation placing all my Glory, | While Tories call me Whig, and Whigs a Tory" (*TE*, IV, p. 11).

11. Isaac Kramnick, *Bolingbroke and his Circle: The Politics of Nostalgia in the Age of Walpole* (Cambridge, MA: Harvard University Press, 1968); Quentin Skinner, "Augustan Party Politics and Renaissance Constitutional Thought," in *Visions of Politics*, 3 vols. (Cambridge: Cambridge University Press, 2002), III, pp. 344–67; Christine Gerrard, *The Patriot Opposition to Walpole: Poetry, Politics, and National Myth 1725–1742* (Oxford: Clarendon, 1994); Brean S. Hammond, *Pope and Bolingbroke: A Study of Friendship and Influence* (Columbia: University of Missouri Press, 1984), pp. 113–4.

12. John Walsh and Stephen Taylor, "Introduction: the Church and Anglicanism in the 'long' Eighteenth Century," in *The Church of England, c.1689–c.1833: From*

*Toleration to Tractarianism*, eds. John Walsh, Stephen Taylor and Colin Haydon (Cambridge: Cambridge University Press, 1993), pp. 1–64 (p. 21).

13. Warburton wrote an exculpatory note, designed to free Pope from the charge made by Crousaz that Pope's work was coloured by fatalism and "*Naturalism*" (cited in *TE*, VI, p. 150).

14. A. D. Nuttall, *Pope's "Essay on Man"* (London: Allen & Unwin, 1984), pp. 191–2.

15. William Warburton, *A Critical and Philosophical Commentary on Mr. Pope's Essay on Man* (London, 1742), pp. xvii, 181, 184.

16. For a fuller statement, see B. W. Young, "'See *Mystery* to *Mathematics* fly!': Pope's *Dunciad* and the Critique of Religious Rationalism," *Eighteenth-Century Studies* 27 (1993): pp. 435–48.

17. Abigail Williams, *Poetry and the Creation of a Whig Literary Culture 1681–1714* (Oxford: Oxford University Press, 2005).

18. Helen Vendler, *Poets Thinking: Pope, Whitman, Dickinson, Yeats* (Cambridge, MA: Harvard University Press, 2004), pp. 9, 12, 35, 36.

# 10

HOWARD ERSKINE-HILL

# Pope and the poetry of opposition

## Introduction

It is long since Pope has been seen as reclining in the bosom of a complacent eighteenth-century establishment. In the middle and later decades of the last century a particular focus was directed on to the Pope of 1729–43 as a poet of political opposition. Pope's target was here seen as the long premiership of Sir Robert Walpole and the generally unenlightened attitudes of King George I and King George II. Then, towards the end of the last century, a sharper focus was directed on to the less overtly political implications of some of Pope's earlier works, notably *Windsor-Forest* and *The Rape of the Lock*, with the result that a concern with, probably a sympathy with, Jacobite attitudes was detected. (Jacobites were those who held that the exiled royal line of the Stuarts, rather than the incumbent line of the Hanoverians, were the true kings of Britain.) One consequence of this later work was to suggest an ideological substructure for Pope's more salient poetry of political opposition in the period 1729–43.

We have abundant discussion of the earlier phase in Pope's career. Whilst it is wrong to impute direct involvement in the Jacobite movement by association, it cannot be without significance that so many of the poet's closest friends among the Catholic gentry and nobility had extensive links to the leaders of the Rising in 1715/16, and several members of their families took an active part in the rebellion. More complex issues arise in the case of the Atterbury Plot, a decade later, and in the later phase when Pope became associated with the Patriot opposition to Robert Walpole in the 1730s. The Atterbury affair (1722–3) saw Walpole and his henchmen uncover a Jacobite conspiracy to invade the country and instal the Pretender, James Edward Stuart, on the throne. It was led by Francis Atterbury (1662–1732), Bishop of Rochester and leader of the High Church party. He also enjoyed a close friendship with Pope, who, as we shall see, was summoned to give evidence at the bishop's trial in the House of Lords. This episode brought the poet's

134

beliefs and alliances more directly into collision with political actualities than any previous event. In what follows I shall be primarily concerned with these later stages in Pope's political life. The main discussion will center on his relations with Walpole, and will reconsider the role of a comparatively neglected figure, the lawyer William Fortescue, who was, for a long time, close to the prime minister. These relationships hold a particular importance for some of Pope's *Imitations of Horace*.

There is now probably a consensus regarding Pope as a poet of political opposition, and in fact the first such poet in English literature, but this consensus remains somewhat blurred at the edges, as different eighteenth-century circumstances emerge into view. Is Pope's attack, when he attacks, cultural rather than political? Is it political as well as cultural, and, if so, is it that of a "loyal opposition" to two uninspiring Hanoverian Kings, or an early part of a long collective trajectory of political thought which would lead away from monarchy altogether towards what many present-day citizens of the USA, and of other states, might think of as an enlightened republicanism?[1] The temptations of a retrospective interpretation which seems to ratify the fortunate present ("Whig History") may, on the other hand, be set aside in favour of a true historicist view which attempts to interpret Pope in terms of the political alternatives apparent in Pope's own time. In particular, if we are to think about political alternatives, we need to remember that in the second decade of the eighteenth century the Whigs themselves were divided into two factions: the Stanhope-Sunderland faction in office, and the Walpole-Townshend faction out of office. Taking a longer view, the salient political alternative to men of Pope's generation was the Jacobite option: a restoration of the exiled Stuart dynasty.

To come to a minor but significant episode in Pope's life, James Craggs the younger (1686–1721), who succeeded Joseph Addison as Secretary of State, offered Pope in 1718 a pension of £300 a year, confidentially, from the secret-service money in his hands (*Anecdotes*, I, pp. 99–100). Both Craggs and Addison were Whigs, but Craggs was a personal friend while Addison had been a known enemy (see *Anecdotes*, I, pp. 66–72.). Pope nevertheless refused the offer, though in polite and grateful terms. Pope needed money at this time. His refusal may have been political – perhaps he would have accepted a subvention from a Tory minister under Queen Anne – or it may have been an assertion of moral independence.

Needing money is one thing, but political danger is another. The general debates sketched in above form a significant background to an important episode in Pope's life and literary biography which has perhaps received insufficient attention, even from Maynard Mack's magisterial biography. I am referring to that strange development, after the trial and expulsion of

Bishop Atterbury in 1723 for Jacobite conspiracy, when Pope, contrary, one would have thought, to every expectation, appeared to have become on social terms with Walpole. I shall argue here that this strange *rapprochement* was probably brought about by Pope's friend William Fortescue, a trusted assistant of Walpole, and a figure in Pope's biography of acknowledged importance but very little explored. Although Fortescue left no records of the negotiation, Pope's letters to him clearly suggest that it was he who instigated the *rapprochement* of Walpole with Pope.

## The Atterbury affair and its aftermath

In 1723 Francis Atterbury was expelled from England following a Bill of Pains and Penalties brought against him by the House of Commons and the House of Lords for Jacobite conspiracy (a condemnation won, it has been suggested, on evidence forged at the behest of Walpole). Pope now stood in considerable danger, derived from several sources.

First, his edition of *The Works of John Sheffield Duke of Buckingham* (1723), which contained, as Pope was well aware, some satirical reflections on the revolution of 1688 and the expulsion of the Stuart, James II, was called in during the Atterbury Plot crisis and expurgated.[2] Only later did the expurgated material creep back into the public realm. Then, in the Atterbury Plot, Pope's kinsfolk, the Rackett family of Hallgrove, near Bagshot, were discovered to have been guilty of "Blacking" (which earlier meant smuggling or stealing deer but, now that the Blacks had been recruited into the Atterbury Plot, also referred to treasonable conspiracy). Third, Pope was not only known as an intimate friend of the condemned Atterbury but had actually given evidence on his behalf at his trial in the House of Lords, although he may have in terror, or in a deliberate bad show, bungled his evidence. Then the Atterbury Plot itself, far from a little blip in the story of the survival of the new Whig establishment, was a very severe international move against the Hanoverian dynasty and its Whig administrations; three attempts were made to exploit disastrous British circumstances and anti-Hanoverian opinion in the period 1721–3. Only the death of the Earl of Sunderland, First Minister in the latest Whig administration, who had been dealing underhand with some of the Jacobite Tories, had prompted the French government to reveal what they knew of the Plot, thus giving Walpole, back in the government after a period out of office, the opportunity to make his career. There was a final point of danger. Walpole wished to intimidate Catholic Jacobites abroad by punitive taxation of Catholic landowners at home, even if the latter had had nothing whatsoever to do with the Plot. This he bluntly admitted at a meeting with some Catholic noblemen and gentlemen who appealed against his new measures.[3] Pope was not a landowner, but he was certainly now a famous poet, known to be a Catholic, and had been attacked as a Jacobite. He too, surely, might have been used in Walpole's campaign of intimidation.

William Fortescue was in an ideal position to reverse any such strategy. It is uncertain when Fortescue first began to assist Walpole in political and family affairs. The first documentary evidence of his being "Secretary to the Right Honble. The Chancellor of the Excheq.ʳ" is dated 27 June 1724. The first evidence of his involvement in Walpole family matters in Devon appears to be of 1722.[4] Pope seems to have known Fortescue (through his friend John Gay) around 1713 (*Corr*, I, p. 195). It is in letters from Pope to Fortescue that we learn of Pope's growing acquaintance with Walpole. One is reduced to hypothesis as to the bargain Fortescue may have brokered at this point, 1723, since no written evidence of it seems to survive. Pope had written to Atterbury that he himself, perhaps, must expect to follow the Bishop into exile (*Corr*, II, p. 167). Fortescue probably wanted to make Pope's position in England safe and permanent. This will have involved trying to save Pope from himself, and from his wide range of disaffected acquaintance. This might be done if Pope and Walpole could be induced to get socially acquainted with one another. What would Walpole gain from such a bargain? (Here one may suspect something of a personal favour granted by Walpole to Fortescue.) However, the bad treatment of a famous poet might well have been represented rather as an opportunity for Jacobite propaganda than a means of intimidating Jacobite Englishmen abroad. This hypothesis is quite well borne out by social and literary evidence to be presented here, but it does remain hypothesis, not proof. Still, so surprising a turn of events demands some explanation.

The epistolary record opens with Pope's letter to Fortescue of 10 May 1725 (*Corr*, II, p. 294). Pope writes:

> I intended to tell you first, how kind Sir R. Walpole has been to me, for you must know he *did* the thing, with more dispatch, than I could use in *acknowledging* or *telling* the News of it. Pray thank him for obliging you, (that is me) so readily: and do it in strong terms, for I was awkward in it, when I first mentioned it to him. He may think me a worse Man than I am, tho' he thinks me a better Poet perhaps: and he may know that I am much more his Servant, than those who would flatter him in their Verses.

Pope adds that he will adhere to his rule to wait until a statesman is out of power before he will say what he thinks of him (in this case that the statesman has been kind and prompt). These are warm terms, even though one plainly detects awkwardness and a residual assertion of moral independence. Walpole must not be allowed to think that he has bought anything, nor that

Pope expects any further favor. What this favor was does depend upon the date of the letter, but George Sherburn's hypothesis that it was Walpole's treasury order for £200 to support the new *Odyssey* translation, signed in April 1725, is convincing. On 23 September 1725, Pope tells Fortescue that Walpole has visited him "spirited thither by Lord Peterborrow . . ." while at Twickenham the great man expressed his support for Mrs. Howard in her land disputes with Vernon, Pope's own landlord (*Corr*, II, p. 323).

On 17 February 1726 Pope writes in a letter to Fortescue with a new tone:

> I told you I din'd 'tother day at Sir Robert Walpole's. A thing has happen'd since which gives me uneasiness, from the indiscretion of one who dined there at the same time; one of the most innocent words that ever I dropped in my life, has been reported out of that conversation, which might reasonably seem *odd*, if ever it comes to Sir R.'s ears. I will tell it you the next time we meet; as I would him if I had seen him since . . . We live in unlucky times, when half one's friends are enemies to the other . . . and consequently care not that any equal moderate man should have more friends than they themselves have.
>
> (*Corr*, II, pp. 368–9)

Walpole could, of course, be terrifying. He would go about Parliament hinting to suspect MPs that he had evidence, or almost enough evidence, of their treason. If Pope had seemed to utter a disaffected word at the great man's own table, that would have been an offense indeed. Pope for the moment clung to the character of an "equal moderate man," which one suspects would have been welcome to Fortescue, and which would be the seed of several poetic affirmations of moderation in Pope's poetry of the 1730s.

Perhaps *rapprochement* was in the air. In April of 1726 Swift revisited England with the manuscript of *Gulliver's Travels* in his luggage. Pope writes to Fortescue that "Lord Peterborrow and Lord Harcourt propose to carry him to Sir R. Walpole" (*Corr*, II, p. 373). Apparently Walpole had already entertained Swift to dinner at Chelsea, but Peterborough secured for Swift a subsequent interview. This Swift used to press the claims of Ireland. Walpole gave him an hour, talked largely of Ireland, but in a manner so "alien" to the assumptions of Swift that the Dean concluded that all his representations were in vain.[5] Stories like these, if in circulation, may attest to a general idea that at this time a *rapprochement* between Walpole and the more militant Scriblerians was a possibility.

In a letter of 5 August 1727 from Pope to Fortescue relations between them seem to have somewhat relaxed: "I returned but 2 days since, but in my Return waited on Sir R. W. and told him, it was you that made me so troublesome at his Sunday-Tables, and disturbing to his Sabbath-days of Rest" (*Corr*, II, p. 441). Pope goes on, in the same paragraph, to mention quite easily "Mr Gulliver's Cousin" and John Gay. Late in 1728 Pope is intending to go to another of Walpole's Sunday dinners (*Corr*, II, p. 530). On 7 June 1730 Pope reports to Fortescue that he has recently been at Sir Robert's but that, apparently seeing Walpole and Fortescue together, "thought men of business should be left to each other" and so did not obtrude. He has accepted an invitation from Walpole "Next Sunday . . . where I therefore desire you would dine." Sherburn comments that Pope may well have wanted "Fortescue as a shield" in view of Swift's recent "Libel on Dr. Delany," which praised Pope as an opposition figure, and about which Pope had complained to Fortescue on 20 February 1730 (*Corr*, III, p. 91). Swift's poem, for which he had but just apologized ("whimsical . . . never intended for the publick"), had been published in London on 9 February and must have made Pope's new Fortescuvian role as "an equal moderate man" almost impossible to play. But, by this time, not without apparently two more remarkable favors to Pope, the *rapprochement* between poet and premier was coming to an end.

## Mending fences

This *rapprochement* was probably at its strongest in 1728–9. In 1728 Pope made his bid to help secure for his old friend and mentor Father Southcott, OSB, the Abbey of St. André at Villeneuve-les-Avignon. This episode does not figure in Pope's correspondence but in the anecdotes preserved by Joseph Spence (*Anecdotes*, II, p. 615). As a result the simple tale that Pope originally told Spence that the priest who had originally saved Pope's life when he was a boy was rewarded, twenty years later, by a beautiful French abbey secured for him by Walpole, begins to look a more complex and very much more interesting affair. In the first place, Southcott was deliberately seeking appointment to this Benedictine abbey. He proposed that he should serve as an absentee (not uncommon) and that all the abbot's income should be devoted not to himself but to funding Alexander Michael Ramsay, the Chevalier Ramsay, the brilliant Jacobite Scot now living in France, whom Southcott had recommended as the tutor to the infant Charles Edward, the Jacobite Prince of Wales.[6] What had Walpole to do with all this? He did not have the Abbey of St. André in his gift. England was, however, in renewed alliance with France, and Walpole might have effectively protested to Cardinal Fleury and the French government if they had allowed the appointment of Southcott to go through. For Southcott was not only a well-known and passionate Jacobite, but it was he above all who had organized what eventuated as the formal protest of the French government against Walpole's punitive taxation of peaceable English Catholics.[7] Pope's move was not to ask Walpole to secure the abbey for Southcott, which obviously the minister could not have done, but rather to ask him not to protest in the event of Southcott being elected. What Pope precisely did was to write a letter to Walpole by Fortescue (*Anecdotes*, I, p. 31).

William Fortescue, then, was continuing in his office of attempting to bind Pope and Walpole together. In this case it was far from a matter of a subscription to Pope's *Odyssey* translation, or invitations to Walpole's Sunday dinners. This was an international affair, and, not only that, but one which involved two active British Jacobites abroad, Southcott and Ramsay. If Walpole wished to grant Pope a favour, this was a very considerable one, and one that will have run against the statesman's strongest prejudices. Pope must have initiated the idea, as Spence recounts, and it is notable that it involved no material advantage to Pope himself. The proposal presupposes a remarkable degree of confidence in Pope that, even with the good offices of Fortescue, such a matter could be raised without throwing Walpole into a fury. What could Fortescue have said in its favour? Perhaps that Walpole had checked the Jacobite threat, at least for the time being, that Atterbury in exile had had no success, that Ramsay had been eased out of his tutorship of Charles Edward and could now be accounted a mere intellectual. By the same token Southcott's ambition to influence indirectly the Jacobite Prince of Wales had been checked too, though not by Walpole. Things seemed to have quietened down. Perhaps "the great man" could afford to grant a favor?

But why would he wish to do so? And, apart from general goodwill to Pope, what would Fortescue's motives be on this particular occasion? Perhaps the most obvious hypothesis is the most convincing. In 1720 Pope's friend Robert Digby had written to him, not without some irony, to congratulate him on "the return of the Golden-age" of which one positive sign was "when I find you frequently with a First-minister" – this was James Craggs the younger (*Corr*, II, p. 51). He alluded to the celebrated Augustan age when political power and the highest arts seemed to have grown freely together: Virgil and Horace under the *princeps* Augustus. Pope had, as a poet who remained a Catholic, struggled up into fame under those laws "by Suffrers thought unjust," as Pope would later put it in one of his Horatian epistles (*TE*, IV, p. 169), and with his *Iliad* translation really seemed the great English poet of the age. Fortescue will have remembered the not entirely straightforward convergence of the Virgil and Horace with Augustus (Horace had fought for Brutus and Cassius at Philippi) but is likely to have thought that there were the greatest precedents for reconciliation. Walpole, less likely to have been seized with classical parallels, would have seen the utility of this one. As Tone Sundt Urstad has shown, Walpole had plenty of his own poets to take his side (not just Edward Young),[8] but to "turn"

Pope, writer of the great modern *Iliad* translation and admirer of Walpole's archenemy, Atterbury, that would be a coup indeed.

## William Fortescue

Whatever the motives, Fortescue must have been in favour of Walpole granting Pope's request in the Southcott affair. It would be good to know more about Fortescue than the bare facts recited above, but it seems that he decided discreetly to destroy the records of his multifarious political, legal, and social activities. He made an exception of a substantial amount of correspondence with Pope (some of which has already been quoted above). From Pope's letters we know that Fortescue was attempting to unravel the financial affairs of the poet's half-sister, Magdalen Rackett, whose family fortune had collapsed as a result of the Atterbury Plot. Her husband, Charles Rackett, and her son Michael, seem to have fled abroad after the discovery of the plot, leaving their affairs in confusion.

Fortescue came of an old Devon landed family and inherited an estate in the north of the county. He was first educated along with John Gay at the little Grammar School in Barnstaple. On the early death of his wife Fortescue resolved upon a public career in law (he never remarried), but his enjoyment of the company of men of letters, particularly (no doubt through Gay) the Scriblerian group, is evident before his Devonian provenance and remote kinship with Walpole's daughter-in-law, Margaret Rolle, drew him into the business circles of Robert Walpole.[9] Quite early Fortescue wrote a literary piece in praise of Pope, while Gay in "Mr. Pope's Welcome from Greece" includes Fortescue among the crowds of friends who, according to the myth of his genial poem, throng the sides of the Thames to celebrate the new *Iliad* translation.[10] Before this Pope and Fortescue collaborated in *Stradling versus Stiles*, one of the funniest satires on law in the eighteenth century, and a delight to read (*Prose*, II, pp. 131–42). Two portraits of Fortescue were painted. The first, by Pope's friend Jervas, was on the occasion in 1730 when Fortescue was appointed Attorney General to Prince Frederick, as the document in his hand begins to proclaim. Though he looks a heavy and important figure a slight smile seems to lurk around his lips, as well it might since it was Jervas who had earlier written of *ridens Fortescuvius*, "laughing Fortescue" (*Corr*, I, pp. 340–1). The later portrait by Thomas Hudson is impressively serious, with challenge, knowledge, and sadness in the face, a good picture of an intelligent and experienced judge.

What was Fortescue's true attitude to Walpole? It was not, I think, that of a timeserver, though he was probably capable of being that. It seems to have been one of admiration and gratitude. A few letters to Walpole from

Fortescue are preserved in Walpole's papers. On 23 August 1734 he wrote a circumstantial letter concerning the possible appointment of the Town Clerk of Newport, Isle of Wight, to the "Sine Cure" of "Master Gunner of Carisbroke Castle." Fortescue has gone through the motions of supporting the Town Clerk's appointment, but thinks he "will Do his majesty more service in the Burrough as a Burgess, than in the Castle as a Gunner." He thus excuses himself for the steps he has taken and rounds off this routine piece of business in a not wholly routine way: "yet you'l Easily I dare say, Sᵣ. believe that in this as Every thing Else my whole dependance is on you."¹¹ Fortescue has been a balanced diplomat in a small affair. Nevertheless his clear advice and complete submission to Walpole are plainly expressed.

On a later occasion, around August 1739, Fortescue begs a place as surveyor for Mr. Scobell, but will not press it if Walpole would rather give it to the nephew of Mr. Scrope. "I would not desire the best Place you could give, either for my self or my Friend, at the Expence of Giving you the least uneasiness." This application failed. A year later, Fortescue again puts Walpole in mind of "poor mr Scobel" who now seeks the post of "collector of Plymouth".¹² Fortescue must have written countless such letters, or on countless occasions spoken to Walpole in this way (including, no doubt, Pope's application on behalf of Father Southcott). His method was to make a case, but then to submit entirely to the great man, who must not be made to feel under pressure. Kindness, perseverance, practicality, and understanding of Walpole, seem to mark his efforts.

Fortescue was one of the two MPs for Newport, Isle of Wight, from 1727–36, in the government interest. The Isle of Wight Record Office shows in what esteem he was held in Newport (high among the burgesses, less high perhaps among the populace). When he gave a political dinner in Newport he sent the bill to Walpole. He was King's Counsel in 1730, Baron of the Exchequer (judge of the Exchequer court) in 1736, Justice of the Common Pleas in 1738, Master of the Rolls and Privy Councillor in 1741.¹³

## The Dunciad and the 1730s

The story of Pope's *rapprochement* with Walpole now passes back into literary history. We come to that extraordinary moment when Walpole appears to have presented Pope's *Dunciad Variorum* to George II. On 17 June 1728 Pope had written to the Earl of Oxford that, like Oxford himself, "the Highest & most Powerful Person in this Kingdom" had commanded a "Key to *The Dunciad*" (*Corr*, II, p. 502). This must of course refer to the unextended 1728 version of the poem. Oxford was involved in the distribution of *The*

*Dunciad Variorum* and, sometime in March 1729, Pope wrote to him to hold in the copies until the two men should next meet. On 13 March he writes to Oxford: "You are now at full liberty to publish all my faults & Enormities; The King & Queen had the book yesterday by the hands of Sir R. W." (*Corr*, III, pp. 25–6). From this it would seem that copies were held back until the royal presentation had been made, on 12 April. The next we hear is a letter to Swift from Dr Arbuthnot, dated 19 March 1729, which avers that "The King upon perusal of the last edition of his Dunciad, Declared he [Pope] was a very honest Man." Later, in 1732, Richard Savage, who was close to Pope at this time, wrote of Walpole's presentation of the 1729 *Dunciad* to the King and Queen "(who had before been pleased to read it)."[14]

This is all the evidence we have for a very unlikely event which may, nevertheless, have actually occurred. We note that the sources are all Pope or those close to him. There is a further question about Arbuthnot's report to Swift. An "honest man" was a cant term for a Jacobite, in circles supporting the Pretender. Since Arbuthnot's family background was Jacobite, and his brother was a Jacobite banker in Paris, he will have known this. Was Arbuthnot sharing with Swift a fictionalizing jest, or, did George II, who may not have been much interested in poetry, but generally knew his enemies, hereby indicate that he knew very well the anti-Hanoverian trend of the work? There are other, related, problems about the story of the presentation of *The Dunciad*. Can George and Caroline really have been sufficiently interested in Pope's anonymous 1728 poem, filled with asterisks, initials and blanks though it was, to have commanded a Key and agreed to a presentation? (Possibly Caroline might have been curious if anyone had drawn her attention to Pope's not very handsome-looking 1728 production.) Another problem is that the anti-Hanoverian innuendo of the 1728 poem was early picked up by Pope's enemies, including the sharp-eyed Matthew Concanen, one of Walpole's coterie of pro-government poets.[15] Fortescue, if he saw the poem, would have immediately recognized its trend, and surely would have warned his friend Walpole to keep clear of it. There are three possibilities here, none of which seems at all probable. Firstly, Walpole did indeed present the poem at court, knowing the nature of the work, and George II did indeed say what was reported (whatever that meant). Secondly, Pope duped Walpole into the presentation, and the great man was perhaps unwarned by Fortescue, Concanen or anyone else. Thirdly – and this is no doubt a long shot – the whole report of the poem's presentation is a fictional practical joke on the part of Pope and his close friends, Arbuthnot, Oxford, and Savage.[16]

Whatever really happened, damage limitation must soon have been the order of the day. The project for reconciliation had overshot its mark. Some of the original poem's innuendo could be brushed off onto the dunces fighting back against Pope. Some spaces and gaps had in the 1729 *Dunciad* been filled in not too offensively. "Still Dunce the Second reigns like Dunce the First?" remained (*Dunciad*, I, 6). As the dust settled, the episode, whether factual or fictional, may seem to have cast a certain air of comedy over the Pope/Fortescue/Walpole triangle of relations. This was an atmosphere different from anything Pope felt at the end of the Atterbury trial. It can be seen in that very daring and various imitation of Horace's *Satire* II.i which Pope had originally considered addressing to Fortescue, and which includes within it Fortescue's own point of view. Pope's letter to Fortescue about the poem was written three days after its publication.

> I wish you a judge, that you may sleep and be quiet; *ut in otia tuta recedas* [so that you may retire into a secure leisure], but *otium dignitate* [leisure with dignity]: have you seen my imitation of Horace? I fancy it will make you smile; but though, when I first begun it, I thought of you; before I came to end it I consider'd it might be too ludicrous, to a man of your situation and grave acquaintance, to make you Trebatius, who was yet one of the most considerable lawyers of his time, and a particular friend of a poet. In both which circumstances I rejoice that you resemble him, but am chiefly pleased that you do it in the latter. (*Corr*, III, p. 351)

The lawyer, Trebatius, was the other participant in the dialogue which was Horace's poem; rather than name Fortescue, Pope in his title refers to "his Learned Council." The secret was well kept. Apparently it was made public only in Warburton's 1751 edition of Pope's *Works*. Pope's letter, to those who know his correspondence well, has unmistakable notes of further damage limitation: "make you smile" may be translated as "I fear you may be annoyed." This, perhaps, because Pope's poem in fact draws laughing Fortescue out of the circles of social humour into the public realm of printed political satire. In the poem, after Pope has ridiculed bad poets who have praised George II as heroic, the "Learned Council" joins the game, and ridicules those who praise the sweet Hanoverian princesses (29–32). "Learned Council" is also drawn into the admission that, since "Laws are explain'd by Men," the approval of Sir Robert would probably be enough to get the poet off a libel charge. This, the conclusion of the satire, is at once funny and frightening. What if Sir Robert does not approve?

This scary edge replicates a balance that Pope maintains throughout his poem within its apparent spontaneity and conversational case. On the one hand the poet likes the idea of being an "equal moderate man." As he puts it here:

My Head and Heart thus flowing thro' my Quill,
Verse-man or Prose-man, term me which you will,
Papist or Protestant, or both between
Like Good *Erasmus* in an honest Mean,
In Moderation placing all my Glory,
While Tories call me Whig, and Whigs a Tory.

(63–8)

On the other hand he sharpens up Horace in his propensity for moral attack: "P. What? Arm'd for Virtue when I point the Pen" (105). This poem has been very much discussed in recent decades, and we have learnt, I believe, that it is in no way a systematically philosophical poem. The two leading attitudes of Pope, the moderate poet and the attacking poet (even if the attacked are the greatest in the land) are psychologically reconciled in the idea of freedom to speak and write. *The Dunciad* and this poem are the public marks, in the second case very plain, that Pope has now shaken off those constraints entailed upon him by his reconciliation with Walpole. It remains a more personal poem than has yet been appreciated, supplying a reprise of those discussions which must have taken place between Fortescue and Pope when the surprising reconciliation was afoot. Even the phrase "Council learned in the Law" – no doubt, then, a general term in law courts – occurs in exactly this form in a Devon deed of 1727 to which Fortescue and Walpole set their signatures.[17]

The darker tones Pope had introduced into his letters to Fortescue about Walpole, recalled in the imitation of *Satire* ii.i, are present also in Pope's epistle *To Augustus* (1737). He was, as he had said to Fortescue, "much more his [Walpole's] servant than those who would flatter him in their Verses" (*Corr*, ii, p. 294). He had, he said, suffered "uneasiness" at having "innocent words" misconstrued and reported (*Corr*, ii, pp. 368–9). Gratitude for favors granted by Walpole had not made him feel easy or secure. In the end the intention of open defiance made him feel more easy, and this led directly to those lines in Pope's *To Augustus* for which there is no full equivalent in Horace:

And when I flatter let my dirty leaves . . .
Befringe the rails of Bedlam and Sohoe.

(415–19; *TE*, iv, p. 231)

In other respects *To Augustus* is a suave poem. It does not display a sustained passage of defiance as does *Sat*, ii.i, though it shows flashes of anger as in the lines which defend Swift (221–5). Generally its polite idiom sharpens its ironies, and this in turn creates a kind of diplomatic comedy which a reader such as Fortescue may well have relished. Pope follows Horace in not lambasting the literary achievement of the present age. He has good things to say, albeit selective and carefully moderated, about a famous poet such as Addison, by whom he personally knew he had been in his literary career betrayed, and about a timeserving poet such as Colley Cibber, whom he now detested. Thus:

> (excuse some Courtly stains)
> No whiter page than Addison's remains.
>
> (215–16)

Note, not only the slightly explicit exception in line 215, but the terms of the second line: "No whiter *page* [my italics]": Pope will not talk of Addison's *deeds*. The poem is also full of glancing reflections on Cibber, who never appears as Poet Laureate of the great George Augustus, but, in diplomatic mode, finds something it can fairly commend: the people's voice is surely wrong if it denies praise to Cibber's *The Careless Husband* (1704), lines 89–92. This comically diplomatic tone slightly reduces the growing gap between Walpole and his friends on the one hand and Pope on the other.

Pope's allusions to Walpole by name continue, as is well-known, from *Satire* II.i into the two 1738 Dialogues which in due course would form the Epilogue to the Satires. Taken out of context they seem half-friendly and it must be remembered that they are found in poems which constitute perhaps the most powerful attack either Swift or Pope ever mounted against Hanoverian Britain with Walpole at the helm. "Go see Sir ROBERT," suggests Pope's *adversarius* in the first dialogue:

> *P.* See Sir ROBERT – hum –
> And never laugh – for all my life to come?
> Seen him I have, but in his happier hour
> Of Social Pleasure, ill-exchang'd for Pow'r;
> Seen him uncumber'd with the Venal tribe,
> Smile without Art, and win without a Bribe.
>
> (27–32; *TE*, IV, pp. 299–300)

The last two lines were, according to the Pope-Warburton footnote of 1751, originally in the poem, dropped from the first edition, then subsequently replaced (*TE*, IV, p. 300). Friendliness of this sort is quite damaging. Line 28 may allude to the danger and discomfort of a man of Pope's sort being within Walpole's circle.

A qualified portrait also occurs in *Dialogue* II. Among Pope's examples of lying, found there, is the allegation that "Sir ROBERT's mighty dull, | Has never made a Friend in private life, | And was, besides, a Tyrant to his Wife"

(133–5; *TE*, IV, pp. 320–1). Walpole's worst enemies knew he was intelligent, had a gift for personal friendship, and had tolerated his wife's infidelities. Pope, writing to Fortescue, on 31 July of this year, seeming to signal that he still held Walpole in high esteem ("I went home, and drank Sir Robert's health with T. Gordon") says also of Walpole in this letter: "You see I have made him a second compliment in print in my second Dialogue, and he ought to take it for no small one, since in it I couple him with Lord Bol –" (*Corr*, IV, p. 114). The paralleling of Walpole's with Bolingbroke's name here is not only provocative but of some significance, since it was Bolingbroke's enterprise, soon after his return to England after the Atterbury Plot, to attempt to build up an united opposition to Walpole: Jacobite Tory, Hanoverian Tory, anti-Walpole Whig. This campaign, conducted chiefly through *The Craftsman* journal, and associated pamphlets and poems, supplied a shield for Pope's poetry of opposition. In the light of Bolingbroke's campaign, Pope's poetry of opposition may have been unwelcome, or seemed ungrateful, but it could not on the face of it be branded as treason. The concept of "treason" was on the one hand wide and terrifying, on the other hand (to those eager to charge political enemies with treason) frustratingly narrow. The great recent example of charges of treason was in the Atterbury Plot, the shadow of which was cast upon the next two decades.[18]

Near the end of the 1743 *Dunciad*, as the last great yawn of Dulness begins to open, which is to bring an end, in Pope's myth, to both England and creation, Pope writes:

> Wide, and more wide, it spread o'er all the realm;
> Ev'n Palinurus nodded at the Helm.
>
> (613–14; *TE*, V, p. 405)

Palinurus, the helmsman of Aeneas, in Virgil's *Aeneid*, was never, in numerous crises, the subject of reproof in that poem, though finally (deceived by the god Somnus) falling asleep at the helm and falling into the sea. Edward Young had praised Walpole as Palinurus, "pilot of the realm" in the seventh satire of his *Universal Passion* (1728). By 1743 Walpole had finally fallen from power. The tone of Pope's allusion is in no way vituperative or triumphant, fuelling charges of ingratitude. Certainly, Pope blamed Walpole and the Hanoverian establishment for the triumph of Dulness and darkness, so Walpole is in a sense victim of himself. On the other hand, the parallel is complimentary, and suffused with Virgilian sadness. Walpole had at least faithfully served the de facto King he recognized. Even Fortescue will have thought this was no ungracious epitaph by Pope on Walpole's two decades of political power, while the ironically barbed "compliments" of the *Epilogue to the Satires* carry, so far as "private life" was concerned, a residual positive charge which was the legacy of Fortescue's attempt to bring Pope and Walpole together.

Pope, then, clearly continued to write "oppositional" poetry throughout the 1730s. But his complicated dealings with Walpole, as mediated by Fortescue, suggest some of the difficulties involved in defining him narrowly as a member of the opposition, *tout court*. As with other aspects of his personality, his political identity was made up of many different components, all registered in the subtle modulations of his poetry.

## NOTES

1. For important modern studies of Pope's political views and the contemporary background, see Further Reading, pp. 237–246 below.

2. John Sheffield, *The Works of John Sheffield Duke of Buckingham*, ed. Alexander Pope 2 vols. (London: Printed by John Barber, 1723). The offending pieces were "Some Account of the Revolution" (vol. II, pp. 70–102) and "A Feast of the Gods" (vol. II, pp. 159–71). In 1722 Pope had written to his Jacobite friend John Caryll that Buckingham's *Works* will contain "many things . . . you will be particularly glad to see in relation to some former reigns" (*Corr*, II, pp. 117).

3. Father Thomas Southcott to Cardinal Fleury, 28 September 1722 (Royal Archives: Stuart Papers [henceforth RASP], 63/128; 64/64). The Catholic Lord Stafford, Southcott's nephew, and other Catholics had a meeting with Walpole to protest at the threat of punitive taxation.

4. Cambridge University Library, Cholmondeley (Houghton) MSS. 57 (henceforth Ch. (H) MSS), Devon Record Office, Z 13/6/9.

5. Irvin Ehrenpreis, *Swift. The Man, His Works, and the Age*, 3 vols. (London: Methuen, 1962–83), vol. III, pp. 479–85. For another version of the meeting, see John Lyon, "Materials for a Life of Dr. Swift," annotations in John Hawksworth's *Life of Swift* (University of Pennsylvania MS., Codex 628).

6. RASP 72/1, 72/14, 72/72, 77/132.

7. RASP 64/64, 67/28, 69/36 (Southcott to James III, 20 September 1723, where he writes: "m$^r$ walpole is going on with his design to extirpate the roman catholicks out of the three kingdoms").

8. Tone Sundt Urstad, *Robert Walpole's Poets* (Newark: University of Delaware Press, 1999). Though Young praised Walpole, he can hardly be reckoned one of his regular supporters.

9. See, for example, Devon Record Office: 49/12/1/23 (19 June 1727), and North Devon Record Office: 2239B/ add 8/86 (3 November 1729).

10. *Life*, pp. 185–6; *John Gay, Poetry and Prose*, ed. Vinton A. Dearing and Charles E. Beckwith, 2 vols. (Oxford: Clarendon, 1974), vol. I, p. 259.

11. Cambridge University Library, Ch. (H) MSS. 2318.

12. Cambridge University Library, Ch. (H) MSS. 2916; Ch. (H) MSS. 2925.

13. Isle of Wight Record Office, Newport: Convocation Book (45 16 b), 1659–1760. On the matter of dinners, see Cambridge University Library, Ch. (H) MSS. 57.

14. Swift *Corr*, III, p. 326; Richard Savage, *A Collection of Pieces Publish'd on Occasion of the Dunciad* (1732), p. vi.

15. Bertrand A. Goldgar, *Walpole and the Wits* (Lincoln: University of Nebraska Press, 1976), pp. 77–8.
16. The fullest account of this strange episode is in Ian Jack, *The Poet and his Audience* (Cambridge: Cambridge University Press, 1984), pp. 42–5.
17. Devon Record Office, 49/12/1/23.
18. On this the most recent treatment is Eveline Cruickshanks and Howard Erskine-Hill, *The Atterbury Plot* (London: Palgrave, 2004). See particularly in this regard Chapters 6–9.

## 11

PAUL BAINES

# Crime and punishment

## Poetry and punishment in the early works

Punishment was more physical, and more visible, in Pope's day than it is in ours. The pillory was still in use at various locations around London, as were public whippings. Eight times a year those condemned to death were taken from Newgate Prison to Tyburn to be hanged: crowds lined the route and gathered for the show. Crime and punishment spawned their own literature, and Pope's lifetime coincided with an explosion in crime-related writing of all kinds. "Proceedings" at the Old Bailey were published regularly from the 1680s. Trials and punishments were widely reported in the newspapers; criminal biography (in both documentary and fictional forms) flourished. On the other side, as it were, there was considerable professional crossover between law and writing: many writers were educated at the Inns of Court, including such notable friends of Pope as Congreve, Rowe, and Warburton. Pope was friendly with several lawyers; one of them was celebrated in "Presentation Verses to Nathaniel Pigott," and another, William Murray, later the Earl of Mansfield, was the addressee of the *Sixth Epistle of the First Book of Horace Imitated*.

Owen Ruffhead, Pope's first official biographer and himself a barrister, declared that Pope intended his work as a "supplement to the public laws," and the metaphorical "lash" of satire was regularly invoked as his model. But Pope's attitude to crime and the law was actually much more complex than this. In an early letter to Henry Cromwell (1 November 1708 [*Corr*, I, pp. 51–2]), Pope jokingly compared his entry into print to a public execution, and likened Tonson's *Miscellanies* to the regular collections of malefactors' lives put out by the Ordinary (Chaplain) of Newgate. In the preface to his *Works* of 1717, he asks "that my youth may be made (as it never fails to be in Executions) a case of compassion" (*Prose*, I, p. 295). The early works themselves often show considerable tolerance towards transgressors, especially female sexual delinquents such as Sapho and the two women (May and the Wife of Bath) updated from Chaucer. Eloisa's motto is "Curse on all laws but those which love has made!" (74; *TE*, II, p. 325) and there is for her, and for the poem, always something sexy in the offence: "I view my crime, but kindle at the view" (185; *TE*, II, p. 335).

Pope can, moreover, position himself as a kind of superior magistrate, acting outside the limited ethics of the law: his "unfortunate lady" is a brave violator of oppressive laws, and indeed a virtuous suicide (then itself still a criminal act); the poet denounces "sudden vengeance" (under the disposition of "eternal justice") against her persecutors (35–7; *TE*, II, p. 365). *The Rape of the Lock* presents a sublimated form of sex crime that requires restitution; Pope's chilling couplet

> The hungry Judges soon the Sentence sign,
> And Wretches hang that Jury-men may Dine.
> (III. 21–2; *TE*, II, p. 170)

is sometimes taken as out of kilter with the palliative tone of the poem, but it reminds us not only that Pope was skeptical about the operations of the ordinary judicial system, but that this is a narrative with an offender and a victim who seeks redress. Jove's golden scales (V.71–2; *TE*, II, p. 206) are emblems not only of fate, but of justice.[1] Though Belinda wins the case, her lock is never restored, and Pope offers her compensation in the form of the poem itself.

The *Essay on Criticism* brings rules and writing together in a different way. Criticism (from κρίνω, to judge – or accuse) enacts a kind of social judgement. It is not only worse to judge badly than to write badly, it is *"more dangerous . . . to the public"* (*TE*, I, p. 237). The ideal critic is Longinus, "An ardent *Judge*, who Zealous in his *Trust*, | With *Warmth* gives Sentence, yet is always *Just*" (677–8; *TE*, I, p. 316). Because of contemporary respect for the "rules," these metaphors are capable of much extension. Pope's sympathy as a writer is (cautiously) with rule-breakers, and he advises writers as if he were their advocate:

> But tho' the *Ancients* thus their *Rules* invade,
> (As *Kings* dispense with *Laws* Themselves have made)
> *Moderns*, beware! Or if you must offend
> Against the *Precept*, ne'er transgress its *End*,
> Let it be *seldom*, and *compell'd by Need*,
> And have, at least, *Their Precedent* to plead.
> The *Critick* else proceeds without Remorse,
> Seizes your Fame, and puts his Laws in force.
> (161–8; *TE*, I, p. 259)

The "plea" of necessity, which Pope italicizes here, was a staple defense in court for criminal offenses, while the critic figures as a sort of implacable policeman. There are, however, particular offenses (blasphemy, obscenity), where the critic (now positioned as the addressee in place of the writer) should behave like an angry magistrate: "Discharge that Rage on more Provoking Crimes, | Nor fear a Dearth in these Flagitious Times" (528–9; *TE*, I, p. 297).

## *The Dunciad* as pillory

One obscene blasphemer was the rogue bookseller Edmund Curll, who in 1716 published a small anthology of poems variously ascribed to Pope, Gay and Lady Mary Wortley Montagu. Not only did Pope slip Curll an emetic by way of punishment, he wrote the results up in a pamphlet which shows how adeptly he could imbibe the tone of criminal literature: *A Full and True Account of a Horrid and Barbarous Revenge by Poison, on the Body of Mr. Edmund Curll, Bookseller* (1716) affects to depict Curll as the victim of Pope's crime, while actually glorying in an act of revenge, itself technically transgressive (*Prose*, I, pp. 257–66).

This amalgam of high juridical pomp and low vendetta underlies *The Dunciad*, a poem shaped in part by the war with Curl. Pope has the law on people, but only in his own way. He is quite explicit about the relationship between his satire and legal enforcement: *The Dunciad* is a vast pillory, one that lasts longer than an uncomfortable hour at Charing Cross. If "Law can pronounce judgment only on open Facts" then for secret offenses "there is no publick punishment left, but what a good writer inflicts" ("Letter to the Publisher," *TE*, v, p. 14). Explaining why mini-biographies of the persons of the poem are appended in the notes, Pope writes:

> If a word or two more are added upon the chief Offenders; 'tis only as a paper pinn'd upon the breast, to mark the Enormities for which they suffer'd; lest the Correction only should be remember'd, and the Crime forgotten.
>
> ("Advertisement"; *TE*, v, p. 9)

An appearance in the poem is the punitive moment (we speak of writers being "put in" the poem, as into the pillory): the explanatory note is the equivalent of the note of offences sometimes pinned to the body of the pilloried criminal. Hence the importance of using individual names in the poem – though these are often slightly mangled for further punitive effect. The crimes that Pope is punishing here consist, ostensibly, of slander against him and his friends, but the True Crime is the anonymity afforded by the popular press. Scriblerus explains:

they would forthwith publish slanders unpunish'd, the authors being anonymous; nay the immediate publishers thereof lay sculking under the wings of an Act of Parliament, assuredly intended for better purposes.

("Martinus Scriblerus of the Poem"; *TE*, v, p. 49)[2]

Having identified the Dunces as a group of malevolent writers operating on the fringes of legality, Pope dismisses the objection that they are too poor for satire: while poverty "might be pleaded as an excuse at the Old Baily for lesser crimes than defamation, for 'tis the case of almost all who are try'd there," it is the "just subject of satyre" when it is the "consequence of vice, prodigality, or neglect of one's lawful calling; for then it increases the publick burden, fills the streets and high-ways with Robbers, and the garrets with Clippers, Coiners, and Weekly Journalists" ("A Letter to the Publisher"; *TE*, v, p. 15). The deft alignment of journalists with the circulators of false coin (they simply make up the slanderous stuff that passes current) shows Pope keen to insinuate a criminal culture for these anonymous individuals to thrive in. His "evidence" consists of contributions from the Dunces themselves, in the form of competing "testimonies" or "witnesses," words which themselves suggest a juridical context (*TE*, v, pp. 23–47). As the poem evolved through attack and counter-attack, the Dunces themselves provided more evidence merely by contesting it.

Pope also wants to establish a criminal pattern to the literary capital. It is from the Grub Street "cave of Poverty and Poetry" that "hymning Tyburn's elegiac lay" emerges, Pope reminds us, noting the characteristic cultural economy: "It is an ancient English custom for the Malefactors to sing a Psalm at their Execution at *Tyburn*; and no less customary to print Elegies on their deaths, at the same time, or before" (I, 39 and n; *TE*, v, pp. 64–5). We are reminded that the hero Lewis Theobald trained as an attorney, an unforgiveable branch of the legal profession in view of Theobald's role in the dubious deathbed marriage of Pope's friend Wycherley and his subsequent role as Wycherley's literary executor (I, 190 and n; *TE*, v, p. 85). Remembering that certain crimes could be pardoned by "benefit of clergy," which had come to mean rote learning of the "necking verse" in order to prove literacy, Pope contends that the standard Grub Street production comes from "less reading than makes felons 'scape" (I, 235; *TE*, v, p. 90). Plagiarism, traditional short-cut of needy poets, is aligned with criminal theft (I, 46 and n; *TE*, v, p. 101). Bards are always on the run from bailiffs because debt landed one in jail (I, 49, II, 57; *TE*, v, pp. 66, 105).[3] Poets fear for their ears, because in theory ears could be cut off (in the pillory) for seditious libel (I, 46, II, 139, III, 212; *TE*, v, pp. 65, 117, 175). The Dunces proceed to the Thames via Bridewell prison, "As morning-pray'r and flagellation end" (II, 258; *TE*, v,

p. 133); Pope locates the mud-diving context by means of a trademark syllep-
sis (a characteristic linkage of two verbs with one subject), that sharply
catches the incongruous play-off between high penitence and low punishment in the state's reformatory regimen.

The pillory was designed to shame offenders and subject them to any kind
of abuse the public cared to shower them with (rotten eggs being the most
notorious); such bathetic physicality afforded many comic opportunities for
Pope to associate his Dunces not only with illegality, but with a filthy, car-
nivalesque violence. Having pilloried his villains, Pope was happy to throw
eggs, in the knowledge that muck sticks. The judicial system had, to help
matters, already prosecuted certain members of the literary profession and
book trade – in particular, Edmund Curll. In listing Curll's moral transgressions, Pope carefully reminds us that he "was taken notice of by the *State*,
the *Church*, and the *Law*, and received particular marks of distinction from
each" (II, 54n; *TE*, V, p. 104). Curll had not only been punished by the vigi-
lante actions of the Westminster scholars, and of Pope himself, but had been
twice reprimanded by the House of Lords for unauthorized publications.
Just a few months before *The Dunciad* appeared, he had been fined by the
court of King's Bench for two obscene publications, and sentenced to stand
in the pillory for publishing an anti-Hanoverian memoir. Dulness awards
him a "shaggy Tap'stry" depicting his own fate amidst those of several other
Dunces:

> Earless on high, stood un-abash'd Defoe,
> And Tutchin flagrant from the scourge, below.
> (II, 139–40; *TE*, V, pp. 117–18)

Defoe had stood in the pillory in 1703 for writing *The Shortest Way with
Dissenters* with insufficiently clear irony; Tutchin had been punished under
James II and died after being beaten up in the street in 1707. Curll celebrates
the violence of these encounters as a matter of pride: "what street, what lane,
but knows | Our purgings, pumpings, blanketings and blows?" (II, 145–6;
*TE*, V, p. 119); but Pope underscores the extent to which such rough justice
coincided with convictions for actual offences.

## "Libels and Satires!"

*The Dunciad* pillories only one non-literary criminal: John Ward, a corrupt
member of parliament who stood in the pillory for forgery in 1727. Pope had
assisted the Duchess of Buckinghamshire in her legal struggle with Ward,
a former agent of her husband's, by calling on the services of his friend,

Lord Harcourt. In the original issue of the poem, near the start of Book III Theobald views the "millions and millions" of unborn books, "As thick as eggs at *W–d* in Pillory" (III, 26; *TE*, v, p. 152). Another pilloried writer, Ned Ward, obligingly complained about this reference, stating that Pope had been bribed by the Duchess to stir up animosity against Ward while he was under the punishment, a barbarous stratagem defeated only by the personal merits of the criminal, which he claimed were sufficient to subdue the rabble. Thanks to the coincidence of surnames, Pope was enabled to install a smart link between degraded white-collar crime and Grub Street journalism:

> But it is evident this verse cou'd not be meant of him; it being notorious that no *Eggs* were thrown at that Gentleman: Perhaps therefore it might be intended of Mr. *Edward Ward* the Poet.                    (III, 26n; *TE*, v, p. 152).

The application of juridical satire to non-literary criminals was Pope's future direction. In the *Epistle to Bathurst* Pope established a set of criminal names to which he would repeatedly return. Wishing to prove that riches are no marker of goodness, Pope reminds us that they are:

> Giv'n to the Fool, the Mad, the Vain, the Evil,
> To Ward, to Waters, Chartres, and the Devil.
> (19–20; *TE*, III.ii, p. 83)

"Ward" is the John Ward of *The Dunciad*, and his dubious financial progress up to and beyond the pillory is acidly summarized in a footnote. "Waters" is Pope's perverted name for Peter Walter, estate manager and moneylender who gained a reputation (partly through Pope) for unscrupulous stewardship of landed estates. Pope claimed he was a "dextrous attorney . . . allowed to be a good, if not a safe, conveyancer," implying without actually stating that Walter sailed very close to the legal wind. The third figure, Francis Charteris, was a cashiered soldier who had amassed a fortune through gaming and moneylending. In 1730 he was convicted at the Old Bailey of raping a servant and sentenced to death, but was pardoned through interest at court. He had died in 1732 and Pope's note includes a mock-epitaph by Dr Arbuthnot celebrating his hideous career. Arbuthnot claims that "having daily deserved the GIBBET for what he *did*, | [he] Was at last condemn'd to it for what he *could* not *do*" (*TE*, III.ii, p. 86); the contention that Charteris was in fact impotent enacts a kind of primal castratory revenge under the sanction of an actual legal condemnation.

Later in the poem, Pope splices the economic and sexual crimes back together, asking whether riches can give "To Chartres, Vigour; Japhet, Nose and Ears?" (*Bathurst*, 88; *TE*, III.ii, p. 95). "Japhet" was Japhet Crook, convicted of forgery in 1731 and sentenced to lose his ears in the pillory and have his nose slit (he died in prison a year later). This bizarre ritual, relic of an already-superseded Elizabethan forgery statute, recommended itself to Pope's attention as an example both of extreme psychology (Crook would in a sense barter bits of his body for gold) and of salutary punishment (which Pope was happy to exacerbate in the poetry). Once again, the spell in the pillory is accompanied by a footnote detailing the offense. Pope adds others to the catalog: Denis Bond, a Director of the "Charitable Corporation for relief of the industrious poor," which collapsed in an embezzlement scandal in 1732 (102; *TE*, III.ii, p. 98), and Sir John Blunt, architect of the South Sea Bubble which ruined many investors in 1720 (135; *TE*, III.ii, p. 104).

All these men, with the exception of Walter, had already been punished by the legal system one way or another: prison, fines, pillory, expulsion from the House of Commons, bills of pains and penalties. But this is not to say that Pope was merely seconding the state line. As we have noted already, Pope evinced much hostility to the way law operated. His ideal economic figure, the charitable Man of Ross, embodies the humane virtues the villains lack in his application of wealth, and manages all disputes without recourse to the courts, rendering "vile Attornies, now an useless race" (274; *TE*, III.ii, p. 116). Law is often a form of contamination. Amongst the fictional examples, the spendthrift "Young Cotta" bankrupts himself in the service of the Hanoverians and is abandoned to his fate in debtor's prison: "His thankless Country leaves him to her Laws" (218; *TE*, III.ii, p. 111). Sir Balaam, another Whig businessman in the vein of Blunt and Ward, is led into treason by the gaming habits of his wife:

> The House impeach him; Coningsby harangues;
> The Court forsake him, and Sir Balaam hangs:
> Wife, son, and daughter, Satan, are thy own,
> His wealth, yet dearer, forfeit to the Crown:
> The Devil and the King divide the prize,
> And sad Sir Balaam curses God and dies.
> (397–402, *TE*, III.ii, pp. 124–5)

The law is followed to the letter, but the forces of law and order (at the top of which stand the Court and King) hardly come out of the process looking disinterested; the real moral justice here is Pope's, and it is characteristically sly. Pope had no time at all for the Coningsby who "harangues" in Balaam's trial: he was a virulent anti-Catholic and one of the managers of the impeachment of Pope's friend Harley in 1715. Pope is here revenging himself on ideal Whig types, indeed the whole Hanoverian edifice, using against itself a system of which, instinctively and politically, he disapproved.

Bond, Ward, Chartres and the rest remained as push-button figures throughout the 1730s (occasionally they acquired another partner, such as Eustace Budgell, the writer strongly suspected of forging a will in 1733).[4] Using convicts did not altogether allay the problem that one of the reasons for Pope's antipathy to the law was the way it could be used to serve political ends: as a Catholic he was by definition a kind of outlaw in his own country, and he had been called as a witness in the show-trial of the Jacobite leader Francis Atterbury in 1723. There was always the risk that satire would be deemed libelous under a hostile regime. This risk Pope addressed early on in his series, in the *First Satire of the Second Book of Horace, Imitated* (1733). For Horace's lawyer-interlocutor, the poet substituted William Fortescue, a lawyer and court insider who nonetheless maintained a friendship with Pope. He advised Pope on legal matters, including the war with Curll, which was increasingly played out under the more straightforward juridical auspices of the Court of Chancery. Shaking his head at the complaint that his satire is too bold towards criminals, "Scarce to wise *Peter* complaisant enough, | And something said of *Chartres* much too rough," Pope approaches "Council learned in the Law" for (free) advice (1–10; *TE*, IV, p. 5). It is a pose, naturally: Pope sets up a mock-trial between the innocent writer and the prudent lawyer that he is bound to win. Fortescue counsels Pope not to write, or to write only the safe side. But using the familiar examples, alongside others, Pope counters that he is ready for any revenge, inside or outside the law, and states that those "who 'scape the laws" will be always subject to his satirical challenge. He is a kind of Unmasked Avenger. Fortescue treats Pope's proposal as something like a defense speech in court, and has recourse to legal jargon:

> F. Your Plea is good. But still I say, beware!
> Laws are explain'd by Men – so have a care.
> It stands on record, that in *Richard*'s Times
> A Man was hang'd for very honest Rhymes.
> Consult the Statute: *quart.* I think it is,
> *Edwardi Sext.* or *prim. & quint. Eliz*:
> See *Libels, Satires* – here you have it – read.
> P. *Libels* and *Satires!* lawless Things indeed!
> But grave *Epistles*, bringing Vice to light,
> Such as a *King* might read, a *Bishop* write,
> Such as Sir *Robert* would approve –
>                    F. Indeed?
> The Case is alter'd – you may then proceed.
> In such a Cause the Plaintiff will be hiss'd,
> My Lords the Judges laugh, and you're dismissed.
>                    (143–57; *TE*, IV, pp. 19–21)

Fortescue cannot really think outside the law, or outside the law as it stands under Walpole; but Pope's position, while it superficially affects to obey the law of libel, actually appears to bamboozle the lawyer merely by mentioning Walpole's name. Poetry's rhetoric is superior to the law-speak it encompasses.

This defensive strand often accompanies the offensive stance of the satire, as if Pope was perennially acting as his own advocate, as well as his own judge and jury. Arbuthnot privately urged Pope to write more cautiously and less punitively in satire, but Pope demurred:

> General Satire in Times of General Vice has no force, & is no Punishment . . . tis only by hunting One or two from the Herd that any Examples can be made. If a man writ all his Life against the Collective Body of the Banditti, or against Lawyers, would it do the least Good, or lessen the Body? But if some are hung up, or pilloryed, it may prevent others. (*Corr*, III, p. 423)

(The sideways shift from "banditti" to "lawyers" perhaps indicates that Pope is keeping a comic tinge to his high-minded address.) While literary satire was supposed to reform people, Pope's view here is closer to one of the traditional principles of judicial punishment: deterrence.

These sentiments underlie the public stance of the *Epistle to Arbuthnot* (1735), though as with *The Dunciad* there is considerable private grievance. In his "Advertisement," Pope declared "This Paper is a Sort of Bill of Complaint," giving it the technical term for beginning an action in the court of Chancery. As in *The Dunciad*, the libels of others are countered by Popean autobiography: but non-writers are now arraigned as well. Arbuthnot counsels "No names – be calm – learn prudence of a friend" in the course of the poem, but Pope will not be silenced: it is the business of satire to tell unpalatable truths, and sometimes it is going to sound like punishment. "A Lash like mine no honest man shall dread" (303; *TE*, IV, p. 117); only the guilty need apply. The lash is wielded fairly lightly against the Dunces, who are back in force – at least, when they can get safely out of the Mint, a debtor's refuge from prosecution and thus, Pope implies, the natural home of (other) poets. Punishment is not the same in all cases. Addison may "give his little Senate laws" (209; *TE*, IV, p. 111) but he refuses the responsibilities that go with power: the lines demolishing him flamboyantly regret the necessity to exercise chastisement. The lines on the over-powerful patron Bufo, by contrast, enjoy the comic inflation they inflict (231–49; *TE*, IV, pp. 112–13). Others, like Hervey/Sporus, are almost too insubstantial for punishment: "Who breaks a Butterfly upon a Wheel?" questions Arbuthnot (308; *TE*, IV, p. 118), alluding to a method of execution used in France; but Pope elects to "flap" him at least, accepting the role of satiric executioner in the controlled violence of the "Sporus" lines, and embedding his response to the alleged excess of punishment in the punishment itself (309–33; *TE*, IV, pp. 118–20) After such variety, Arbuthnot's last question is easily answered: satire has a duty to punish in appropriate ways whatever the crime and whoever the criminal.

> "But why insult the Poor, affront the Great?"
> A Knave's a Knave, to me, in ev'ry State,
> Alike my scorn, if he succeed or fail,
> *Sporus* at Court, or *Japhet* in a Jayl,
> A hireling Scribler, or a hireling Peer,
> Knight of the Post corrupt, or of the Shire;
> If on a Pillory, or near a Throne,
> He gain his Prince's Ear, or lose his own.
>
> (360–7; *TE*, IV, p. 122)

The law is politically compromised; satire calls out crime wherever it lurks, and calls it crime whether or not it has been identified as such by the mechanisms of the state.

## The "edge of Law"

Despite the awesome dexterity of these lines, it was a troubled position, and one continually open to the challenge of Pope's enemies, who scorned such arrogation of power, especially in one effectively disenfranchised under anti-Catholic legislation. In 1738 Pope returned to self-defense in the two dialogs later known as the *Epilogue to the Satires*. In the first, Pope lists his favourite criminal targets and berates the world for admiring "Crimes that scape, or triumph o'er the Law" (168; *TE*, IV, p. 309). The second has the interlocutor warn Pope that Nicholas Paxton (treasury solicitor and Walpole's agent in identifying seditious publications) will find Pope's satire libelous. He advises that Pope stop using individual names, reaching once more for the criminal comparison:

> Yet none but you by Name the Guilty lash;
> Ev'n *Guthry* saves half *Newgate* by a Dash.
>
> (10–11; *TE*, IV, p. 313)

James Guthrie was Ordinary of Newgate, "who publishes the memoirs of the Malefactors," sometimes with names replaced by dashes. Pope offends a judicial prudence which would rule out all targets except convicts like the notorious thief-catcher and receiver of stolen goods Jonathan Wild:

> *Fr.* Yes, strike that *Wild*, I'll justify the blow.
> *P.* Strike? why the man was hang'd ten years ago:
> Who now that obsolete Example fears?
> Ev'n *Peter* trembles only for his Ears.
> <div align="right">(54–7; <i>TE</i>, iv, p. 315)</div>

Pope notes that Peter Walter had, "the year before this, narrowly escaped the Pillory for forgery: and got off with a severe rebuke only from the bench" – an allegation not corroborated, but a significant hardening of Pope's own punitive line, even as the villain appears about to escape.

At times Pope aligns his position as satiric enforcer with the traditional rights of communal punishment around the pillory:

> And must no Egg in *Japhet's* Face be thrown,
> Because the Deed he forg'd was not my own?
> <div align="right">(189–90; <i>TE</i>, iv, p. 324)</div>

But in the end – or what seems to be the end – Pope declaims from the highest possible moral ground, that of a precipice:

> Yes, the last Pen for Freedom let me draw,
> When Truth stands trembling on the edge of Law.
> <div align="right">(248–9; <i>TE</i>, iv, p. 327)</div>

On this brink he laid down the attempt to present poetry as the highest of all tribunals, citing the actual power of his opponents as a reason to desist. A further poem, the unfinished "1740," was written partly in code, apparently in fear of censorship. Yet the analogy between satire and punishment, which had offered Pope such imaginative richness and rhetorical power, was not quite done. In the final version of *The Dunciad*, Pope leaves Dulness holding court, a mocking combination of royal levee and court of appeal from which no one escapes – except perhaps the poet who (at risk of prosecution) frames the scene.

## NOTES

1. As in Pope's *Messiah*: "All Crimes shall cease, and ancient Fraud shall fail; | Returning Justice lift aloft her Scale" (17–18; *TE*, i, p. 114). *Windsor-Forest* (1713) is another text that demonstrates much animus against the abuse of legal power.
2. Pope refers to legislation requiring all pamphlets to carry the name and address of the figure responsible for publication, a stipulation widely evaded.
3. The "Index" jokingly confirms this: *TE*, v, p. 240.
4. See for example *Arbuthnot*, 378–9 and note; *TE*, iv, pp. 124–5.

# 12

## MALCOLM KELSALL

# Landscapes and estates

Pope had a key role in the development and the interpretation of the land-scape garden and the country-house estate in the eighteenth century. He has been seen as one of the last Renaissance humanists for whom both the garden and all Nature were speaking pictures, emblems which the humanist used to convey moral meanings.[1] He has been interpreted also as one of the first Romantics, a fundamental influence on the development of the late eighteenth-century picturesque garden.[2] His association with the landed aristocracy led him to co-operate with them in the planning of their demesnes and he made of his own villa and garden at Twickenham, near London, an emblem of his personal principles, horticultural, ethical, and political. His expression of these principles in his writings, when read empathetically, set the highest standards of taste and morality for his society.[3] On the other hand, the whole landscape movement with which he is associated, when read unsympathetically, has been criticized as exploitative and a mystifica-tion of power.[4] Seen from this viewpoint, Pope was a lackey of the rich and an apologist for the dark side of British imperialism.

Such diversity of interpretation is indicative of the complexity of the sub-ject and the variation which comes from changing one's viewpoint. The tensions between these readings suggest, perhaps, that there may have been similar tensions (ambiguities, even contradictions) in Pope's personal posi-tions in relation to his society. This is a possibility which will be developed in this essay. It will be claimed, ultimately, that there emerges from these tensions an element of visionary radicalism in Pope's iconology which trans-cends the limitations of the historical moment.

## Pope's villa at Twickenham

First a few matters of fact. Pope's early taste in landscape was shaped by the rural scenery of Binfield in Berkshire, where he grew up. The family came within the circle of patronage of Lord Burlington who was instrumental in the revival of the classical style of the Roman Augustan theorist, Vitruvius, and his disciples, the Venetian Andrea Palladio (1508–80) and the architect of the early Stuart court, Inigo Jones (1573–1652). Burlington's villa and gardens at Chiswick, west of London, were models for Pope when he came to lease, and develop, his own villa nearby at Twickenham after 1718. Pope's gardens became a show-place and the exterior of the villa, seen from the Thames, was frequently portrayed, although access to the interior was a privilege reserved for personal friends. John Serle, Pope's gardener, produced a guidebook.

Pope's increasing hostility to the Hanoverian monarchy and especially to the government of the First Minister, Sir Robert Walpole, drew him progressively into opposition politics and many of the great estates within the circle of his acquaintance can be associated with those alienated from the regime: Lord Peterborough at Bevis Mount, Lord Bathurst at Cirencester Park and Riskins, Viscount Bolingbroke at Dawley Farm, Viscount Cobham's "patriot" circle at Stowe, and, more generally, Ralph Allen at Prior Park, Mrs Henrietta Howard at Marble Hill, and the Digby family at Sherborne Castle.

Gardens are transitory things. Pope's home at Twickenham was demolished in 1807. There remain only traces of his grotto, reduced to the subterranean passage which Samuel Johnson mocked in his life of Pope (Johnson, *LOP*, III, pp. 134–5). Elsewhere the landscape has become a palimpsest, as at Stowe, the garden which Pope knew overlaid by generations of subsequent development. Even when the original remains, for instance the great woods of Cirencester, Nature does not remain the same. Trees take generations to grow, more transient vegetation disappears; remove the gardener's hand and, as Milton wrote, even Paradise grows wild. Nor do Pope's own generalizations about his ideal forms of garden convey precise information. We do not have a seedsman's catalogue for Twickenham, nor an equivalent of a planting plan, only some gnomic statements to consider "the genius of the place," to make a garden like a painting or to order contrast, to surprise and to conceal the boundaries (*Anecdotes*, I, pp. 252–4) – advice repeated in the *Epistle to Burlington*, lines 47–70, with the additional injunction to "call the country in." We know he disliked topiary work (*Guardian*, no.173; *Prose*, I, pp. 148–51) and the excessive formality displayed in Timon's garden (*Burlington*, 99–176). Such views, however, might fit numerous scenarios, "classic," "picturesque" or "romantic." Twickenham itself had some kind of transitional role between the old "formal" and the new "landscape" garden,[5] but the terminology of description and the historical evidence are imprecise.

Nonetheless, a would-be definitive iconography of Twickenham was created for the contemporary public. Consider, for example, Nathaniel Parr's engraving after Peter Andreas Rysbrack, 1735 (Figure 3). Pope is depicted

Figure 3. Pope's villa at Twickenham, after the painting by Peter Andreas Rysbrack, engraved by Nathaniel Parr (1735)

standing with his dog, Bounce, at what appears to be the entrance to his villa, but what is, in fact, the entrance to his grotto which led (under the Hampton road) to his garden beyond. As an act of especial courtesy Pope has gone out to meet his visitors who have arrived on the Thames. The façade of the villa has been ornamented with a neo-Palladian portico in imitation of Lord Burlington's Chiswick. This was a compliment to Burlington's taste and a sign of Pope's allegiance to the "villa culture" of the ancients (Cicero's Tusculum or the younger Pliny's Laurentum). The lawn and boundary hedge are "formally" cut; behind the villa the maturing trees grow in "natural" profusion. Against the villa's wall the frames indicate the practical development of horticulture.

The subsequent inscription is promiscuously drawn from the *Imitations of Horace*:

> Know, all the distant din the World can keep
> Rolls o'er my Grotto, and but Sooths my Sleep.
> Content with Little, I can piddle here
> On Broccoli and Mutton round the year;
> But ancient Friends (tho' poor or out of play)
> That touch my Bell, I cannot turn away.
> 'Tis true, no Turbots dignify my boards,
> But Gudgeons, Flounders what my Thames affords:
> To Hounslow-Heath I point, and Banstead Down;
> Thence comes your Mutton, & these Chicks my own:
> From yon old Walnut Tree a Show'r shall fall;
> And Grapes long-lingring on my only Wall,
> And Figs from Standard and Espalier join:
> The Devil's in you if you cannot dine.
> Then chearful healths (your Mistres's shall have place)
> And what's more rare, a Poet shall say Grace.
>
> A. Pope

The obvious emphasis is on retirement from "the World" (meaning the social, political, and business world of the new Rome, London); on hospitality and friendship (without regard to wealth or status); and on the self-sufficient and simple (non-luxurious) productivity of the garden/estate (*dapes inemtas*: unbought feasts) rather than the way of the world of Rome/London (*omnia Romae/ Cum pretio*: all things at Rome have their [high] price). These are standard classical motifs and were unexceptional commonplaces of "villa culture."[6]

Two things, however, may strike a modern reader as odd. The first is the emphasis on poverty and upon the "little" on which one may "piddle" here. Although Pope began with an artisan's dwelling, nonetheless the construction of a four-storey villa (with five acres of ground) was neither cheap nor small, then or now. Considered in abstract, philosophical terms, Pope is alluding to the philosophical "mean" between, for instance, the contemporary grandiloquence of Marlborough's Blenheim Palace or Walpole's Houghton Hall, and the poverty of the wind-chilled attic of a Grub Street hack. But there is a politics to that "mean." "The ancient Friends (tho' poor or out of play)" in the *Imitations* are "Chiefs, out of War, and Statesmen out of Place" (*Sat*, II.i, 126): men like Peterborough or the attainted Bolingbroke. These "ancient" friends constitute the opposition to the "world" of modern London.

The second oddity is the synecdoche by which "my Grotto" stands for the estate. The extended passageway contained both a virtuoso's collection of minerals and the materials of an actual mine. Architecturally, it is an equivalent to the "rustication" of the lower floor of great houses, the domain of "Nature" (and of servants/slaves) from which architectural form arose. Aesthetically, the grotto is a commonplace of humanistic garden tradition derived from the ancients, manifest in the Renaissance palaces of Italy and France, and which may still be seen in England at Woburn and Stourhead. For Pope, however, the opposition between "the World" and "the grotto" seems to have acquired psychological associations. William Kent (garden designer and friend) depicted Pope, in a phantasmagorical sketch, as an inspired poet composing in the grotto, and Pope himself wrote of it as a camera obscura, a place into which external images are projected, as if it were the mind itself. Or, closed to the world, it became another world of self-reflexive mirrors, lit only by its own internal illumination. Maynard Mack has interpreted the grotto, therefore, as combining both the mirror of memory with the lamp of creative imagination.[7]

Contemporary verses, collected in John Serle's plan of the estate, celebrated the grotto as a sacred place, a shrine of true patriot virtue, and, as Pope claimed, a poetic mine uncorrupted by the lust for gold. Deeper historical tradition associated classical grottoes with prophetic caves and with the nymph Egeria, who taught wisdom to Numa, an early Roman king. Christian iconography appropriated the grotto as a religious site, even the birthplace of Christ. Pope would have been aware of the religious overtones, although it is uncertain whether he, or later Catholic incumbents, embellished the site with the icons of the crown of thorns and the five wounds of Christ. But "A. Pope" was a man not ashamed of his (persecuted) faith. Much depends upon the ambiguous Horatian motto he inscribed on the private (inner garden) side of the grotto: *Secretum iter et fallentis semita vitae* (*Ep*, I.xviii, 103). One might render this innocuously, with Mack, as "a secluded journey along the pathway of life unnoticed," or, provocatively, using Abraham Cowley's idea of the "innocent deceiver" (*Essays in Verse and Prose*, 1668) as "a secret journey through a straight gate by an innocent deceiver." Catholicism was notorious for its "equivocations" by which the faithful survived.

Thus, the meanings which may be derived from the grotto depend upon a range of associations. In this respect it is the richest emblematic site on Pope's miniaturized estate. How far we should extend the associations is uncertain, and the same uncertainty extends to the main garden beyond. Serle's plan shows an extended lawn and bowling green (there is no "formal" parterre). These are entered from the grotto and set with regular alleys of trees dissolving into "wildernesses" traversed by pathways offering diverse views of the garden and its architectural ornaments (Figure 4). There is also a kitchen garden, an orangery, and a vineyard. The whole offers an Horatian mixture of the *utile et dulce*, the useful and the pleasant (*Ars Poetica*, 343).

What further significations might be read into the garden? Serle records three "mounts" and a temple of shells, the latter whimsically sketched by Kent with the pagan deities descending on a watery rainbow. The climactic feature of the garden was (ultimately) an obelisk dedicated to the memory of Pope's mother, *matrum optima*, best of mothers, which was raised in a narrowing cypress grove which, by optical illusion, seemed to extend the garden, like a vista in Palladio's Teatro Olympico in Vicenza. Perhaps the shell temple alludes back to the grotto and to "the great chain of being" in which mineral substance becomes living form; perhaps the mounts are both viewpoints and allusions to the lost mount of paradise (*paradeisos* originally meant a garden in Greek). One is on more definite ground in reading the obelisk both as a sign of the transitoriness of life, of the immortality of the soul, and of Pope's *pietas*, his (Christian) reverence for his parents. But there is a more provocative reading of the garden.[8] Pope had written about constructing a cathedral from trees, and Serle's diagram resembles the floor plan of a Palladian church (hence Roman Catholic) with columnar aisles, central dome, and either lady chapel or high altar marked by the obelisk. *Matrum optima* may allude to another mother, blessed among women. Catholics were forbidden to erect places of worship, but here A. Pope has built his church to Nature's God. If so, here is a hidden sign, *fallentis semita vitae*. Perhaps – but John Rocque's map (1746) shows a curvilinear, not rectangular, site.

To emphasize the elements of moral allegory in the Popeian landscape is not to deny the keen sensitivity of his eye for natural beauty. It was this exquisite sensibility which led his friends to value his contribution to the planning of greater demesnes. But, in this kind of co-operation, Pope's specific contribution is absorbed into a complex (and irretrievable) interplay between the poet, the taste (and financial resources) of great patrons, and the work of professional landscape gardeners such as Charles Bridgeman and Kent. What is unique, in Pope, is the moral expression of his obsession

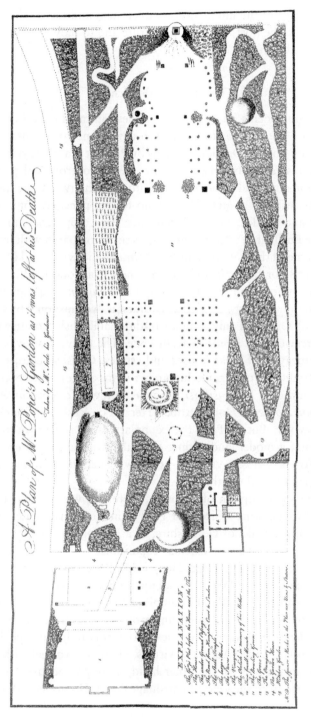

Figure 4. A plan of Pope's garden at Twickenham by John Serle, his gardener (1745)

with the meanings of the interaction between man and estate, the "use of riches" to restore the (lost) paradise of Nature and to move human society closer towards ideal form.

## The estates of the rich

Pope's two major poems on "the use of riches" in making and managing great estates are the *Epistles* to Burlington (1731) and to Bathurst (1732). Possibly another poem, "Dawley Farm" is by Pope. It is a panegyric on Bolingbroke and his estate, but the addressee was so controversial politically that the author remained anonymous. Neither of the two authentic Epistles praises his friends' estates. There is no formal panegyric of Chiswick House, Villa and garden, nor of Cirencester Park. Pope goes no further than to praise Burlington's "taste" in architecture (compared with imitating fools), to commend those who plant like Bathurst and who build like Boyle (*Burlington*, 178), or, by implication, to link them to a model landlord whose tenants "owe" more to him than to the soil (*Burlington*, 184), an ambiguous commendation, as is the claim that Bathurst is "yet unspoil'd by wealth" (*Bathurst*, 226). One need only compare traditional English "country house" poetry to perceive what is *not* there in Pope. The convention was one of exemplary panegyric of great houses and estates. Classical culture blends with feudal traditions of organic hierarchy: witness, from the seventeenth century, Ben Jonson's *To Penshurst*, Thomas Carew's *To Saxham*, Andrew Marvell's *Upon Appleton House*, Robert Herrick on Rushden, Charles Cotton on Chatsworth. But for Pope the exemplary estate is his own five acres at Twickenham, a model landholding equivalent to the few acres of King Alcinous in Pope's *Odyssey*, VII, 142–75. Now a linen-draper's son provides the touchstone of moral worth.

This is a major disruption of tradition, therefore, whether one takes as paragons of "villa culture" Cicero or Pliny from antiquity, or Lorenzo the Magnificent, or the Duke of Devonshire, or a Burlington from the modern world. This disruption gives particular significance to Pope's choice of the Roman poet Horace as his alter ego. Horace, like Pope, was of modest origins (he was the son of a freed slave). He had fought in civil war in defense of the republic and lost (at the battle of Philippi) just as Pope's co-religionists had been crushed by William III's "thundring arm" in the civil war of the 1690s. Horace made peace with victorious Caesar Augustus and, like Pope, became a spokesman for so-called Augustan virtues. He was rewarded with a farm in Sabine territory. Pope, on the other hand, more provocatively, declared his independence from the kind of patronage which Horace enjoyed:

... (thanks to Homer) since I live and thrive,
Indebted to no Prince or Peer alive.

(*Ep*, ii.ii, 68–9)

He alludes to the humanistic tradition embodied in the founding father of
European poetry, and he celebrates also the material property he has earned
by poetry and which gives him his liberty. It is this which enables him to
make his personal declaration of independence: "Unplac'd, unpension'd, no
Man's Heir or Slave" (*Sat*, ii.i, 116). It may seem tendentious to link Pope to
the American Declaration of 4 July 1776, but the country-house gentry of the
American revolution (men like George Washington of Mount Vernon and
Thomas Jefferson of Monticello) drew inspiration from the discourse of the
English opposition to the corruption, tending to "tyranny", of the monarcho-
aristocratic system of the Hanoverian regime. Pope was the major poetic
voice of that opposition.

Both of Pope's *Epistles* on "the use of riches" are ferocious attacks on
the misuse of wealth, but paradoxically (and protectively and provocatively)
addressed to two of the wealthiest men in the country. The corruption he
depicts is extreme. From the Court downwards the aristocracy is debauched
by the pursuit of power, place and pecuniary greed, poxed by promiscuity,
a High Society of pimps and gamesters, flatterers and fools. The economic
order of the City is a prey to the unregulated excesses of capitalist speculation.
The entire culture is indifferent to the exploitation of the poor; while the rich
riot, the laborer starves (*Bathurst*, 24). The paradox of Pope's position is that
he is both a personal friend of landed aristocrats, and yet a virulent critic
of the misappropriated and misapplied wealth of the powerhouses which
controlled the realm. "Timon," the notorious archetype in the *Epistle to
Burlington*, is not a mere individual, but representative: "A hundred smart
in *Timon*" (*Sat*, ii.i, 42). If the *Epistle to Burlington* had been written in
the 1790s, one would call Timon's villa (or Cotta's inhospitable "hall" in
*Bathurst*) examples of the *ancien régime*. Even Pope's friendship with the
great might not have protected him from prosecution for the "Jacobinical"
implications of his attack on the powers that were. The "radical" and the
dangerously "constructive tendency" of the satire would be apparent. Which
is not to suggest that his praise for his great friends is insincere. In a letter to
Burlington he described Chiswick as "the finest thing this glorious sun has
shin'd on," and he wrote a glowing account to Martha Blount of the Digbys'
estate at Sherborne. (*Corr*, iii, pp. 313–14; ii, pp. 236–9) Consider, on the
other hand, his moralization in public verse of the tentacular extension of
Bathurst's planting at Cirencester:

> All vast Possessions (just the same the case
> Whether you call them Villa, Park or Chase)
> Alas, my BATHURST! what will they avail?
> Join *Cotswold* Hills to *Saperton's* fair Dale,
> Let rising Granaries and Temples here,
> There mingled Farms and Pyramids appear,
> Link Towns to Towns with Avenues of Oak,
> Enclose whole Downs in Walls, 'tis all a joke!
> Inexorable Death shall level all,
> And Trees, and Stones, and Farms, and Farmer Fall.
>
> (*Ep*, II.ii, 254–63)

The emphasis is ethical, on the vanity of grandeur, but the lines might be construed also as (gentle) mockery of Bathurst's "taste" in mingling woods and pyramids, granaries and temples, and the gigantic (Brobdingnagian) linking of towns with avenues. (Pope's correspondence with Bathurst often mocks the magnitude of these projects and Pope's Lilliputian status.) Is there not, as well, a hint of criticism, flickering by implication, of the enclosure of common land walled in as unproductive park, or restricted "chase"? Compare the modest utility of Twickenham.

It has been suggested that there is an uncertain demarcation between the Timonesque tendencies of Pope's super-rich friends and the Brobdingnagian Timon.[9] If there is clear blue water between, it depends upon nice definitions of esthetic "taste" and the morality of the "use" of riches. Timon, ostentatiously, is an example of bad taste, and his landscape is a perversion of the ideal of the *ingenium loci*, the spirit of the place.[10] Timon's parterre is "a Down," his lake "an Ocean"; trees are cut as statues (and statues are thick as trees). Unnatural formality constrains everything:

> Grove nods at grove; each Alley has his brother,
> And half the platform just reflects the other.
>
> (117–18)

Compare the ideal of Twickenham. The implication of Pope's argument is that bad taste (formal gardening) is indicative of bad morality, whereas good taste, as shown at Twickenham, Chiswick or Cirencester, coincides with virtue. Philosophically this has been claimed to be a fundamental tenet of civic humanism, for the proper practice of the "liberal" arts (*cultus*: culture/ cultivation) is a sign of the superior viewpoint of the aristocracy empowered by land to govern.[11] But the linkage of taste with virtue is a non sequitur, as apparent to Henry James in his country-house fiction as to a Marxist critic. Among the country-house order itself one might turn to Jefferson and John Adams, who on their English garden tour of 1786 admired the esthetic landscape, but condemned the misapplication of aristocratic wealth. Like-wise, the early chapters of *The Absentee* (1812) by Maria Edgeworth of Edgeworthstown House, eviscerate the competitive use of standards of taste by which the wealthier of the "ins" excluded those they would keep "out" (and Edgeworth had no use for absentee landlords, of which Burlington had been a spendthrift example). Taste and power functioned together in the competitive world of the rich in which Pope was a privileged, but impuissant, visitor.[12]

Although an historical perspective is necessary to understand Pope's social position, it can be reductive of poetry. Something is "far more deeply inter-fused" into his landscape (Wordsworth, *Tintern Abbey* [1798], 96). Consider a typical couplet, expressive of how "Nature" has been forgotten at Timon's villa:

> Un-water'd see the drooping sea-horse mourn,
> And swallows roost in Nilus' dusty Urn.
>
> (125–6)

This melancholy evocation might come from some Byronic lament on the ruins of Hadrian's villa, and there is an extraordinary, almost Keatsian, beauty of sound and imagery. What the imagination perceives is, as it were, an emblem of a lost civilization in which no streams of living water flow (such as Moses and the Man of Ross called forth). Nothing fertilizes this waste land. For Pope the meaning of the landscape depends upon its relation to consonant architectural form, and forms are textualized as icons which become meaningful here from their association with the river of life, the Nile, and the sea itself into which all waters flow. Timon's dry fountains are unnatural, and what is unnatural is contrary to the ideal order of Nature's God.

## A visionary landscape

The movement of Pope's imagination is from the historical (Walpole's Houghton, Marlborough's Blenheim) to the archetype (Timon's villa) to an implied visionary ideal (the good, which is realized through the imagination). Our imperfect world is a realm of shadows, but beyond is the realm of light – to adopt a Platonic image. The third Earl of Shaftesbury is the authoritative voice on Platonism and the landscape in Pope's lifetime, but Pope's English poetic forefathers, Milton and Spenser, are Platonists also: one the tragic poet of paradise lost, the other the creator of a chivalric order which exists only in faerie land, while this world is prey to ineluctable mutability. Beyond these lie the Platonic gardens of Renaissance humanism where, in an ideal landscape, true philosophers enjoy "the Feast of Reason and the Flow of Soul" (*Sat*, II.i, 128), to which one may join the Christian Platonism of St. Paul. Now we see "as in a glass darkly"; only in God's kingdom shall we see the light "face to face".

In Pope, the ideal belongs to what the Platonist Philip Sidney called the "golden world" of poetry. It is something which the poet creates, mirroring a perfect idea, by which the imperfections of this world are found wanting. Compare, in Pope's verse, the ideal of hospitality and friendship at Twickenham with the "hecatomb" of Timon's banquet, a hell for the guests where they find themselves "In plenty starving, tantaliz'd in state" (*Burlington*, 163); or compare that rarity, a poet saying grace, at Twickenham with "the Pride of Pray'r" of Timon's chapel (*Burlington*, 142). Timon's vanity and folly ultimately feed on intellectual ignorance, for his library is noted for its bindings, not for the contents of the books: "For all his Lordship knows . . . they are [but] wood" (*Burlington*, 138). Compare Pope's verse, steeped in catholic, humanistic learning. The two modern authors whose absence from Timon's collection Pope notes are John Locke, the philosopher of those rights to life, liberty, and property which the American revolutionary vision demanded for "the new world" (in the teeth of militant Hanoverian opposition); and Milton, the poet of *Paradise Lost* and champion of freedom of speech and republican liberty.

Timon is, thus, the antitype of the good, the true, and the beautiful, a representative of the "Corruption" which like the Biblical "Flood" inundates Britain (so Pope argues). No means is offered by Pope by which Timon's corrupt power can be overborne, except by some undefined process of Nature.

> Another age shall see the golden Ear
> Imbrown the Slope, and nod on the Parterre,
> Deep Harvests bury all his pride had plann'd,
> And laughing Ceres re-assume the land.
> (*Burlington*, 173–6)

Past and future are imaginatively present here. "Laughing Ceres" recalls the Virgilian *laetas segetes*, joyful cornfields, of the *Georgics* (I, I): the future will see the pleasure garden replaced by the culture of the land which reaches the very walls of the villa. But by what specific means? It is not customary to link Pope with the visionary tradition in English art, but what else is this idealization of the future but a vatic prophecy?

Equally vatic is the Augustan ending of the poem which envisages the Vitruvian "Ideas" of Burlington's mind calling forth in some undefined future "Imperial Works." Three times Pope bids the imperium (the power of government) to build harbors, raise temples, and constrain the "dangerous

Flood." It is as if to will were to achieve. A similar aspiration was to inspire Jefferson envisaging the imperial city of Washington, C.-N. Ledoux's visionary architecture in France, or Sir John Soane's (unbuilt) London. This is the unfulfilled Romanticism of the Enlightenment: "To hope, 'til Hope creates . . . the thing it contemplates" (Shelley, *Prometheus Unbound* [1820], 573–4).

What then of the poet piddling at Twickenham? In comparison with the great, it is apparent that he must be "content with little." His five acres of leased land are less even than the (normative) fifty acres of the American freeholders whom Jefferson saw as "the chosen people of God." Imitating Horace's epode, *Beatus ille*, Pope wrote:

> Happy the man whose wish and care
> A few paternal acres bound . . .

But Pope's idealism is touched by irony. Are men happy when bound to a *few* paternal acres? Horace, in the epode, thought not, and Pope neither had paternal land, nor could he bequeath his five acres. Nor was his "wish and care" limited by his tiny Elysium. On the contrary, Twickenham was the base for what he described as his "Heav'n directed" mission to use the "sacred Weapon" of satire in "Truth's defence," and reinterpreting Timon's pride, he wrote of himself:

> Yes, I am proud; I must be proud to see
> Men not afraid of God, afraid of me.
> (*Epilogue to the Satires*, II, 208–9)

It is a gigantic claim, perhaps only equaled in English satire by Byron's adoption of the persona of Satan in *The Vision of Judgment* (1822) to voice a divine opposition, not unlike Pope's, to the corruption of the Hanoverian regime.

Pope's great friends (out of office) separated themselves from the targets of his satire by recruiting him into their landscapes as an exponent of their ideals. There are seats dedicated to Pope at Cirencester and Sherborne, and most significantly of all, in the ideal world of the great landscape garden of Stowe, his bust is placed in the quasi-paradisiacal region known as the "Elysian Fields." In this golden world of the imagination (a secluded dell) Pope looks out to a circular mount on which is raised the Temple of Ancient Virtue. His companions in a shrine of British Worthies are great statesmen, philosophers, and poets. They include John Hampden, who defied tyrannical taxation (an inspiration to the American revolutionaries) and those two champions of freedom, whom Pope noted were absent from Timon's library: Locke and Milton.

Looking to the future, one might add to this company men like William Wordsworth, Samuel Palmer, and William Morris of Kelmscott. Like Pope and the Renaissance humanists, these visionaries were to find inspiration in Nature's "green shade" (Marvell, "The Garden," 48) and believed that even in our fallen world, through the idealism of memory and desire, one might aspire to build Jerusalem in England's green and pleasant land.

## NOTES

1. For major studies in this area, see Further Reading, pp. 237–246 below.
2. Morris R. Brownell, *Alexander Pope and the Arts of Georgian England* (Oxford: Clarendon Press, 1978).
3. Howard Erskine-Hill, *The Social Milieu of Alexander Pope: Lives, Example and the Poetic Response* (New Haven: Yale University Press, 1975).
4. Raymond Williams, *The Country and the City* (London: Chatto and Windus, 1973).
5. Peter Martin, *Pursuing Innocent Pleasures: The Gardening World of Alexander Pope* (Hamden, CT: Archon Books, 1984).
6. See J. S. Ackerman, *The Villa: Form and Ideology of the Country House* (London: Thames and Hudson, 1990); as well as Horace, *Epodes*, II, 48; Juvenal, *Satires*, III, 183–4.
7. Maynard Mack, *The Garden and the City: Retirement and Politics in the later Poetry of Pope* (Toronto: University of Toronto Press, 1969), p. 60.
8. Michael Charlesworth, "Alexander Pope's Garden at Twickenham: An Architectural Design Proposed," *Journal of Garden History* 7:1 (1987), pp. 56–68.
9. Malcolm Kelsall, *The Great Good Place: The Country House and English Literature* (Hemel Hempstead: Harvester Wheatsheaf, 1993).
10. Terry Comito, "The Humanist Garden," in *The Architecture of Western Gardens*, ed. Monique Moiser and George Tyssot (Cambridge, MA: MIT Press, 1991), pp. 37–44.
11. John Barrell, "The Public Prospect and the Private View: The Politics of Taste in Eighteenth-century Britain," in *Reading the Landscape: Country – City – Capital*, ed. Simon Pugh (Manchester: Manchester University Press, 1990), pp. 19–40.
12. Stephen Bending, "One among the Many: Popular Aesthetics, Polite Culture and the Country-house Landscape," in *The Georgian Villa: Landscape – Society*, ed. Dana Arnold (Stroud: Sutton, 1998), pp. 61–78.

# 13

CATHERINE INGRASSIA

# Money

When Alexander Pope recounts the onslaught of impecunious writers who seek him out at Twickenham, he describes their typical "modest wish" for "My Friendship, and a Prologue, and ten Pound" (*TE*, IV, p. 99). That triad of desires captures the basic types of currency in which Pope regularly traded: professional friendship, literary commodities or words, and, of course, money. Pope dwells on these currencies in *Epistle to Arbuthnot* (1735) because they define the symbolic system of investment and exchange that shapes his personal and professional relationships, his poetic career, and his financial activities. These three currencies are deeply imbricated and mutually reinforcing: as Pope's professional success increased, aided in part by an ad hoc system of patronage and his savvy determination to control the publication of his texts, his financial gains outstripped those of most of his poetic contemporaries. From the earliest stages of his career, Pope realized the value of ongoing relationships (sometimes collaborative, sometime adversarial) with his colleagues in the print trade: "A mutual commerce makes Poetry flourish" (*Corr*, I, p. 20). By skillfully deploying printed rejoinders, financial assistance, or well-placed advice, he contributed to his consistent "fame" in the marketplace and enhanced his ability to control the production and distribution of his own texts (and the attendant socio-poetic image). That control – which ranged from holding the copyrights to his poems to determining the quality of ink and paper and the appearance of the text on the page – simultaneously enriched Pope's poetic persona and his financial accounts. Pope cultivated his image of the gentleman author, removed from the concerns of the trade, while he was unapologetically writing for money. He relished the personal comforts and independence it provided: "(thanks to *Homer*) since I live and thrive, | Indebted to no Prince or Peer alive" (*Ep*, II.ii, 68–9; *TE*, IV, p. 169). That wealth enabled Pope, in turn, to strategically assist colleagues, and, more importantly, to create a life of retirement at Twickenham that obscured his dependence on the urban print marketplace and the new financial systems he decried in his poems. While he repeatedly and rather proudly refused any pensions, even those offered secretly, ("Un-plac'd, un-pension'd, no Man's Heir, or Slave," [*Sat*, ii.i, 116; *TE*, iv, p. 17]), he recognized the value of friendly relationships with select members of the aristocracy which in turn enhanced his marketability and his prestige.

Pope's colleagues, like modern critics, often view him as hypocritical in his attitude toward money, and depict him as mercenary and self-interested. Indeed, Pope's relationship with money is complicated and fraught with ambiguities. How can the wealthiest poet of his day condemn those who write for money? How can someone who enthusiastically invested in the South Sea Company and other speculative ventures denounce "paper credit"? How can the poet who became wealthy by creating his own type of literary factory when translating Homer represent the commercialization of the trade in the excoriating terms of *The Dunciad*? By entering "this idle trade" (*Arbuthnot*, 129; *TE*, iv, p. 105), Pope participated in the three currencies he identifies and retained an acute awareness of his own financial situation and the symbolic value with which his culture invested words and money. Indeed, money – both as real and symbolic currency – profoundly shaped Pope's poetic career (thematically and materially), and all his major poems address, in some measure, financial issues and the use and gain of riches. He used his poetry and his heavily revised correspondence to dissemble about his own financial experiences, his earnings, and his position within the print trade.

### "this Age of Hope and Golden Mountains"

With this line, Pope captures the spirit of possibility that characterized early eighteenth-century British culture. Almost contemporaneously with Pope's birth in 1688, the economic landscape of England changed dramatically, moving from the traditionally land-based model of wealth to a world shaped by the possibilities and contingencies of the "paper credit" Pope describes in *Epistle to Bathurst* (1733). The financial and concomitant socio-economic changes that occurred during this period mark a perceived transition from a culture that, in idealized representations, embodied a devotion to a patrician ethos of generosity and morality to a financially driven, avaricious society where "A Man of wealth is dubb'd a Man of worth" (*Ep*, i.vi, 81; *TE*, iv, p. 243). The development of a system of symbolic financial instruments (stocks, lottery tickets, and other forms of speculative investment), credit-based institutions, and new banking practices (the Bank of England was established in 1694) that have come to be known as the "financial revolution" emerged in the 1690s and reached an apex with the rise and then

Money

ultimate collapse of the so-called "South Sea Bubble."[1] The term "paper credit" suggests the insubstantial and intangible forms of property and negotiable paper circulating in society: lottery tickets, stocks, bills of exchange, and letters of credit. Paper credit and the mechanisms of speculative investment shifted the nature of property from material, immovable, and stable forms such as land to fluid, immaterial, and diffuse symbolic instruments. The new financial instruments, in many ways, could be realized only imaginatively in the sense that individuals received paper, not goods, for their investment. As was often recounted, the market could rise or fall based on rumor, suspicion, and the word on the street. A semiotic confusion threatened to erupt as investors attempted to anticipate the market or adjust to their new-found wealth or loss.

While Pope aggressively critiqued the dangers of "paper credit" (and money generally) in the *Moral Essays*, particularly *Epistle to Burlington* (1731) and *Epistle to Bathurst* (1733), before 1720 he, like most of his contemporaries, took advantage of the opportunities the new financial instruments afforded when investing both his own money and that of Martha Blount. (He also gave Lady Mary Wortley Montagu advice on her South Sea Company investments.) As early as 1716, Pope invested in the South Sea Company, whose status was favorably affected by the Treaty of Utrecht celebrated in *Windsor-Forest* (1713). Depending on the "general Opinion" and the advice of others, "those whose judgement I myself most depend upon," between 1716 and 1720 Pope consistently invested in South Sea stock. Throughout 1720 he attempted to time the market as he describes to Martha Blount: "it is thought the South Sea will rather fall than rise . . . and upon this belief I have myself kept a thousand five hundred pounds lying by me, to buy at such a juncture . . . I have given orders to buy 500ll for myself as soon as South Sea falls to 103: which you shall have if you have a mind to it. It will amount so to near 6 per cent: And my Broker tells me he thinks it will fall to that" (*Corr*, I, p. 379). Pope does not want his money to be "lying dead." The talk of brokers and inside information bespeaks a culture where the actions of speculative investment are increasingly naturalized. Subsequent letters similarly capture the temper of the age and reveal Pope's infatuation with the possibilities presented by speculation:

> I daily hear such reports of advantages to be gaind by one project or other in the Stocks, that my Spirit is Up with double Zeal, in the desires of our trying to enrich ourselves . . . I hope you have sold the Lottery orders, that the want of ready mony may be no longer an Impediment to our buying in the Stock . . . I hear the S. Sea fell since, & should be glad we were in: I also hear there is considerably to be got by Subscribing to the new African Stock, Pray let us do something or other, which you judge the fairest Prospect, I am equal as to what

Stock, so you do but like it. Let but Fortune favor us, & the World will be sure to admire our Prudence. If we fail, let's e'en keep the mishap to ourselves; But tis Ignominious (in this Age of Hope and Golden Mountains) not to Venture.

(*Corr*, II, p. 33)

He throws his lot to "Fortuna" and enters the unstable and highly volatile world of speculative investment. More strikingly, the letter evinces his confidence in nonspecific, unverified information ("I hear"), his desire to invest regardless of the fund ("let us do something or other"), and his willingness to abdicate responsibility for the decision ("I am equal as to what Stock, so you do but like it") – all characteristics he resoundingly criticized in others. At the same time Pope is aggressively and meticulously negotiating the continued terms for the translation of Homer, he rather insouciantly invests large sums of money (£1,500) in stock. Howard Erskine-Hill has suggested that Pope, like other "British papists or Jacobites, living beyond their means with estates double-taxed, or in jeopardy, or forfeited," was susceptible to his friend John Caryll's encouragement to invest: "the prospect of successful speculation was perhaps an especially potent and fatal temptation . . . the point evidently put to the poet must have been what many families in his position were thinking: hitherto he had always been on the losing side; now perhaps he could win."[2] That, of course, did not happen. While Pope had sold some of his stock (at a profit) in July, he was still holding at least £500 worth of stock when the bubble burst in August 1720.

Immediately following the collapse of the bubble, Pope projects a rather sanguine attitude that belies the renewed financial pressures such a loss created for him:

The fate of the South-sea Scheme has much sooner than I expected verify'd what you told me. Most people thought the time wou'd come, but no man prepar'd for it . . . Methinks God has punish'd the avaritious as he often punishes sinners, in their own way, in the very sin itself: the thirst of gain was their crime, that thirst continued became their punishment and ruin. As for the few who have the good fortune to remain with half of what they imagined they had, (among whom is your humble servant) I would have them sensible of their felicity . . . Indeed the universal poverty, which is the consequence of universal avarice, and which will fall hardest upon the guiltless and industrious part of mankind, is truly lamentable. The universal deluge of the S. Sea, contrary to the old deluge, has drowned all except a few *Unrighteous* men: but it is some comfort to me that I am not one of them, even tho' I were to survive and rule the world by it.

(*Corr*, II, p. 53)

In this rather self-serving letter, Pope distinguishes himself from the "unrighteous," ignoring the pecuniary desires – the "thirst of gain" – that drove him in the first place. He had invested with enthusiasm, expressing pleasure at "adventuring in so good company" (*Corr*, II, p. 32), yet he extricates himself from full blame: he claims not to be among the too "avaritious" who are doubly punished. Despite his loss, Pope continued to invest throughout his lifetime, amassing what Colin Nicholson terms a "considerable record of investment experience."[3]

In poetic representations, Pope's attitude toward speculative investment becomes markedly less generous, coloured perhaps by both the additional information related to government involvement in the South Sea Bubble and his own subsequent financial challenges. John Gay observed that Pope "engag'd to translate the *Odyssey* in three years, I believe rather out of a prospect of Gain than inclination, for I am persuaded he bore his part in the loss of the South Sea."[4] The stock collapse occurred at the time when Pope was spending large sums renovating the villa and gardens at Twickenham where he had moved in 1719, a project that occupied his time, imagination and money for the following decade.[5] The 1720s also marked a period when he felt the pressure of additional taxes on Catholics. Pope laments to Caryll how the tax increases will cause him to "lose a good part of my income" and, "in this expectation," Pope plans to purchase an advantageous "annuity . . . to enable me to keep myself that man of honour which I trust in God ever to be." (*Corr*, II, p. 173). (The larger context for that letter is his attempt to get back £200 he lent Caryll "as soon as 'tis convenient for you to pay it.") Throughout his life, he regularly invested in annuities and later wrote "So bought an Annual Rent or two. | And liv'd – just as you see I do" (*Ep*, I.vii, 71–2; *TE*, IV, p. 273); indeed, he owned thirty-one shares of the Sun Fire Insurance Company when he died. Despite his involvement, the intensity of his language regarding speculative financial activity increased. The "deluge" of the South Sea Bubble becomes "an ocean of avarice and corruption" that threatens to drown every aspect of society. By 1723, he writes "Every valuable, every pleasant thing is sunk in an ocean of avarice and corruption . . . so money upon money increases, copulates, and multiplies, and guineas beget guineas in *saecula saeculorum*." In this same letter, his personal assessment is similarly bleak: "My body is sick, my soul is troubled, my pockets are empty, my time is lost, my trees are withered, my grass is burned! So ends my history" (*Corr*, II, pp. 182–3).

## "I could write for my bread"

If Pope realized only limited profits with his South Sea Company investments, he had marked success in his literary "investments" during a period when similar opportunities to "venture" presented themselves in the increasingly open print trade. The 1690s saw the relaxing of licensing laws which enabled the nearly exponential expansion of the print trade. While in *The Dunciad* (1728, 1729, 1742), Pope specifically satirizes the dangers of the commercial literary marketplace, he recognizes it also provided a chance for financial gain and cultural authority otherwise unavailable to a disabled, Catholic poet. His attacks on authors preoccupied with popularity, frequency of publication, and profit strategically ignore his own dependence on those same market forces. The opportunities Pope had in the print trade were multiple and remunerative. Although early in his career he, like most professional writers, sold his copyright and made limited amounts on each text, he quickly learned how to negotiate financially advantageous terms. David Foxon estimates that Pope earned at least £5,000 for the *Iliad* between 1715 and 1720, and almost that much for the *Odyssey* (a veritable fortune at a time when the average laborer earned only £12 per year). Indeed, Foxon marvels at "the contrast between the 30 guineas or so a year that Pope received in those early years and the 800 a year or more that the *Iliad* produced."[6] The profits of the print trade were particularly welcome during a period when Pope needed money. He signed an agreement to translate the *Iliad* within weeks of the 1714 publication of *Rape of the Lock*, the very moment his family's income had been diminished by a royal edict in France that resulted in a 25 percent reduction in interest on French annuities. Pope consistently expresses his concern about lost revenue and the potential for additional anti-Catholic measures that would restrict his income: "if I had money and they took it away, I could write for my bread (as much better men than I have been often suffered to do)" (*Corr*, I, p. 242). Though Pope was never poor like the "hacks" he dismisses, he needed a consistent cash flow, especially after his father's death in 1717. He had to support his mother. He assumed considerable financial responsibility for Martha Blount, investing her funds. And he aspired to create a life of gentlemanly retirement for himself that definitely required money.

Consequently, when Pope was in the midst of translating the *Iliad*, he was also securing subscribers for the volumes, something he always denied doing. The mechanisms of speculative investment and selling books by subscription share some structural similarities: both required "investors" to pay for a product they, initially, could only conceive imaginatively. It enabled the individual offering the (literary or financial) stock to secure monies up front with merely the promise of a return on the investment. Certainly Pope fulfilled his promise and satisfied his subscribers (even if he swelled his translation to six volumes to secure the desired profit); yet Pope intuitively recognized that a poet, like a stockjobber, doesn't do "real" work or produce a "real" product – only words and paper.[7] While he solicited subscribers himself, he also convinced his friends to work on his behalf (and offered detailed advice toward their efforts). His letters during this period are filled not with the process of writing poetry but with the business of selling it. "While I am engaged in the fight" of translating, he wrote to Caryll, "I find you are concerned how I shall be paid, and are soliciting [for subscribers] with all your might" (*Corr*, I, p. 220). A representative letter notes: "You mentioned a gentleman who was ready to subscribe to you; be pleased to receive the subscription, and let me know his name, which was torn out by the seal of your letters, that I may transmit him a receipt. Do the same also in regard to my Lord Cornwallis's, or any others you may find." (*Corr*, I, p. 270). He urges Caryll to promote the project to an interested buyer "with what speed is convenient, since I know the danger there is of letting an affair of this nature cool too much" (*Corr*, I, p. 204). As with his previous attempt to time the stock market, he also recognizes the need to "time" the sale of subscriptions.

Much of his urgency in attracting subscribers stems from the financial arrangements he made for the translation. Pope essentially became his own publisher, a pattern he continued throughout his career. By usually holding his own copyrights, dealing directly with a printer, and, in the case of Homer, selling his texts by subscription, he eliminated the middleman bookseller. This arrangement tremendously increased his share of the profits (or the return on the investment of his intellectual capital). It also exposed him to additional financial risk. Pope was vulnerable to piracies – while the booksellers typically respected their colleagues' copyrights, they did not necessarily honor those of a poet like Pope. He also had to remain financially solvent so he had the money to fund the publishing of his words. He must essentially speculate on the future value of his own work. In letters, Pope notes amounts he owes to various publishers for the paper or ink purchased. Firmly believing that an "An author who is at all the expenses of publishing ought to clear two thirds of the whole profit into his own pocket," Pope calculated the exact amount to be charged for each text. "For instance, as he explained it," writes Spence, "in a piece of one thousand copies at 3s each to the common buyer, the whole sale at that rate will bring in £150. The expense therefore to the author for printing, paper, publishing, selling and advertising, should be but £50, and his clear gains should be £100" (*Anecdotes*, I, p. 85). Pope also made considered publishing decisions regarding everything from the appearance of the text on the page or the quality of the paper and ink, to the size of the volume itself – all decisions designed to increase his "cultural capital." The aesthetic value of the material text enhanced Pope's poetic image (another commodity) and thus his potential for financial gain.

Pope's wealth seemed enormous in relation to his colleagues in the print trade who earned little beyond the initial payment (£10–25) they received when they sold their work to a publisher. What is notable about the money is not only the deliberate way Pope earned it, or the ways he worked to obscure his strategic financial plans, but what it enabled him to do professionally. He could secretly hire Elijah Fenton and William Broome (whose collaboration he subsequently denied) to help him translate Homer; he could set up Robert Dodsley and Lawton Gilliver as booksellers and then have them distribute his works; he could offer financial assistance to less successful authors who had been his enemies (John Dennis) or friends (Richard Savage). He could create an elaborate series of professional relationships that enabled him to keep his name in the marketplace, to enhance his poetic image, and to get others to write about him and his words. The money he accumulated also enabled him to resist the system of patronage and flattery that seduced many of his contemporary authors. "South-sea Subscriptions take who please, | Leave me but Liberty and Ease . . . | Give me, I cry'd, (enough for me) | My Bread, and Independency!" (*Ep*, I.vii, 65–6, 69–70; *TE*, IV, p. 273). He profited in the print trade through his financial acuity, his skilful negotiations, and, of course, the marketability of his own newly minted words.

## Poetic response

Much of Pope's poetry, particularly the *Moral Epistles* and *Imitations of Horace* that contribute to the discursive creation of professional friendships, directly addresses the issue of money. As he acknowledges in *Epistle to Bathurst*, money is the sine qua non of life – "Useful, I grant, it serves what life requires" (27; *TE*, III.ii, p. 88). No one can ignore its importance: "A wise man always | . . . makes a diff'rence in his thought | Betwixt a Guinea and a Groat" (*Ep*, I.vii, 35–8; *TE*, IV, p. 271). It has the potential to command ("It raises Armies in a Nation's aid") or to corrupt ("But bribes a Senate, and the Land's betrayed," *Epistle to Bathurst*, 33–4; *TE*, III.ii, p. 88), help or hurt. Yet increasingly (and inappropriately) money becomes the sole measure of the man in a culture where new financial instruments and opportunities for investment create the illusion that one can and should profit: ". . . to the world, no bugbear is so great, | As want of figure, and a small Estate" (*Ep*, I.i, 67–8; *TE*, IV, p. 283). Pope records an avaricious society where individuals will endure "pains of body" and "pangs of soul" to avoid "the spectre of pale Poverty" (*Ep*, I.i, 70–1; *TE*, IV, p. 283); yet no one suffers to increase virtue or wisdom. The common London advice is "Get Mony, Mony still! | And then let Virtue follow, if she will" (*Ep*, I.i, 79–80; *TE*, IV, p. 285). The portrait of Sir Balaam in the *Epistle to Bathurst* enacts in miniature the dangers Pope sees as systemic. The "plain good man," the "religious, punctual, frugal," Balaam gains tremendous wealth ("Stocks and

Subscriptions pour on ev'ry side," [*Bathurst*, 370; *TE*, III.ii, p. 123]), but loses his faith – "What late he call'd a Blessing, now was Wit, | And God's good Providence, a lucky Hit | . . . Seldom at Church ('twas such a busy life)" (*Bathurst*, 377–81; *TE*, III.ii, pp. 123–4) – and ultimately his life. Seduced by the trappings of money, he enters a devalued and ultimately oppressive world; for Balaam, wealth begets death, debt, and loss. Money can realign social relationships and create another kind of hierarchical confusion with classes and genders mixing inappropriately: "Statesman and Patriot ply alike the stocks, | Peeress and Butler share alike the Box" (*Bathurst*, 141–2; *TE*, III.ii, p. 105). The fashionable activities of "polite" society – cards, opera, court life – perpetuate that interpretative quagmire that Pope attempts to correct. Money ushers in linguistic confusion, a corruption of the currency of words. The cacophony that originates in the City – specifically in Grub Street and Exchange Alley – infiltrates the Court. Rumor, word of mouth, and (mis)information that guide the buying and selling of stocks and literary commodities now become the "modern language of corrupted Peers" and "this new Court jargon" that advances the wrong advice (*Ep*, I.i, 98–9; *TE*, IV, p. 287).

If the "wrong advice" is troubling, at least it can be heard (even if whispered) and potentially corrected. The loud environs of Grub Street and Exchange Alley bespeak the compromised nature of their enterprise; the action is noticeable. Similarly money as coin necessarily draws attention to itself. As the *Epistle to Bathurst* makes clear, with "incumber'd Villainy" of old, corruption is noisy – "the crack'd bag the dropping Guinea spoke, | . . . gingling down the back-stairs"; "A hundred oxen at your levee roar" (*Bathurst*, 36, 66–7, 46; *TE*, III.ii, pp. 88–9, 92–3). But the movement from noise to silence is particularly dangerous. The cultural dullness apocalyptically depicted in *The Dunciad* is marked by a transition from aural confusion to silence, darkness, and lacuna. Silent too is paper credit, the pervasive currency which exists unnoticed and grows unchecked as it "silent sells a King, or buys a Queen" (*Bathurst*, 78; *TE*, III.ii, p. 93). It reproduces, "copulates, and multiplies," giving individuals money they did not "earn": "While with the silent growth of ten per Cent, | In Dirt and darkness hundreds stink content" (*Ep*, I.i, 132–3; *TE*, IV, p. 289).

Though poetry may be an "idle trade," for Pope it is real work that richly justifies the money he earns. As Samuel Johnson observed "He was one of those few whose labour is their pleasure."[8] His profits undercut claims to financial disinterest ("I can be content with a bare saving gain," [*Corr*, I, p. 236]), yet he also describes poetry as a diversion from avarice and envisages a kind of poetic economy that can assuage the pangs of greed which threatens to subsume cultural expectations. Words can replace coins as a desired currency. Pope envisages the "raging fit" to write that overtakes so many men actually providing a kind of balm to more dangerous impulses: "And rarely Av'rice taints the tuneful mind" (*Ep*, ii.i, 192; *TE*, iv, p. 211). Those who "ryme, and scrawl, and scribble" (while they fall into the semiotic confusion Pope abhors) do not indulge in great mischief; indeed "Sometimes the Folly benefits mankind" (*Ep*, ii.i, 188, 191; *TE*, iv, p. 211). The poetic economy of words (even if one is just "scribbling") supplants the material economy – "The good man heaps up nothing but mere metre" (*Ep*, ii.i, 198; *TE*, iv, p. 211). The profits offered by language compensate for the losses in the marketplace or for threats of political instability that might result: "Flight of Cashiers, or Mobs," the writer will "never mind" (*Ep*, ii.i, 195; *TE*, iv, p. 211). Pope, of course, is a poet and not just a "Man of Rymes" (*Ep*, ii.i, 341). The palliative effects of the poetic economy are greatly idealized and the description serves perhaps as a compensatory claim for Pope's indifference to money. Certainly one could argue Pope cared primarily for profit and heaped up meter largely because it enabled him to heap up money. The poetic economy may be profound for Pope the poet, but largely because it is inextricably linked to monetary gain for Pope the man. Because of his carefully achieved wealth, he does not have to become "the bard . . . | Who rhymed for hire" (*Dunciad*, iv, 101–2). "He was never reduced to the necessity of soliciting the sun to shine upon a birthday," writes Johnson, "of calling the Graces and Virtues to a wedding, or of saying what multitudes have said before him. When he could produce nothing new, he was at liberty to be silent."[9] Because he never offered his words in exchange for money to one individual, "Above a Patron" (*Arbuthnot*, 265; *TE*, iv, p. 114), he determined the supply and value of his words, set the rate of exchange, and labeled counterfeit the work of those who did otherwise.

## Final accounting

It is difficult to extricate Pope's personal attitudes toward money from his discursive representations. A master of dissembling, Pope worked carefully to obscure the professional acts that provided evidence of inconsistencies in the poetic persona he created. Thus, in the carefully revised version of his life, the gentleman author does not grub for subscribers; the poet in retirement does not fund city booksellers' shops; the critic of "paper credit" does not invest speculatively. His professional friendships enabled him to control the publication of his letters and, through William Warburton, ensure (for a while) his poetic legacy. His poems strategically ignored his complicity with the print trade, his experience in the financial marketplace, and his relentless desire for profit. The contradictions exist on a personal level as well.

According to Mack, most of Pope's colleagues regarded him as notoriously parsimonious, yet his sister insisted "'Tis most certain that nobody ever loved money so little as my brother." (*Anecdotes*, I, p. 156). Samuel Johnson describes Pope as a man obsessed with money: "it would be hard to find a man, so well entitled to notice by his wit, that ever delighted so much in talking of his money . . . [i]n his Letters and in his Poems, his garden and his grotto, his *quincunx* and his vines, some hints of his opulence, are always to be found."[10] Certainly, he was focused on cultivating his five acres, what Maynard Mack describes as "his miniature Twickenham estate" (*Life*, p. 349). The grotto and gardens were a bit of extravagance by his own description. By contrast, the inventory of his house upon his death suggests Pope's frugality in terms of acquiring things: his furniture was extremely modest and the only real signs of self-indulgence were the fifty-six portraits he acquired.[11] Perhaps it is not avarice but rather pragmatism that prompts Pope to be of the opinion, "not very uncommon in the world," as Johnson observed, "that to want money is to want every thing."[12]

## NOTES

1. For major works on the financial revolution and the South Sea Bubble, see Further Reading, pp. 237–246 below. For discussions of the ideological significance of these financial changes, see amongst others J. G. A. Pocock, *The Machiavellian Moment* (Princeton: Princeton University Press, 1974) and *Virtue, Commerce, and History* (Cambridge: Cambridge University Press, 1985).
2. Howard Erskine-Hill, *The Social Milieu of Alexander Pope* (New Haven: Yale University Press, 1975), p. 84.
3. Colin Nicholson, *Writing and the Rise of Finance* (Cambridge: Cambridge University Press, 1994), p. 67.
4. John Gay, *Letters*, ed. C. F. Burgess (Oxford: Clarendon Press, 1966), p. 43.
5. For a discussion of Twickenham, see Maynard Mack, *The Garden and the City* (Toronto: University of Toronto Press, 1969).
6. David Foxon, *Pope and the Early Eighteenth-Century Book Trade*, ed. James McLaverty (Oxford: Clarendon Press, 1991), p. 39.
7. This aspect of literary authorship produced a larger anxiety for Pope about what Catherine Gallagher describes as "the minimal materiality inherent in signifying systems." See Gallagher, "Raymond Williams and Cultural Studies," *Social Text* 30 (1992): p. 87.
8. Johnson, *LOP*, III, p .218.
9. Ibid., p. 219.
10. Johnson, *LOP*, III: 204.
11. Mack, *Garden and City*, Appendix B, pp. 244–58.
12. Johnson, *LOP*, III, p. 219.

# 14

## JAMES MCLAVERTY

# Pope and the book trade

## Introduction

Pope's absorption in the book trade is remarkable. Always fascinated by typography, he was commenting on trade practices and condemning some of them by the time he was thirty. But paradoxically the tricks he observed, particularly author and bookseller anonymity, serialization, reissues, and manipulation of formats, all fed positively into the second half of his career, in which he was, in the modern sense, his own publisher, financing and designing his own books, and supervising their distribution. Pope made a lot of money from the publication of his own work – around £10,000 from his translations of Homer alone – but he also made the book trade his subject and its resources a means of self-expression. In ways that are characteristic of him, he seems at times the most unequivocal of insiders, with a detailed knowledge of contracting, designing, advertising, and distribution, while at other times, he is merely the bibliographer or book historian, wryly recording curious practices and displaying them for our disapproval. Complex social pressures lie behind these stances – a growing public sphere in which reputations were to be earned and maintained, the possibilities of large financial rewards for writing, the slow replacement of patronage by the market – and Pope undoubtedly regarded his own times and their changes as hostile to his success. Ironically, this very awareness became integral to his achievement.

## The Jacob Tonsons and William Lewis

Pope made his first appearance in print in Tonson's *Poetical Miscellanies, The Sixth Part* (2 May 1709). It was a distinguished start because Jacob Tonson, Sr. was the leading London bookseller.[1] The surviving invitation suggests the smoothest of transitions from the private to the public sphere: "I have lately seen a pastoral of yours in mr. Walsh's & mr Congreves hands, which is extreamly ffine & is generally approv'd off by the best Judges in poetry . . . If you design your Poem for the Press no person shall be more Carefull in the printing of it, nor no one can give a greater Incouragement to it" (*Corr*, I, p. 17).[2] Bookseller and writer move in the same circles; public and private judgments coincide.

> But why then publish? *Granville* the polite,
> And knowing *Walsh*, would tell me I could write.
>            (*Epistle to Arbuthnot*, 135–6).

The circulating manuscript of the "Pastorals" had already been prepared for the transition, providing one of Pope's closest imitations of print, with exquisite dropped heads, careful contrasts of italic and roman, and footnotes below a rule, conventions largely followed by Tonson in printing the poem.[3]

The Tonsons remain a shadowy presence in Pope's dealings with the trade as the tantalizing might-have-been. They were Pope's preferred booksellers, it seems, but his interest was not reciprocated, at least not enough to offer the rewards he sought. His second major poem, *An Essay on Criticism* (15 May 1711), was published by an old schoolfriend William Lewis, even though it was printed by the elder Tonson's partner and printer, John Watts.[4] The Tonsons had paid Pope well for the material he contributed to their collections (13 guineas for the sixth part of the *Miscellanies* and 15 guineas for Steele's *Miscellany*) but perhaps they declined to make an offer for *An Essay on Criticism* – a single poem offering a much more doubtful prospect than a miscellany – and suggested that Pope publish at his own expense. (A guinea was worth 21 shillings or £1.05 in modern terms.) Pope's response might then have been to turn to his friend Lewis as a better way of handling the process.

The surviving manuscript of *An Essay on Criticism* was the one that went to the printer and provides an insight into the control Pope exercised over the trade at this stage of his career and later. It was issued as a quarto pamphlet, a format produced by folding a sheet into four leaves, making a square book, that Pope was to use for the subscription editions of Homer and for his *Works*. Pope plots the printing, page by page. He was always interested in sophisticated typographical effects, even if in his later quartos that sophistication showed itself in plainness. In this essay he uses italic very heavily, following Creech's translation of Horace's *Art of Poetry*, in adopting an emphatic tone and highlighting topics for the eager student:

> Those RULES of old *discover'd*, not *devis'd*,
> Are *Nature* still, but *Nature Methodiz'd*;
> *Nature*, like *Monarchy*, is but restrain'd
> By the same Laws which first *herself* ordain'd.
>            (*Essay on Criticism*, 88–91)

This italic was dropped for the third and subsequent editions. The movement in Pope's career is towards a more chaste typography, without italics, ornaments or capitalized nouns, though he will later revive italic in smaller octavo editions (eight leaves per sheet) he prepares for the general public.[5]

## Bernard Lintot

An *Essay on Criticism* had appeared a week before Pope's birthday, 21 May, in 1711. Just over a year later the publication of *Miscellaneous Poems and Translations* (20 May 1712) marked the start of his extraordinarily successful alliance with Bernard Lintot.[6] Lintot aimed to rival the Tonsons as the major literary publisher of the early years of the eighteenth century, and Pope enabled him to make a success of the project. Lintot came from Horsham in Sussex and he and Pope may have been brought together by the Carylls of West Grinstead, the two families having some connections. Caryll had an interest in *Miscellaneous Poems and Translations* through "The Rape of the Locke" ("This Verse to C—l, Muse! is due") and the Chaucer translations supposedly by the actor Thomas Betterton (*Corr*, I, p. 142). Lintot's status as a country gentleman as well as a stationer may explain Pope's pleasure in depicting him as something of an oaf who had to trick others into checking his translations because he had no languages (*Corr*, I, pp. 371–5). Lintot clearly valued Pope (I suspect he thought he was a great writer), but Pope did not reciprocate.

John Gay and Nicholas Rowe also moved to Lintot's stable at the time of *Miscellaneous Poems and Translations*, and there is a strong sense of excitement at the new relationship. Pope's "Verses to be Prefix'd before Bernard Lintot's New Miscellany" are a playful expression of such excitement:

> Some *Colinæus* praise, some *Bleau*,
> Others account 'em but so so;
> Some *Plantin* to the rest prefer,
> And some esteem *Old-Elzevir*;
> Others with *Aldus* would besot us;
> I, for my part, admire *Lintottus*. —
>                     (*TE*, VI, pp. 82–3)

Lintot takes his place as the culmination of this little history of printing, and Pope shows intimate knowledge of his business, picking out "LINTOT"'s regular appearance in capitals, the cleanness of the printing, and Lintot's willingness to pay for his copy. Lintot certainly paid Pope well for his poems, though not over generously. John Nichols's extracts from his accounts show payments for these works: *Essay on Criticism* (£15), *Miscellaneous Poems* (15 guineas, £7, £3.16.6), *Windsor-Forest* (30 guineas), *Ode for Musick* (£15), additions to *Rape of the Lock* (£15), *Temple of Fame* (30 guineas), *Key to the Lock* (10 guineas). These payments are in line with top payments to other writers: Richard Barford's *The Assembly: A Poem*, for example, got 15 guineas and Gay's *Trivia* £43. But it was the *Iliad* that set Pope up as a major earner from his writing (around £5,000 from the six volumes), and the contrast with his other earnings is quite remarkable. The *Iliad* translation was designed from the start as an income-generating venture. In a revealing conversation with Spence, Pope said, "What led me into that [*The Iliad*] . . . was purely the want of money. I had then none – not even to buy books" (*Anecdotes*, I, p. 82).

Subscription allowed the author to benefit both from the trade, through a copyright payment, and from a form of collective patronage (especially if some subscribers paid for multiple copies without collecting them). Lintot generously not only paid for the copyright but also subsidized the subscription by providing free copies. (Tickell, translating for Tonson, paid for his at cost.) The contract was signed on 23 March 1714 and the surviving copies, in the British Library and the Bodleian, show that there was a dramatic last-minute change in the arrangements from an octavo to a quarto edition, which was a bigger, riskier deal for Lintot. In order to meet the increased cost of the subscription copies (the expenditure on paper would have doubled), Lintot decided he must sell even larger-format copies himself (which meant folios, with the sheet folded only once) and print a combination of large-paper (250) and small folios, called "pott" from the watermark sometimes used (1,750). The result is the strange arrangement, with repercussions throughout Pope's career, whereby the subscription copies were in the smaller cheaper format, though they had illustrations, and the trade editions were in the grander folio. As David Foxon has explained, Lintot miscalculated. If he could have sold the 2,000 folios, he might have had a profit of £728, divided equally between himself and Pope, but after the first edition he reduced the order for pott folios from 1,750 to 1,000, thereby limiting his own potential profit to £111 per volume.[7] There were other problems for Lintot – about how the subscribers were to get their copies and about when the trade edition could be launched – which led to him sending Pope a somewhat desperate note on 10 June, pleading for co-operation:

> All your Books were deliverd pursuant to your direction the middle of the Week after you left Us . . . Pray detain me not from publishing my Own Book having deliverd the greatest part of the Subscribers allready, upwards of four hundred.

> I designd to publish Monday sevennight pray interrupt me not by an Errata.
> I doubt not the Sale of Homer if you do not dissapoint me by delaying the
> Publication.
>
> (*Corr*, I, p. 295)

Pope would have resented these disputes, but he had every reason to be pleased. He had 657 subscribers rather than the anticipated 750, but they paid him 6 guineas each and he already had his copy money. His profit from *The Iliad* is usually estimated at around £5,000.

Lintot was not so dissatisfied with the arrangement for *The Iliad* that he was unwilling to make a similar agreement with Pope for *The Odyssey*. Tonson lurks in the background here, later to serve as a cause of the breach between them. Fenton told Broome: "Tonson does not care to contract for the copy, and application has been made to Lintot, upon which he exerts the true spirit of a scoundrel, believing he has Pope entirely at his mercy" (*Corr*, II, p. 214). Lintot did reduce the copy money from 1200 to 350 guineas, or 70 guineas a volume, around a third of the payment for *The Iliad*. The generous arrangement for the subscribers' copies, however, remained essentially unchanged. The delivery problem was solved by issuing the five volumes in two blocks, with Pope responsible for deliveries. The time between subscription and trade publication was shortened to one week. All seemed set fair, with good rewards promised for author and bookseller. But there was, nevertheless, a serious quarrel. Perhaps Lintot had been unaware of the significance of a change in the wording of the two Homer contracts. In the first Pope intended to "translate Homer's Iliads"; in the second he had "undertaken a Translation of Homer's Odysses." For *The Odyssey*, he had two collaborators, Fenton (four out of twenty-four books) and Broome (eight). The collaboration was subsequently the source of adverse publicity, but there is no evidence that Lintot was ignorant of this arrangement, or that he objected. The problem, more likely, lay with Tonson. Pope had agreed to edit Shakespeare for Tonson for £100, and unfortunately the Shakespeare was advertised at the same time as *The Odyssey*. The Shakespeare was also a subscription edition, but the subscription was for the benefit of Tonson, not Pope. Advertisements for both books appeared in the journals on 23 January 1725.[8] Here was a rival publication with Pope's name attached, and at the very moment that Lintot was taking in subscriptions for Pope at his shop, Tonson was using Pope's name to take in subscriptions for himself at his. In retaliation, Lintot decided to advertise his own subscription edition of *The Odyssey* and undercut Pope by offering the five volumes for 4 guineas. The terms closely echoed those Tonson was offering for the Shakespeare. I doubt whether Lintot damaged Pope's subscription by this offer, and he may have succeeded in shifting his own stock more quickly, but he undoubtedly offended Pope, who resolved to have nothing more to do with him. But Lintot held the copyright to the early poems, and within ten years Pope was co-operating with him again.

## Edmund Curll

Lintot now changed character among Pope's book trade personae, becoming a villain. Hitherto he had played a comic-solemn role, subsidiary to Edmund Curll's villain. Curll had first come into serious conflict with Pope over *Court Poems* in 1716, suggesting they might be written by Pope, or Gay, or a "Lady of Quality," a reference to Lady Mary Wortley Montagu. The reference to Montagu probably made Pope feel entitled to behave in the way he did, which was to give Curll an emetic/laxative and then publicize his action; it was, as Norman Ault suggests, the only form of chivalric action open to an invalid (*Prose*, I, pp. xcvi–xcvii). The resulting pamphlets show a curious mixture of intimacy and contempt: *A Full and True Account of a Horrid and Barbarous Revenge by Poison on the Body of Mr. Edmund Curll, Bookseller, With a Faithful Copy of his Last Will and Testament* (1716) and *A Further Account of the Most Deplorable Condition of Mr. Edmund Curll* (1716). Pope's knowledge of Curll's business is astonishing, a combination of personal enthusiasm and good information from Tonson, who identified Curll as the publisher of *Court Poems*. Curll embodies the failings of the trade, confessions of malpractice tumbling from his mouth: "I do sincerely pray Forgiveness for those indirect Methods I have pursued in inventing new Titles to old Books, putting Authors Names to Things they never saw, publishing private Quarrels for publick Entertainment" (*Prose*, I, p. 262). He takes no responsibility for his publications, hides behind the name of other booksellers, vilifies great men of either party, distorts the facts, puts out works under the names of famous authors when they are not theirs, publishes incorrect editions, abuses great authors, and publishes pornography as a major source of income.

"A Further Account" equals its predecessor in its account of the trade, but the emphasis shifts from the bookseller to his authors. Pat Rogers has observed that this "Account" provides "practically a working gazetteer" of the Grub Street subculture.[9] Curll, summoning all his authors for their final instructions, gives his porter descriptions and addresses: "At the Bedsted and Bolster, a Musick House in *Morefields*, two Translators in a Bed together," "At the *Hercules* and *Still* in *Vinegar-yard*, a School-Master with Carbuncles on his Nose," and so on (*Prose*, I, p. 278). Some of these figures may be identified, others may be merely plausible, but the effect is of capturing precisely a needy and disaffected group in their habitats. When they stand before Curll on his close-stool, Curll tells them they are to be the libellers of Pope, who is to become the direct as well as indirect victim of the corruptions of the trade. Curll's own role, energetically accepted, was to become for Pope the antithesis of respectable publication. As such he is given a vivid role in the poetry, but Pope also learnt much by imitation. Curll's interest in biography led to publication of the letters; his miscellanies provoked the Pope-Swift miscellanies; his notes were developed into official notes; and his guile in publication stimulated Pope into ruses of his own. In some respects Curll was the master and Pope his apprentice.

## The Dunciad

The book trade promises to loom larger in *The Dunciad* (1728) than it actually does. Martinus Scriblerus in the *Variorum* edition (1729) offers us the prospect of a vision of technological determinism that the poem never realizes. Pope's cultural commentary, of course, remains reticent in ascribing responsibility for the cultural malaise it identifies – social action is transformed by a mythology that obscures human agency – but the Court, the monarchy, the aristocracy, and educational institutions are responsible for the reign of Dulness, not the printing press. Scriblerus, as so often in his "Of the Poem" gives us a false lead.

> We shall next declare the occasion and the cause which moved our Poet to this particular work. He lived in those days, when (after providence had permitted the Invention of Printing as a scourge for the Sins of the learned) Paper also became so cheap, and printers so numerous, that a deluge of authors cover'd the land: Whereby not only the peace of the honest unwriting subject was daily molested, but unmerciful demands were made of his applause, yea of his money, by such as would neither earn the one, or deserve the other.
>
> (*TE*, v, p. 49)

The idea that printing is a scourge for the learned is not a view Pope himself endorses elsewhere in the poem. Consequently, we find uncreative individuals rather than processes: no paper-making, no harassed compositors and pressmen, no contracts, no distribution, and, of course, very few sales. The poem, though its notes draw on extensive knowledge of the trade, evinces much less detailed knowledge than the two accounts of Curll's sufferings.

That said, the action in the first two books focuses on the piecework-slaves of the book trade and their masters. Tibbald's lodgings in the first book might well be Vinegar-yard, and the two sisters, Poverty and Poetry, lying shivering together in one bed (i, 32), recollect the two translators together in Moorfields and represent the Grub Street from which the material of "Curl's chaste press, and Lintot's rubric post" (I, 38) springs. In the second book these booksellers become actors in the narrative, and Dulness's games reveal their natures and demonstrate their prowess. Excrement is again deployed as a motif, though in more diverse ways than in the scenes of Curll's discomfiture, its associations with money-making and with scandal being made plain. The first scene of the games is the Strand, an important book trade centre, but Pope does not use book trade patterns of distribution as a way of showing the extension of Dulness's influence. The first race is for the phantom poet, with Curll and Lintot the two challengers. The treatment of these two figures is surprisingly generous and comic, with a nice contrast between Lintot's lumbering self-assertion and Curll's impudence. As so often, particulars (Lintot's payments to James Moore Smythe) underlie the action. Lintot immediately claims the prize, but Curll quickly responds:

> Alone untaught to fear,
> Stood dauntless Curl, "Behold that rival here!
> The race by vigor, not by vaunts is won;
> So take the hindmost Hell." – He said, and run.
> Swift as a bard the bailiff leaves behind,
> He left huge Lintot, and out-stript the wind.
> As when a dab-chick waddles thro' the copse,
> On feet and wings, and flies, and wades, and hops;
> So lab'ring on, with shoulders, hand, and head,
> Wide as a windmill all his figure spread,
> With legs expanded Bernard urg'd the race,
> And seem'd to emulate great Jacob's pace.
> (*Dunciad*, II, 53–64)

Lintot's clumsiness is finally made to stand as a metaphor for his rivalry with Tonson. Even in his competition with Curll he is outstripped by his swifter rival, who, strengthened by the ordure into which he falls (specifically publication of Pope's letters), goes on to win. He also wins a second, urinating competition, for Eliza Haywood, in which he challenges the novelist's publisher, Chetwood. The attack is not inappropriately directed at Curll the pornographer, but it otherwise tells us little about his business.

The urinating contest ends the detailed examination of book trade figures in *The Dunciad*. In the four-book revision of the contest (1743–4), Chetwood is simply replaced by Osborne, who is accused in the notes of having sold *Iliad* folios as subscription quartos. The one book trade incident in the new Book IV of the poem neatly represents the movement of Pope's thought, which is away from ridicule of Grub Street towards a critique of high culture and learning. Sir Thomas Hanmer presents the goddess with his luxurious edition of Shakespeare, but this is not a trade edition. It is an expensive product of Oxford University Press, and, as Pope insists, it is not even marketed, being distributed to gentleman commoners gratis. The responsibility of the book trade for the advance of the reign of Dulness remains a minor one.

## Wright, Gilliver, and Dodsley

For *The Dunciad Variorum* Pope needed a new bookseller and printer he could supervise closely. He chose a manipulable young bookseller, Lawton Gilliver, just out of his apprenticeship, and an experienced printer, John Wright, who had been foreman to the Tory printer John Barber. A skilled printer was needed for the *Variorum* and for some of Pope's other experiments over the next six or seven years, and the playing with many-layered notes, parallel texts, black letter or Gothic type, and varied typographical styles, were expressive of Pope's new control over his printer. John Dennis reports that work on the *Variorum* did not go altogether easily:

> Does not half the Town know, that honest *J. W.* was the only Dunce that was persecuted and plagu'd by this Impression? that Twenty times the Rhapsodist alter'd every thing that he gave the Printer? and that Twenty times, *W.* in his Rage and in Fury, threaten'd to turn the Rhapsody back upon the Rhapsodist's Hands? (*TE*, v, p. xxvii)

Nevertheless, *The Dunciad Variorum* is an able printing job. The types are not new and there is some heavy inking to compensate, but a complicated design is realized with some aplomb: a mock-epic in quarto is created to sit alongside the Homer translations.

Relations with Gilliver were even more perplexed, with Pope facing up to a problem that was to haunt the second half of his career – that of copyright. In order to claim copyright, the work had to be entered in the Stationers' Register; such entries were usually made by members of the Company and for a while Pope seems to have thought that they had to be. That created problems when he wanted to keep his identity secret or declined to give a proper assignment to a bookseller, as was the case with the *Variorum*. Instead he assigned the copyright to Lords Bathurst, Burlington, and Oxford in order to protect himself, and they eventually assigned the copyright to Gilliver. As a result, Gilliver's case against the pirates of the first edition failed because he could not establish his property. Pope later brought cases in Chancery over his letters (Curll), over the *Essay on Man* (Bickerton), and over *The Dunciad* (Lintot) in an attempt to secure his property.

Pope's plans for the second half of his career were fairly clear at the time of *The Dunciad*: using Gilliver and Wright, he would publish first *The Dunciad* and then a great philosophical poem in several epistles; the two would then be combined as a new volume of works. The *Essay on Man* would be the first section of the great poem and each of its four books would have a corresponding illustrative epistle or epistles. Gilliver would hold the copyright to *The Dunciad*, but Pope would retain the rights to his philosophical magnum opus. The scheme was completed in outline, and a publishing success. The Lords paid Pope £100 for *The Dunciad*. For each of the epistles Gilliver agreed to pay £50 for the copyright for one year, taking on the responsibility of entering them in the Stationers' Register. Gilliver knew that at the end of the scheme of publication he would have a half share in the second volume of *Works*, as a result of *The Dunciad*.

In addition to the publication of his own works, Pope sent other business to Gilliver and Wright. It seems likely, for example, that he had an investment in the *Grub-street Journal*, and used Gilliver, who was its leading proprietor, as an agent who would occasionally influence policy. He also helped move the work of friends and protégés along the road to publication. Additional printers and publishers involved in these arrangements could also assist Pope when anonymity was needed. The first epistle of an *Essay on Man* was printed by John Huggonson, who was then the printer of the *Grub-street Journal*, and the name that appeared on the title page and in the Stationers' Register was that of the *Journal*'s publisher, John Wilford.

As one might anticipate, Pope and Gilliver fell out over the profits from sale of the *Works*. Pope had to pay for his half of the edition and then sell those copies. He clearly expected that Gilliver would take care of that for him, but Gilliver offered 13s. a copy, rather than 17s., and as a result lost his place as Pope's bookseller to Robert Dodsley, who set up shop with Pope's help in Spring 1735. If Pope had remained on good terms with Gilliver, we might know less of the affair of the publication of the *Letters*, which so damaged Pope's reputation. When in 1729 Pope prepared an edition of the *Posthumous Works of William Wycherley II* (an edition aborted for copyright reasons) as a riposte to Theobald's edition of Wycherley, he printed extra copies of his own correspondence with Wycherley on better paper and added some other letters. He then kept them, waiting for an occasion on which they might be used. Such an opportunity seemed to occur in 1735, just as a new copyright bill was going through Parliament. Writing as "PT," an enemy of Pope, Pope managed to persuade Curll that he had authentic letters that he already had printed. There was an elaborate charade, with James Worsdale, the painter, dressed as a clergyman, acting as Pope's agent, but eventually Curll received two batches of letters, only to be brought before the bar of the House of Lords on a charge of printing the letters of peers. Pope may have been trying to give Curll a fright, and to influence the copyright bill (which was in fact lost), but it seems unlikely that he was trying to injure him seriously. Curll responded to his accusers by telling the truth, and, having worked out most of the story, published it along with the letters.

> The Plot is now discover'd: Lawton Gilliver has declared that you [Pope] bought of him the Remainder of the Impression of Wycherley's letters, which he printed, by your Direction, in 1728, and have printed, Six Hundred of the additional Letters, with those to Mr. Cromwell, to make up the volume.[10]

Pope, protesting at the evil of publication of his letters, published his subscription edition in 1737. Later, in a landmark case against Curll (1741), he established copyright in private letters.[11]

From *Works* (1735) onwards Pope regularly brought out new volumes of his octavo works, collecting new material and re-presenting old. These volumes were printed by Wright or Henry Woodfall and marketed by Robert Dodsley (who made entries in the Stationers' Register) and by Thomas and Mary Cooper (who handled the distribution). With the advice of Nathaniel Cole, solicitor to the Stationers' Company, and his friend William Murray, he brought or threatened legal action against those who pirated material. Only in his final years, under the influence of William Warburton, who had become his commentator, did he return again to quarto editions with a chaste typography, a project that was to be interrupted by his death.

Although, with his attacks on Grub Street, his hostility to individual booksellers, and his sense of the unreliability of print, Pope can be thought of as an enemy to the book trade, few writers made better use of its resources. Most often when planning a work, he thought of it as a book, and began to plot its appearance, manufacture, and marketing. To a significant degree, these plans succeeded and set the patterns of presentation and debate that have persisted to the present day.

## NOTES

1. The best account of Tonson is Kathleen M. Lynch, *Jacob Tonson: Kit-Cat Publisher* (Knoxville: University of Tennessee Press, 1971).
2. Margaret J. M. Ezell treats Pope's manuscript circulation in *Social Authorship and the Advent of Print* (Baltimore: Johns Hopkins University Press, 1999).
3. The manuscript is reproduced with others in Maynard Mack, *The Last and Greatest Art: Some Unpublished Poetical Manuscripts of Alexander Pope* (Newark: University of Delaware Press, 1984).
4. John Nichols, *Literary Anecdotes of the Eighteenth Century*, 8 vols. (London: Printed for the author by Nichols, Son, and Bentley, 1812–16), VIII, p. 300, suggests that Lintot paid Pope rather than Lewis for the copyright.

5. This is one of the themes of David Foxon's *Pope and the Early Eighteenth-Century Book Trade* (Oxford: Clarendon Press, 1991), especially in the final two chapters. *An Essay on Criticism* is treated on pp. 162–80.
6. Summer was not a good time to publish. I wonder whether Pope sometimes arranged publication to coincide with his birthday. His final poem *The Dunciad in Four Books* was published on 29 October 1743, the eve of George II's sixtieth birthday.
7. Foxon, *Pope and the Book Trade*, pp. 51–63. My account of this whole episode is heavily indebted to Foxon, with further detail drawn from my "The Contract for Pope's Translation of Homer's *Iliad*: An Introduction and Transcription," *The Library* 6:15 (1993): pp. 206–25.
8. The proposals make the nature of the translation and subscriptions clear. Pope quotes them in *The Dunciad Variorum* (*TE*, v, p. 31); it is unlikely he would have risked seriously misrepresenting them.
9. Pat Rogers, *Grub Street: Studies in a Subculture* (London: Methuen, 1972), pp. 82–3.
10. Alexander Pope, *Mr Pope's Literary Correspondence. Volume the Second* (London: Printed for Edmond Curll, 1735), p. xiv. I provide further details in my "The First Printing and Publication of Pope's Letters," *Library* 6:2 (1980): pp. 264–80.
11. Pat Rogers, "The Case of Pope *v.* Curll," *The Library*, 5:27 (1972): pp. 326–31; and Harry Ransom, "The Personal Letter as Literary Property," *Studies in English* 30 (1951): pp. 116–31.

# 15

VALERIE RUMBOLD

# Pope and gender

Pope's work was both energized and constrained by gender; but evaluating its effects is far from straightforward, since gender in Pope's time was neither a monolithic system nor an entirely stable one, and major shifts were under way that would have far-reaching effects on understandings of what it meant to live as a man or a woman.[1] For instance, the progress of normative heterosexual masculinity in stigmatizing its homosexual other was gradually ruling out the possibility both that boys might be counted among the objects of a manly passion, and that excessive infatuation with women might itself be counted as effeminacy. Meanwhile, the older model of elite femininity associated with intellectual culture, public sociability and household authority was being eclipsed by an emphasis on female domesticity that emanated from the middle ranks of society. These are just two instances, but sufficient to indicate the scale and importance of some of the changes at work. For Pope, marked as different by his disability, his Catholic religion, and his Tory loyalties, gender would entail a particularly difficult interface between challenge and conventionality, one that stimulated some kinds of imaginative work while it closed down others.[2]

## Sociability and sexuality

Pope was the child of elderly parents, and was brought up at home with the help of a wet nurse, an old aunt who taught him his letters, and, later, a Catholic priest who acted as tutor.[3] In response to anti-Catholic legislation his parents retired to the Thames valley village of Binfield, where he spent his teenage years; and here he had the benefit of meeting among his retired neighbours men who had in their time been notable wits and statesmen. At the same time, having contracted spinal tuberculosis, most probably from his wet nurse, Pope began to suffer noticeably from stunted growth, curvature of the spine, and a range of debilitating symptoms; and this, together with his Catholic family's civil disabilities, increasingly barred him from crucial masculine activities.[4] Forbidden to attend school or university (with the exception of an unrewarding spell at a small illegal Catholic establishment), to own land (and consequently his own home) or to work in the service of the crown (for instance as Poet Laureate), he was also barred by physical disability from active sports, and, in his own judgment (if we credit his various remarks on the topic), from marriage.[5] As a boy he used his relative isolation to read voraciously, and he learned all he could from the literary men among his retired neighbours, but, having only a much older half-sister by his father's first marriage, he suffered many of the disadvantages of the only child, exacerbated by the preponderance of the elderly in his immediate circle, and by his exclusion from the masculine peer group of school and college. He learned early to occupy the role of promising youngster, basking in the attention of accomplished older men, a dynamic which would underlie several of his most important adult friendships: Atterbury and Swift were his elders by two decades, and Bolingbroke by one.

Pope's combination of civil and medical disabilities entailed restrictions in many ways close to those within which women had to operate; but he also lived strenuously, insofar as his health permitted, as a member of a masculine cultural and intellectual world. The privileges of this homosocial milieu were vital to him; and he pursued masculine sociability and friendship by entertaining friends at home, by undertaking long-distance visits, and by keeping up a voluminous correspondence. Such masculine friendship could reach the pitch of hero worship: in the case of the charismatic Bolingbroke, Brean Hammond describes him as adopting an admiring role of "quasi-feminine passivity."[6] Yet Pope bid fair for his own standing in this masculine world: building on the success of his translation of Homer's epics of war and heroism an unprecedented commercial career as poet, he projected the image of a manly spokesman for traditional values, independent both of patron and of party. So effective, apparently, was the masculine allure with which he played the role of published poet that he found himself embarrassed by the attentions of an infatuated woman who called herself "Amica," probably the first female fan in literary history to make such a nuisance of herself that she had to be asked to desist (*Life*, pp. 796–801).

Observers at the time and since have seemed puzzled by the fact that Pope cherished a life-long friendship with Martha Blount without ever, apparently, proposing marriage – leading to allegations that they were lovers or were secretly married (we are reminded of similar speculations about Swift and Esther Johnson).[7] Pope spoke of himself as a ludicrous partner for any presentable woman, a theme that his enemy Colley Cibber would develop in painful detail when he described how he had forcibly dragged "the little-tiny Manhood of Mr. *Pope*" off a prostitute for his own good (the alleged motive being even more suspect than the anecdote itself).[8] Yet it also has to be said that Pope's largely celibate life suited him in important ways: living in tender companionship with his widowed mother, he retained a large degree of control over his time and his domestic space, and could often manage long visits to the homes of friends. To imagine a counterfactual Pope with a wife and children is not easy, given the extreme commitment and professionalism that marked his writing career. In *An Epistle to Arbuthnot*, where "The Muse but serv'd to ease some Friend, not Wife, | To help me thro' this long Disease, my Life," he even fashions for himself a role as mother to his own mother's senility, setting himself "to Rock the Cradle of reposing Age" (131–2, 409).[9] The vignette certainly emphasizes how good a son he is (itself an important manly role), but also suggests that the dynastic dead end in which he finds himself entails, along with a loss of manly scope, a marginality in some sense crucial to his poetic career. Finding his friends principally among the political opposition, committed to a minority religious community whose values and assumptions often irritated him, without house or land to transmit to the next generation, and relatively free of implication in the patriarchal politics of ruling a family, he arguably had an ideal position from which to launch the frequently oppositional work that would characterize his career: with regard to gender, this would include, alongside much that exploited in one way or another the customary tropes of masculine authority and feminine contingency, poems explicitly critical of the patriarchal limitations imposed on women, notably *Elegy to the Memory of an Unfortunate Lady*, *Eloisa to Abelard*, and "To a Lady with the Works of Voiture."

Pope was drawn to witty, outspoken women – people who to some extent shared his talents and interests – but tended to fall out with them in the longer term. He flirted with the outgoing Teresa Blount only in the end to quarrel with her in favour of lifelong devotion to her shy sister Martha.[10] His fascination with Lady Mary Wortley Montagu ended in obsessive attacks on her as a filthy and avaricious whore.[11] Isobel Grundy sees even in his early letters to her "the hostility already immanent in the adoration": that is, "he constructs her as a beautiful body – implicitly a nude body – while she is busy constructing herself as doing and seeing and writing."[12] His basic prejudices about women made it impossible to integrate into a stable friendship the boldness and autonomy that attracted him. This was a period when, despite the actual ferment around notions of gender, many assumed that the characteristics and proper roles of the sexes were timeless and unchanging. The male was associated with strength of body and of mind, along with the moral and rational capacities that conferred authority in family and public life, while the female was marked as inferior by a problematic combination of poor judgment and weak self-discipline with a body dominated by its sexual functions. Women were not to be trusted with autonomy, and the chastity that could alone ensure that a husband's children were his own was preached to them as the sine qua non of virtue. Pope comments (not necessarily sympathetically) on one of the belittling effects for women of the resulting double standard:

> What is generally accepted as Virtue in women, is very different from what is thought so in men: A very good woman would make but a paltry man.
>
> (*Prose*, I, p. 161)

Yet particularly since the word "man" was unabashedly used in this period to denote both the species and the sex, it was hard for women to challenge such a masculinist account of the human condition without giving up the claim either to womanhood or to virtue. The excluded shadow of Pope's "paltry man" thus haunts the margins of a professedly generalizing poem like the *Essay on Man*, where the examples are preponderantly male:

> Shame to the virgin, to the matron pride,
> Fear to the statesman, rashness to the chief,
> To kings presumption, and to crowds belief.
>
> (*Essay on Man*, II, 242–4)

Men are assumed to manifest various public characters in a way that is unavailable to women: they, allotted only to private life, are distinguished only by marital status.[13] Later in the poem Pope moves from an account of procreation, where women are specifically mentioned as mothers, to speculations on political origins that are derived entirely from relations between fathers and sons: there is no felt need to spell out the place of women in the political hierarchies that result (III, 119–26, 211–34). The masculine in fact appropriates so much of the human that the feminine is left with no viable standpoint. Although at first glance the pairings and contrasts typical of the heroic couplet may seem straightforwardly mimetic of a system in which the sexes are defined as balanced and freestanding opposites, slippages and non sequiturs tell a different story.[14]

Pope's letters and poems show him inhabiting a range of established modes of masculinity: rather than seeing these as spurious or contradictory, we might consider each as in its way reflecting, at least provisionally, an aspect of the manly competence to which he aspired. As a young man he wrote to the established man-about-town Henry Cromwell in the style of a rake, which later caused embarrassment when the letters were published without his consent.[15] To ladies he knows and likes early in life he presents himself as a slyly accomplished practitioner of conventionally gallant double-entendre.[16] He also warms to the Ovidian tradition of sympathy for women suffering at the hands of ungrateful or disloyal men. This harmonised with his characteristic emotional impulse to cast himself as champion of women friends who found themselves in marital and financial difficulty, an impulse that on occasion made him enemies.[17] In his mature correspondence there is a characteristically intimate manly style that stresses friendship and familial duty, sharing the concern for his widowed mother and for his friends' well-being in this world and the next that he would fashion into the climax of his self-presentation in the *Epistle to Arbuthnot*. Yet in the 1730s he also presents himself as an outrageously indecent imitator of Horace's advocacy of safe sex with boys and prostitutes (safe, that is, insofar as they have no husbands to take revenge): *Sober Advice from Horace* adds to the original a plethora of slurs on women in general and on his friend-turned-antagonist Lady Mary in particular; and the performance is crowned with a mock-scholarly commentary designed to embarrass his classicist *bête noire* Richard Bentley.

*Sober Advice* is a salutary reminder that the education in Latin and Greek that boys entered upon once separated from female tutelage was a key factor in forming elite male identity. Carolyn Williams has shown how Pope used his translation of Homer to vindicate his own manliness, in an important sense compromised by his exclusion from the educational establishment in which such manly learning was traditionally acquired; and she indicates how this classical context is crucial to a whole range of his negotiations of gender.[18] The caricature of Lord Hervey as Sporus in the *Epistle to Arbuthnot* is after all rooted in allusion to the sexual tyranny of a Roman emperor, while the Atticus portrait taunts Addison with allusion to the Roman hero Cato and Atticus the friend of Cicero. Yet the "manly ways" on which the poet congratulates himself cannot necessarily be quite so straightforwardly understood as modern notions of normative heterosexual masculinity might suggest. James McLaverty presents *To Arbuthnot* and *Sober Advice from Horace* as twin responses to the attacks Hervey and Lady Mary had published against Pope, and discerns in the latter a strategy of teasing the reader with the pederastic assumptions of Horace's original, which are largely neutralized in the text, only to be gratuitously highlighted in the mock-scholarly commentary: in this account the contrast between Pope and Hervey would not be that one is heterosexual and the other bisexual, but that one is manly in his passions, and the other passively venal.[19] Whatever the reader's judgment, the classical context of masculine education and its tradition of reading the gender formations of antiquity through a Christianizing lens is too important to ignore. *Sober Advice* also reminds us that for a balanced view of Pope and gender we must be prepared to explore even the poems least attractive and accessible to modern readers.

## The Rape of the Lock

Few of Pope's poems are as explicit in their concern with gender as *The Rape of the Lock*, published in substantially different versions in 1712 and 1714, and with the addition of Clarissa's speech in 1717.[20] At its heart is a failed courtship, modeled on a quarrel in a Catholic circle connected with Pope's. Belinda is initially constructed as the hyperbolic divinity of traditional male gallantry, and is compared to the sun (I, 14; II, 1–14). (Compare the moon-like women who in practice preserved Pope's esteem the longest.)[21] She dresses in a parody of the arming of the epic hero (enabling Pope to combine traditional gibes at female vanity with celebration of the imperial commerce that brings "the various Off'rings of the World" to her dressing table); and she conquers "two adventrous Knights" – her loud exultation over her victory signaling aspirations far beyond what her society sanctions for women (I, 121–48; III, 26).

Polarised on either side of her are two extreme examples of female types between which, after the cutting of the lock, she has to choose (although both, in line with anti-feminist stereotypes, are male-focused women of questionable integrity who have no real solidarity with Belinda). Her supposed friend, "fierce *Thalestris*," who instigates the heroine's campaign to regain the severed lock, has an Amazonian name; but far from defying subordination on Belinda's behalf, she turns out to value even the outward appearance of gender decorum, however deceptive, far more than she values her (IV, 89–120). If the Baron does succeed in keeping the lock he has stolen, Thalestris will feel obliged to drop her: "'Twill then be Infamy to seem your Friend!" At the opposite pole, Clarissa, whose name connotes brightness and the clarity of truth, speaks for feminine self-restraint; but no-one in the poem applauds what she says ("*Thalestris* call'd her Prude"), and we are not likely to forget that it was she who had put the scissors into the Baron's hand when she first saw him gazing at Belinda's hair (III, 127–8; V, 35). Pope puts into her mouth a conventional exhortation to good-humored acceptance of male power and the transience of female beauty; but it is arguably undermined by the speaker's duplicity, and by the accomplished complacency with which Pope makes her deliver her truisms. (The familiar note that Clarissa's speech was added "to open more clearly the MORAL of the Poem" is not Pope's: it was added by his authorized editor Warburton, who consistently preferred moral orthodoxy to ambiguity or ambivalence in the texts he annotated.)

The male sex as represented by Sir Plume and the Baron is deeply compromised, leaving Belinda arguably "the most virile figure in the poem."[22] Sir Plume, for all the designer artefacts that bedeck his person, is a henpecked nonentity: his resentful original "could not bear that Sir Plume should talk *nothing* but nonsense" (*Anecdotes*, I, pp. 444–5). When Sir Plume tries to assert Belinda's rights his words are utterly ineffectual:

> "Plague on't! 'tis past a jest – nay prithee, pox!
> Give her the hair" – he spoke, and rapp'd his box.
> It grieves me much (reply'd the Peer again)
> Who speaks so well shou'd ever speak in vain.
>
> (IV, 129–32)

The Baron's courteous but intransigent response may seem, in contrast, to lay down the law to some effect; but any pretence to masculine authority is undermined by the wider context. The poem had begun in affected awe at the risk to "Little Men" of engaging in "Tasks so bold" as to prompt the "mighty Rage" of "soft Bosoms"; and at the end of the poem the Baron is felled by Belinda; and whatever his prophecies of her eventual submission to another, he fails in his attempt to keep hold of the lock (I, 11–12; V, 75–122).

Belinda, however, does not get it back either, for framing the whole action is a narrative voice which in its power to make things happen, and in its allusions to the heroic realm of epic and of manly learning, demonstrates a masculine potency beyond anything achieved by the male characters themselves: bringing the action to a close by instructing us to "trust the Muse" (the female vehicle for writerly mastery to which Pope nominally defers), he takes it upon himself to put Belinda in her place, a place which he defines by the superiority of masculine art (which is for eternity) to feminine beauty (which is ephemeral) (V, 123–50). In the context of Pope's exclusion from so many of the masculine roles that his society offered, this performance constitutes a triumphantly masculine command of the classical heritage. Yet in the face of this apparent gender triumphalism it is worth remembering how teasingly the miniaturized divine machinery that flitters around Belinda and the Baron has been represented as a bevy of highly sexual but only provisionally gendered creatures (I, 19–104). For the sylphs, adopting the body of one sex or the other is merely a stratagem. Subversively adapted from Milton's angels, these miniaturized replacements for the tutelary gods of epic leave hovering the suggestion that gender is after all only a performance, and one that is undertaken principally for erotic pleasure.[23]

## Eloisa to Abelard

*Eloisa to Abelard* is another story of lost love that puts the emphasis on the woman's experience; but it is conceived in the radically different idiom of Ovidian erotic tenderness (deriving from Ovid's *Heroides*, with their heroines' laments over lost lovers), and is related to the tradition of heroic love which had at the Restoration helped to voice, in the erotic mode, royalist aspirations to commitments so absolute that only souls prepared to defy death and fate could sustain them. It is in this vein of melting yet rigorously idealistic love that Eloisa offers, for example, a defence of free love that defies everything eighteenth-century women were taught to hold dear (lines 73–98). Also part of the generic appeal to unbridled feeling is the Gothic atmosphere of Eloisa's haunted convent and its gloomy setting, constituting an appeal to subjectivity that finds its context in notions of the female as impressionable and lacking in rational self-discipline. The tone recalls in part the letters of natural description and mood painting that Pope wrote to his friend Martha Blount: one function of such notions of feminine sensibility in his creative life was evidently to channel esthetic and emotional interests less easily aligned with the masculine.[24]

Lovers in the heroic letter are generically absent and unfaithful; but Abelard's castration on the orders of Eloisa's indignant family makes his case both more complex and more absolute. Indeed, it is clear that his readers included many women who found that the poem spoke to them in compelling but disturbing ways, making it the most responded-to of Pope's poems by contemporary women poets.[25] They typically took up the poem not to embrace the relative freedom and sensuality that the mode might seem to license, but to reassert the chastity and piety that Eloisa defies. Recognizing in Pope's ventriloquism the kind of libertine discourse that female honor depended on resisting, they vindicated the grounds of self-worth they had been brought up to hold dear. The *Rape* was in contrast very little answered or imitated by women poets.[26]

### *Epistle to a Lady. Of the Characters of Women*

In 1734 Pope published his *Epistle to Cobham. Of the Knowledge and Characters of Men*, and in the following year his *Epistle to a Lady. Of the Characters of Women. Characters of Men* presents a very few examples of female behavior and casts human concerns in a distinctively masculine mold; but *Characters of Women* focuses on women as a puzzling group, best defined by contrast and comparison with the male. This is a rich and complex poem whose arbitrariness and inconsistencies Pope is unable to resolve; and its poignancy lies in the fact that although he is writing it for a very much loved friend, he still has enormous difficulty in formulating praise for her as a woman that does not hinge either on contrasting her with the allegedly deplorable norms of her own sex or on likening her to the other. Furthermore, in satirizing women's characters as unstable he projects onto women what he was prone on other occasions to diagnose in himself; and while this compromises any claim to balance or objective analysis, the struggle between distrust and identification in his construction of the female renders the representation of character in this second poem intrinsically more compelling than the relatively bland formulations of *Characters of Men*, where Pope seems perhaps too relaxed on the familiar masculine terrain of respectful frankness between author and aristocratic friend.

Having started with the damaging claim that "Most Women have no Characters at all" (2), strategically attributed to Martha herself, and thus initiating a divide-and-rule policy that will throughout the poem undermine her identification with her sex, Pope introduces a gallery of female perversities that comes close to suggesting that femaleness is simply a matter of masquerade, an implication that begs comparison with the provisionality of gender attributed to the sylphs in the *Rape*:[27]

> How many pictures of one Nymph we view,
> All how unlike each other, all how true!
> (5–6)

Yet the ideal character he draws for Martha, herself unmarried and childless, includes both a husband and a daughter, arguably undermining this representation just as much as the inconsistent portraits satirized at the beginning of the poem, and suggesting that despite the virtues she could have brought to marriage and motherhood, she falls short of being a fully achieved exemplar of her sex (7–14; 257–68). Even as the poem moves to its most convincing testimony of esteem, addressing her as "Friend," "the one word in the language that denotes relationships of equality and permanence" (*Life*, p. 632), any potential for transcending the constraints of gender is countered by the tender implausibility with which Pope seeks to persuade her that the "Virgin Modesty" of "the Moon's more sober light" really does draw the eye more than a flaming sunset (249–56). Unlike those sun-identified beauties Belinda, Lady Mary Wortley Montagu, and Martha's own sister Teresa, she holds a place in his affections that is sustainable precisely because she lacks their wit, confidence, and autonomy. Throughout the poem that culminates in constructing the ideal woman as "a softer Man," his difficulties in conceiving fully achieved humanity as female are palpable (272–80).

## The Dunciad in Four Books

Dulness, the goddess of the *Dunciad*s, is a female personification rather unusually constructed around a distinctly physical, self-indulgent notion of motherhood, an overt threat to the adult masculinity enforced by taking boys away from their mothers and nurses and sending them to school. Yet among all the writers attacked in the *Dunciad*s, very few are women. Nurturance, not utterance, is emphasized as the female role, with Dulness (subversively reminiscent of Queen Caroline) developed as a seductively comfortable mother who lulls the nation into perpetual babyhood. Eliza Haywood, the woman writer who is satirized at greatest length, is imaged as the breast-feeding mother of bastards: she never utters a word (II, 157–98).[28] Susanna Centlivre appears only for the moment in which she "felt her voice to fail" (II, 411). Allegedly bad women's writing is never allowed to perform itself as allegedly bad men's writing repeatedly does in the poem.[29]

Thus it is hardly surprising that although Pope labored over a women's caterwauling section for the noise-making contest of Book II, he never published it.[30] One of the competitors, Mary Pix, was a successful dramatist; but Pope fails to engage with her plays in any specific or interesting way. The other, a venomous satirist called "N—," does not match any known woman writer of the time. The badly chosen victims resist integration into any coherent cultural critique. In contrast, the male monkey-jabberers are identified in a sequence of tightly interlocked units that level author and output in a meaningless babble associated with the university disputations from which Pope's religion excluded him: the passage effectively targets men whose Protestantism underlay their privilege as it underlay their Whiggish hostility to a Tory and Catholic poet (II, 235–42).

It is Blackmore, however, much-ridiculed author of Whig epics, who best highlights the limitations set by gender on Pope's writing about women writers. The episode in which Blackmore wins the prize engages in detail with Pope's specific resentments: Protestant dissent and Whig avarice are clearly engaged as the passage reaches its climax in a reverberating crescendo of carefully orchestrated noise (II, 247–68). The discarded caterwauling episode, which makes no case at all for women writers' cultural significance, remains a very thin joke in comparison with the symphonically coded "o" sounds that render Blackmore's performance so paradoxically impressive. Despite the fascination of reading the fissures and negotiations with which gender challenged Pope, the gap in the *Dunciad*s where this women's episode might have been remains a poignant reminder of the constricting power of gender – constricting to the person gendering as well as the person gendered.

## NOTES

1. For important studies in this area, see Further Reading, pp. 237–246 below.
2. For a reading focused on connections between gender and Pope's physical and other disabilities, see Helen Deutsch, *Resemblance and Disgrace: Alexander Pope*

and the Deformation of Culture (Cambridge, MA: Harvard University Press, 1996). Chapters 2 and 3 carry particular weight in this regard.

3. For Pope's childhood, see Anecdotes, I, pp. 3–32; Valerie Rumbold, Women's Place in Pope's World (Cambridge: Cambridge University Press, 1989), pp. 24–47.

4. Rumbold, Women's Place, pp. 2–6.

5. Ibid., pp. 4, 255.

6. Brean S. Hammond, Pope and Bolingbroke: A Study in Friendship and Influence (Columbia: University of Missouri Press, 1984), pp. 3, 11–12, 13.

7. Rumbold, Women's Place, pp. 128–9.

8. Colley Cibber, A Letter from Mr. Cibber, To Mr. Pope (London: Printed and sold by W. Lewis, 1742), pp. 47–9; Laura J. Rosenthal, "'Trials of Manhood': Cibber, The Dunciad, and the Masculine Self," in "More Solid Learning": New Perspectives on Alexander Pope's "Dunciad", ed. C. Ingrassia and C. N. Thomas (London: Associated University Presses, 2000), pp. 101–4.

9. For the evolution of the phrase "not Wife," see J. McLaverty, Pope, Print, and Meaning (Oxford: Oxford University Press, 2001), p. 207.

10. Rumbold, Women's Place, pp. 110–30.

11. Ibid., pp. 131–67.

12. Isobel Grundy, Lady Mary Wortley Montagu: Comet of the Enlightenment (Oxford: Oxford University Press, 1999), p. xviii.

13. See also Epistle to a Lady, 207–18 (TE, III.ii, pp. 67–8).

14. See Carole Fabricant, "Defining Self and Others: Pope and Eighteenth-Century Gender Ideology," Criticism 39 (1997): pp. 523–6; Laura Brown, Alexander Pope (Oxford: Basil Blackwell, 1985), p. 106.

15. Rumbold, Women's Place, pp. 48–51, 163–4.

16. Ibid., pp. 51–3.

17. Ibid., pp. 3–109.

18. Carolyn D. Williams, Pope, Homer, and Manliness: Some Aspects of Eighteenth-Century Classical Learning (London: Routledge, 1993).

19. McLaverty, Pope, Print, and Meaning, pp. 173–208.

20. For the poem's origins and versions, see Rumbold, Women's Place, pp. 48–82.

21. Ibid., pp. 148–9, 277.

22. S. Clark, "'Let Blood and Body bear the fault': Pope and Misogyny," in Pope: New Contexts, ed. D. Fairer (Hemel Hempstead: Harvester Wheatsheaf, 1990), p. 93.

23. See John Milton, Paradise Lost, ed. A. Fowler, 2nd edn. (Harlow: Addison Wesley Longman, 1998), vol. VIII, 614–29.

24. Rumbold, Women's Place, p. 253.

25. Claudia N. Thomas, Alexander Pope and his Eighteenth-Century Women Readers (Carbondale: Southern Illinois University Press, 1994), pp. 190–3.

26. Except for Maria Edgeworth's novelistic use of the Rape: see Susan Matthews, "'Matter too soft': Pope and the Women's Novel", in Pope: New Contexts, ed. D. Fairer (Hemel Hempstead: Harvester Wheatsheat, 1990), pp. 103–20 (116–19).

27. Matthews, "Matter too Soft," p. 105, notes in these lines a subversive potential assimilable to Lacanian feminism. See also Judith Butler, Gender Trouble: Feminism and the Subversion of Identity, 2nd edn. (London: Routledge, 1999), pp. 171–80.

28. Line references are to *Alexander Pope: The Dunciad in Four Books*, ed. Valerie Rumbold (London: Addison Wesley Longman, 1999).
29. Cf. Fabricant on the politics of representation, "Defining Self," pp. 503–7.
30. Valerie Rumbold, "Cut the Caterwauling," *Review of English Studies* 52 (2001): pp. 524–39.

# 16

GEORGE ROUSSEAU

# Medicine and the body

Alexander Pope's body, as most readers know, was severely deformed. Although he was trampled by a cow as a child of eight in a Berkshire field, as his sister reported (*Anecdotes*, 1, pp. 3–4), his deformity sprang from an incurable tuberculosis of the spine, later called Pott's Disease, which produces curvature of the spine and a markedly humped back. By the time he entered puberty, he began to shrink rather than grow tall, eventually dwindling to no more than four and a half feet tall as an adult, and the fact that one leg was significantly shorter than the other caused him to develop his hump back. The protrusion was painful as well as noticeable, and in time forced him to walk with a stick (cane) and to wear specially fitted shoes. The accident he sustained as a child may also have contributed to genital difficulties he suffered from throughout his life: difficulty in urinating, painful testicles, and urethral pain so bad that he begged the surgeons for frequent operations to ease it. He also suffered from chronically poor eyesight, occasionally so acute that his parents and early doctors erroneously attributed his curved spine and humped back to excessive reading that wrecked his eyes.[1] Voltaire epitomized him as "protuberant before and behind" and Pope himself later claimed that his "Crazy Constitution" had amounted to "this long Disease, my Life."[2] He was prone to quipping, often disparagingly, about his miserable body which he likened to vermin and other small animals (especially to spiders and toads), and on one such occasion he referred to himself anonymously as "a lively little Creature, with long Arms and Legs: a Spider is no ill Emblem of him."[3] He was so precocious in boyhood – a prodigy – and composing such remarkable poetry by the age of ten that he seemed to take on the attributes of adulthood long before he arrived there, and if the medicine of his time had been more advanced he might have been declared a victim of progeria (the malady of growing old while still juvenescent).

The fact that "Little Alexander," as he was often called, was also a Catholic, persecuted when grown for his religion – as Catholics then routinely were – and a lifelong bachelor (marriage would have been difficult for someone in his condition and its lack shrank his heart), further added to his perception that his was a life endured in pain caused primarily by his monstrous body. But as he matured two or three images of his body began to form – as monstrous, grotesque, even freakish – which (understandably) produced anger as his "ruling passion" (as he would call these in *An Essay on Man*). Eventually he grasped that these views were not as monolithically straightforward as they seemed: a sick body in a sound mind. The nocturnal phantasmagoria in Canto IV of *The Rape of the Lock* (53–4) in which Belinda imagines abortive freak creatures when "Men prove with Child, as pow'rful Fancy works, | And Maids turn'd Bottels, call aloud for Corks" – would not be far off the mark as a description of his psychomachia (warfare) between the parts of his body that impelled the world to mock him as "a caricature of a man."

It is unthinkable that such a "Carcase" (as he metonymically often referred to his deformed body) would not take a psychological toll on his selfhood and literary identity. Yet if in one region of his mind he was a monstrous creature of the "vermin spider kind," in another he was the seducer enticing and tempting the very creatures who had spurned him. The seducer lies at the opposite end of the spectrum from the monster: adroit in arts of persuasion and smooth in tempting his victims, he slyly coerces them to conjoin with him despite apparent monstrosity. Yet the freakish monster who fails to learn the seducer's tricks is far worse off, and such a fate seemed to Pope, even if unconsciously so, a destiny far worse than the one he had actually inherited. Furthermore, if seducers were proverbially male (the warrior or prince carrying off his bride), temptresses were female, as Eve the "mother of men" had been; and Pope came to construe himself, especially his literary persona, in this role as temptress who had disguised his gender to thrill in joys denied to him, as had the historical Eloisa in *Eloisa to Abelard* and the biographical Lady Mary Wortley Montagu ("Sapho") who Pope imagines saying "I too could write, and I am twice as tall" in the *Epistle to Arbuthnot* (103). Yet no matter how direly Pope found himself represented by these illicit temptresses, he also enjoyed friendships with other women – young and old – which were playful, anything *but* seductive in this illicit way. In this sense, he managed to remain energized by curbing his impulses to excess. Even so, it is hard to imagine that in his friendships with women he waxed amnesiac about his dwarfish size and protuberances.

He was far too young to be suffering from enlarged prostate syndrome when the problems in his genitals began to affect him. These were likely to have been the fallout of the time he was possibly trampled by the cow, and as he grew into manhood they complicated his ill health. First, he had difficulty passing water, then pains in the kidney area of his back, and was finally told that his genital apparatus (probably the shaft of the penis itself) was in some way compromised. He appealed to the best surgeons, especially the illustrious William Cheselden, who operated on him numerous times and were able to alleviate the discomfort and helped him edit Shakespeare (see *Corr*, II, pp. 100, 106, 177; V, p. 78). But the symbolic fallout was more consequential than the medical for a poet searching for literary identity in an era when the reins of gender identification were tightening. And by the time he set out to translate the Homeric epics in 1713–15 as a young man of just twenty-five (even before his romantic advances were rejected by Lady Mary), he had recognized that no matter how famous a poet he had by then become the die was cast: deformed and dwarfed, unmarried and Catholic, he would not be able to prove his manhood in reproductive ways. Small wonder that he resorted to defenses located primarily in the pen: "let me draw the last pen for freedom" (*Epilogue to the Satires*, I, 3).

The Pope who draws the "last pen," as it were, is not merely commenting on his commitment to moral truth and the integrity of the honest man, but also on the pen as metonymy for selfhood, masculinity, and penis – the components of identity about which he was sensitive, even nervous. It is of course difficult to construct a case for symbolic genitals as signifiers in contrast to anatomic ones: anyway the former is almost impossible to prove.[4] Yet no psychoanalytic training is required (not that I advocate it retrospectively anyway) to recognize the metonymy of the one for the other, especially in the cases of patients (Pope, like Coleridge, was a lifelong patient). During his lifetime endless stories circulated about his forlorn escapades to prove his masculinity – not just the outrageous one Cibber recounts about a visit Pope made to a London brothel,[5] but others in the various homosocial clubs to which he belonged, including the Scriblerians – and even if these exaggerate his attempts he himself revealed to his mostly male correspondents (John Gay, Swift, the good Dr. Arbuthnot) to what degree he was a "soft kind of man" nervous about his masculinity.[6] Dwarfdom and deformity had combined to produce a series of other literal infirmities, which, in turn, took a toll on his romantic aspirations. Maynard Mack has captured the essence of this emotional toll when demonstrating how it shrunk his heart. If Pope were homosexual (in our sense), which I strongly doubt, his deformity would have impaired him anyway from acting this role to any degree: physically in view of his various body defects, psychologically because he was so fraught about his masculinity, no matter how much it was commodified among his contemporaries.

Pope was not of course the only writer in British literary history to turn his "pen" on the world, no matter how angry that life's lottery had dealt him such a physique; and it is additionally simplistic to think this was his only reason for lashing out: his war with the dunces also had undeniable esthetic and intellectual bases. Yet it is also unimaginable that he would have developed as he did, personally and poetically, without "this little, tender, crazy Carcase [sic]," as William Wycherley and others among his early homosocial set often referred to his physical body (*Corr*, I, p. 55).

Jonathan Goldberg has traced the way the human hand has acted as a surrogate penis for certain writers since the Renaissance and Raymond Stephanson has expanded this view to book-length describing how it also incorporated Pope's masculinity and creativity. "I can think of no author before Pope whose poetic stature, reputation, and accomplishment were publicly imaged as questions about his privy members, with public speculation about the actual conditions of his yard." Speculations about a poet's penis – yard – may seem odd in our era of sanitized discourse that does not give offence, yet in the Restoration and early Augustan world in which Pope matured, the codes of both the male imagination and the sexualised body were vastly different from what they have become today. As Stephanson continues to comment, "although we [today] are more accustomed, perhaps, to thinking of this gifted hunchback as sadly unique or unfortunately deformed, in fact Pope's dwarfed body and literary fame became emblems of the new marketplace of letters."[7]

Pope had indeed been novel here and firmly within this tradition, yet he could have triumphed over his deformity and turned bodily defect around into partial benignity, as does Clifford Chatterley in D. H. Lawrence's *Lady Chatterley's Lover* (1928) and the many Catholic clerics (several personally known to Pope) forbidden by doctrine to marry. Besides, whereas Pope raged against the dunces – his "warfare on earth" – other deformed persons in his own time turned their defect to virtue: used it to endear themselves, marry, and bear children. Pope's inescapable deformity, on the other hand, intrigued his contemporaries to the point of obsession – even Edmund Curll's new print shop in Covent Garden was called "Pope's Head" – and predisposed him to a way of life that relied on surrogate strengths, especially creative outlets in poetry and the arts of drawing, gardening, and landscape architecture. And it had the additional consequence of causing him to draw close to other literary bachelors, notably Swift and John Gay, but also many other older married males – John Caryll and William Wycherley – with whom he existed in a state of near Carlylean hero worship.[8] It also motivated him simultaneously into a state where he used his ill health to endear himself to older men while launching into hyperactivity in fields other than poetry: architecture, landscape gardening, and grottology. The pride propelling him to vent his spleen against the dunces was rarely at stake in these other activities. The main points here, easy to overlook or trivialize, are firstly that Pope labored under *two* physical deformities – dwarfism with its protrusions and, later on, a genital dysfunction – and, secondly, that he was unable to contain his rage arising from perceived assaults to his manhood. What his contemporaries often expressed as prurient interest in his body, he construed as attack of one kind or another: if not for the suggestion that physical deformity correlated to inner moral defect, then for the sense he derived that insult to his body was tantamount to the spurning of his character and the quality of his poetry itself. The result was a pitch of rage that would have concerned the psychoanalysts of his age had there been any. As Allen Tate, the modern American poet, has so poignantly asked: "What . . . rage between his teeth?"[9] What rage indeed? The subject is no longer easily addressed in a milieu (ours) when terror of every type, it seems, compels us to mediate rage culturally and reduce it to the realm of the "appropriate" to render it bearable.[10] The astonishing development is that Pope should have been so self-conscious about the implications of assault to his physical body as to coin lines that echo far beyond their literal truth for full poetic effect: "Let me draw the last pen for freedom."[11] This was not merely the literal "pen" in his hand.

Deformity and heightened rage exist in proximity in the life and works of Pope, even if they continue to surprise his readers by the number of biographical sites from which they are absent. For example, his associations in gardening (the world of Bathurst and Cirencester) and landscape architecture (Kent and Burlington) – all those men with whom he interacted when consulting "the Genius of the place" – were pre-eminently decorous if also largely homosocial, and it is hard to imagine that the same "Pope" who advised these figures also lashed out wildly at the dunces. A modern psychoanalyst might purport that Pope, having channeled most of his ego-strength into his pen – especially the perfection of his couplet art – struck whenever his niche there was imperiled. Outrage had of course been a main component of satiric inspiration ever since the Homeric bards sang of "the wrath of Achilles" and the Roman satirist Juvenal grew indignant over the moral vices he found widespread in his Rome. Pope in the state of blinding rage recognized that his *body* as well as mind was implicated. Spinal tuberculosis had not merely removed him from the ranks of star-studded manhood; it also configured him for public consumption – especially by his detractors – as impotent and lame: as he himself pathetically conceded to a friend, "I live like an Insect, in hope of reviving with the Spring." Or, as he confessed to Lord Bathurst, "I do not think I shall ever enjoy any health four days together, for the remaining Sand I have to run" (*Corr*, IV, 499; II, 525). Even the reliable Samuel Johnson reported in his *Lives of the Poets* (1779–81) that "his legs were so slender that he enlarged their bulk with three pair of stockings."[12] Hardly a "Carcase" whose physique was cause for celebration.

Nevertheless, what commands attention is not that Pope was aware of his bodily states but that he should have grasped them as commercial and marketing assets *despite* the personal injury and insult they gave him. As a lifelong patient (from youth he artfully manipulated his near-invalidism so as to render it attractive to his homosocial set of older men) he forged a hypochondriacal style of life capable of enthralling his curious contemporaries – the body as the site of fascination in its own right had made vast strides since the English Restoration. Hence it is not excessive to contend that Pope's contemporaries were as curious about his body – his *afflicted* body in *pain* – as they were about his sequestration in Twickenham. And it falsifies the evidence to think Pope merely monitored his bodily signs and vigilantly commented upon their aberrations in his expansive correspondence, as if merely a compulsive hypochondriac. Patientdom and near-invalidism notwithstanding, as his best biographer has claimed (*Life*, p. 153), he also lived in an era of revolutionary theories about the body – from static to nervous and fluid – which piqued his contemporaries to ascertain how a "poet's body" differed from theirs, or, you could say, how the new poetics of subjectivity were incorporating bodily states, for the two were interconnected in the collective Augustan mindset of Pope's maturity.

If Pope's was an Age of John Locke for the association of primary sensations into higher abstract ideas, his was also an Age of Thomas Willis (1621–1675) for the first modern view of the body as a nervous self. Willis's revolutionary brain theory placed the anatomical nerves at the centre of the human frame and guided its motions.[13] As Willis wrote, "it will plainly appear that I have not trod the paths of footsteps of others, nor repeated what hath been before told."[14] Locke was the generation's philosopher of mind par excellence; but Dr Willis was the modern philosopher of the body, as William Wotton in *Reflections upon Antient and Modern Learning* (1697) and others acknowledged, having rendered it an object for experimentation and verbalization. Willis, neurologist *and* psychologist, taught that the brain and nervous system preside over mind. For a poet of selfhood like Pope, whose infirm body was paradoxically the source of *both* pain and power, blemish and asset, the "doctors" of medicine had taught him much, not least about the words needed to describe his own body. No wonder he courted them avidly, from youth to maturity: if not surgeon William Cheselden then "nerve doctor" George Cheyne whose *Essay of Health* Pope seems to have read around 1725.[15] He had lived among the doctors, and his body, far more than his mind, preoccupied him for the range of its paradoxes: his "long Disease, my Life" may have been caused by his "crazy Carcase", but in time he also realized how anatomic difference converted to curiosity, keeping his flame alive with the reading public. It is thus simplistic to think that what Pope lacked in the groin he more than compensated for in the head. The truth is more complex and disturbing: he promoted himself as a cultural icon whose poetic identity was based, in significant part, on anatomical difference. No wonder then that he read widely in those subjects – anatomy and physiology – as the great passages about the human passions ("Each vital humour which should feed the whole, | Soon flows to this, in body and in soul") demonstrate in the second epistle of *An Essay on Man* (lines 139–40).

Pope's knowledge of Richard Blackmore's theories of "nervous gout" in the *Critical Dissertation upon the Spleen* (1725) and *Discourses on the Gout* (1726) arose, in part, from embittered feuds with the doctor-author about poetic art. The acclaim for Blackmore's works shocked Pope (*Creation*, which had drawn on the new nervous anatomy, was widely read in its day) and sensitized him to the degree that views other than his own held sway. He was certainly aware of, and had probably read, parts of *The English Malady* (1733) by the "inimitable Doctor Cheyne" (Pope's own phrase). A best-seller in 1733 just as Pope was composing the last epistle of his *Essay on Man* and various of his *Imitations of Horace*, *The English Malady* explained the anatomical nerves to laymen and demonstrated how physical bodies – even Pope's – became nervously aroused. Cheyne surveyed the spectrum from arousal and rapture to "low spirits" leading to melancholy and "self-murder." All, according to him, were *nervously* determined. Sans nerves, neither cognition nor memory served (the brain's directions obeyed only when the nerves functioned), let alone the states of high heroic passion (anger, jealousy, lust, revenge) found in epic and – inversely – in mock-epic.

Yet, even before Cheyne's books became bestsellers in the 1720s and 1730s, Pope had versified the nerves, making it plain that the Willisian revolution filtered down to his gaze. And if he could have hung on few more months after his death in May 1744 he would have seen how Mark Akenside – judged a prodigious talent by Pope – further elevated the role of nerves in the imaginative process in the *Pleasures of Imagination* (1744). That same year John Armstrong stressed their importance in "the art of preserving health" in his long poem of this title, as did Malcolm Flemyng two years later when he composed an epic in hexameters on neurotic disorders.[16] These poets of the 1740s could not have focused so vividly on the nerves if the body had not already been culturally mediated and sufficiently popularized. Pope tapped into the body's new commodification before they did, partly for selfish reasons having to do with his public persona.

Pope's poetry captures the range of these nervous tropes. "Rapture warms the mind" in *An Essay on Criticism* (236) in just the way Willis had described in his brain treatises: as heating up the vital spirits that expand the nerves. And in *The Odyssey* it will warm Ulysses' "raptured soul" too (1, 558), as it will "the Happy Man" of *Windsor-Forest* – and equally the poet who finds his soul possessed by the nine Muses and his imagination fired in "Raptures" (259–60). Conversely, negative "rapture" describes Bayes's state of mind as he (the King of Dulness, Colley Cibber in the later version) lies in Dulness's lap at the opening of Book III of *The Dunciad*:

> Him close she curtain'd round with Vapours blue,
> And soft besprinkles with Cimmerian dew.
> Then raptures high the seat of Sense o'erflow.
>
> (III, 4–5)

Rapture is the word Pope chooses when Helen follows Achilles at their climactic moment of love in *The Iliad*:

> Him *Helen* follow'd slow with bashful Charms,
> And clasp'd the looming Hero in her Arms.
> While these to Love's delicious Rapture yield . . .
>
> (III, 557–9)

Rapture is also rife in Pope's *Odyssey*, as when Ulysses – far from Troy – first sees the coast of Greece ("With rapture oft the verge of *Greece* reviews"), or when Alcinous' palace and kingdom are described as beyond all expectation ("Th' unwonted scene surprize and rapture drew"), or when Ulysses' old nurse Eurycleia first sees the great hero after he lands at Ithaca at the opening of Book XXIII:

> Then to the Queen, as in repose she lay,
> The Nurse with eager rapture speeds her way![17]

For good reason Pope sustains the use of "rapture" in Book XXIII more than anywhere else in his Homeric translations, despite the frequency of its appearances there as well. "Rapture" is a favourite word of Pope's, used dozens of times in his poetry, most often to describe heightened anatomical states leading to passion and imagination.

He himself was no stranger to "enraptured" nervous states and the romantic energizing they brought to his own verse, even if that state was not entirely "romantic" in the way some Pope critics have decreed. Looking back on his literary career in 1737, he nostalgically reminisced on the memory of composing poetry in the flush of manhood, when words rhapsodically flowed because his imagination was fully fired up: "You grow *correct* that once with Rapture writ" (*Epilogue to the Satires*, I, 3; *TE*, IV, p. 297). Such "rapture" incorporates the poet's own bodily states as well as his firebrand imagination working at high temperature. Willis had explained how these moments arise: "The brain doth produce a type of fire which transfixes the imagination."[18] During maturity and senescence this nervous "fire" (pictured as fluid flowing through hollow tubes) flickers, as it did for Pope. The most enraptured creative states occur when the nerves are "taut and tonic"[19] – the words are Cheyne's – when the brain concentrates attentively without the slightest dissipation, and ruddy animal spirits flow quickly and regularly rather than feebly or haphazardly in their tubes, as they would in the "hey-go-mad" Tristram Shandy's nerves, the erratic flow of which had been the primary cause of his downfall:

> – you have all, I dare say, heard of the animal spirits, as how they are transfused from father to son, &c., &c. – and a great deal to that purpose: – Well, you may take my word, that nine parts in ten of a man's sense or his nonsense, his successes and miscarriages in this world depend upon their motions and activity, and the different tracks and trains you put them into, so that when they are once set a-going, whether right or wrong, 'tis not a halfpenny matter, – away they go cluttering like hey-go-mad.[20]

Cheyne and other "nerve doctors," building on Willis's legacy, had explained how these "high imaginative states" occur. When Pope experienced them, in "rapture writ," it consoled him to think he was not so completely deformed after all, but free to create as other great poets had been; masculine and without the anxieties and tensions that plagued him throughout the "long disease, my life." He could imagine there was nothing flaccid or effeminate, soft or weak, in his body, let alone lacking the masculinity he sought. In rapture he had produced great poetry, much of it rhapsodic – "warm and romantic" – even if he did not formally label his works rhapsodies.[21]

Pope did not compose in trances, nor was his imagination organically "esemplastic" in the way Coleridge describes in the *Biographia Literaria* (1817). Nevertheless, Pope's poetry demonstrates why he, and some of his modern critics, have detected in him anticipations of romanticism: if not of the rhapsodic glow associated with Romantic poets – the Byrons and Coleridges who valued Pope's poetry so highly – then not entirely alien to the enraptured lyricism of the poets of the 1740s.

Pope's attitudes to contemporary medical theory were not uniformly enthusiastic. He exposed the practices of many medical doctors and lambasted their theories. His verses abound in blistering assaults on their defective logic and limited wit. Even author-doctors – Garth, Mead, Blackmore,

Hartley – are often butterflies on Pope's satiric wheel, as much for their petty "projects" and risible "experiments" as for their personal pedantry and puffery. Pope's critique of the new scientific knowledge extended to the "Newton craze" of his era ("And shew'd a NEWTON as we shew an Ape," he chided his contemporaries in *An Essay on Man*, II, 34).[22] It nevertheless goes too far to think Pope's *satiric* treatment of medicine the predominant one. He possessed more understanding of medicine than science, as any lifelong patient would, and was well aware of recent theories of the nervous body: especially those conducing towards a poet's definition of himself. He had felt comfortable with most doctors: routinely taken to them as a child, operated on by them for his genital afflictions, and often relying on them – as friends – for "sober advice," none more so than the wise Dr. Arbuthnot, rewarded by Pope with a great poem named for him. Pope may not have lived in the houses of doctors, as did Coleridge for many years in the Highgate home of Dr James Gilman, but he kept *au courant* of their comings and goings "in the Town," a further reason he facilely refers to them, especially in *The Dunciad*.[23] Medicine – the science that theorizes the body in healthy and pathological states – was the one branch of natural philosophy Pope had good reason to cultivate.

Pope's adulthood in 1725–44 coincided with the decades when the medical arts were being culturally mediated: first, owing to a thirst for new knowledge among the growing reading classes; and then in response to the Restoration paradigm shift in the conception of the body itself – the latter specially as the result of Willis's nervous legacy, but also in response to then contemporary anatomists charting the new nervous body along its fault lines from brain to the smallest nerve. This was an organic body in which each part – each motion – responded to the other. As such it also gave rise to new verbal possibilities for explication, and versifying, of the body connections. The old Galenic model of humors, determined by solids and fluids, was gone; a new body arose constructed along nervous fault lines.

The anatomical revolution took a toll in diagnosis and also opened up possibilities for mind-body interaction. Mind and body were being "*nervously* defined," as Willis and, later, Cheyne claimed.[24] As they were, it became difficult to label diagnoses, like Pope's, as located entirely in the one or other. Diagnosis in Pope's case is difficult to assess in its original context: he was certainly deformed and impaired in the ways described but psychologically speaking it is more difficult to affix a just diagnosis. Despite chronic ailments in addition to his two impairments – dwarfism and genital dysfunction – he was hypochondriac in some degree without being (in our sense) depressive or suicidal. His heart was romantically starved, and suspicion – as well as the lust to engage in literary warfare – dominated his psyche to a degree that it does not go too far to classify him (diagnosis again) as paranoid despite the word not having been invented at that time.

The concept of paranoia that forms a cornerstone of Freudian psychoanalysis was not available in Pope's time except as extrapolations made from actions judged as prone to excessive combat. Pope certainly cultivated enemies, as studies of *The Dunciad* have long documented. Yet a psychoanalysis of his life still appears gratuitous because treatment is irrelevant. If the facts of Pope's life are gathered and interpreted, as they have been by biographers from Samuel Johnson to Maynard Mack, we can see how Pope's self-constructed poetic identity played itself out: marginalizing and isolating him in childhood; sensitizing him after a life of embattled fracas; isolating him into volitional seclusion while concurrently energizing him to compose great poetry; annihilating the possibility of his making peace with the "dunces" or forgiving them for transgressions made to his "person", while concurrently inspiring him to keep composing in retirement. When the first major revaluation of Pope's poetry occurred in the second decade of the nineteenth century, its participants (including Byron, Hazlitt, and William Lisle Bowles) asked questions about his couplet art.[25] They also wondered what weight to give to his enemies and feuds, Pope's "warfare on earth." Extreme displays of cantankerous behaviour in life and literature are viewed negatively in our era, often as the sign of maladjustment. This may be a further reason why our generation has been so recalcitrant to reassess Pope's literal body – his "Crazy Constitution" – and speculate about the consequences of the new anatomy on his art.

## NOTES

1. The classic treatment of his medical case history is Marjorie H. Nicolson and G. S. Rousseau, *"This Long Disease, My Life": Alexander Pope and the Sciences* (Princeton: Princeton University Press, 1968). Mack claims (*Life*, p. 153) that "the chances are good that it [Pott's Disease] was contracted during infancy from the milk of Mary Beach his nurse; less probably, from cow's milk," but this cannot have been the case as Pott's disease cannot be transmitted from human to human.
2. Voltaire, *Oeuvres*, LXII (Paris, 1819–1825), p. 157; *TE*, IV, p. 105.
3. Pope, *The Guardian* no. 92 (26 June 1713), in *Prose*, I, p. 125.
4. Raymond Stephanson has made a strong case in *The Yard of Wit: Male Creativity and Sexuality 1650–1750* (Philadelphia: University of Pennsylvania Press, 2004).
5. Colley Cibber, *A Letter from Mr. Cibber, to Mr. Pope* (London: W. Lewis, 1742), pp. 47–9.
6. See Stephanson, *Yard of Wit*, pp. 1–9, 25–92.
7. See Jonathan Goldberg, *Shakespeare's Hand* (Minneapolis: University of Minnesota Press, 2003); Stephanson, *Yard of Wit*, pp. 23–4.

8. Bachelordom was common in his era and should not be interpreted as the coverup for an illicit sexuality; the point here is not merely the apparent homosociability of these bachelor-writers but their affinities and emotional ties they had developed in relying on one another for moral support.
9. Allen Tate, *Mr Pope and Other Poems* (New York: Minton, Balch & Company, 1928).
10. For Pope's "rage" see G. S. Rousseau in *The Enduring Legacy: Alexander Pope Tercentenary Essays*, ed. G. S. Rousseau and P. Rogers (Cambridge: Cambridge University Press, 1988), pp. 199–239.
11. For the full range of Pope's poetic images of pens, quills, and other writing instruments see Stephanson, *Yard of Wit*, p. 285 (index entry).
12. Johnson, *LOP*, III, p. 197.
13. Willis's best-known treatise on the brain, *Cerebri Anatome* (London, 1664), was translated into English by Samuel Pordage and contained plates by Sir Christopher Wren; see Thomas Willis, *The Anatomy of the Brain and Nerves* (Montreal: McGill University Press, 1965). The case for Dr Willis in relation to Pope has most recently been made by G. S. Rousseau in *Nervous Acts: Essays on Literature, Culture and Sensibility* (Basingstoke: Palgrave, 2004).
14. Willis, *Anatomy*, p. 235.
15. For the full range of reading, see Nicolson and Rousseau, *Disease*, pp. 55–72.
16. Malcolm Flemyng, *Neuropathia; sive de morbis hypochondriacis et hystericis* [The pathway of the nerves, or hypochondriacal and hysterical disorders] (York, 1746).
17. See respectively *Odyssey*, IV, 697; VI, 179; XXIII, 2.
18. William Feindel, ed., *Thomas Willis: The Anatomy of the Brain and Nerves: Tercentenary Edition*, 2 vols. (Montreal: McGill University Press, 1965), vol. I, p. 123.
19. George Cheyne, *The English Malady* (London: G. Strahan, 1733), p. 6.
20. See Melvyn New, ed., *The Florida Edition of the Works of Laurence Sterne: Tristram Shandy*, 2 vols. (Gainesville: University of Florida Press, 1978–84), vol. I, pp. 1–2.
21. For "rhapsodic aesthetics" see Pat Rogers, "Shaftesbury and the Aesthetics of Rhapsody," *British Journal of Aesthetics* 12 (1972): pp. 244–57. The rhapsody as a poetic topos flourished in this era although often as a satiric subspecies.
22. Newton, who was heavily indebted to both Willis and Locke for his bodily metaphors, wrote no medical works but drew heavily on the language of neural transmission in his *Opticks* (London: Royal Society, 1704).
23. For the range of medical references in his poetry see U. C. Knopflmacher, "The Poet as Physician: Pope's *Epistle to Dr. Arbuthnot*," *Modern Language Quarterly* 31 (1970): pp. 440–9.
24. Cheyne, *The English Malady*, p. 6.
25. See William Hazlitt, "Pope, Lord Byron and Mr. Bowles," *London Magazine* (June 1821), reprinted in *The Works of William Hazlitt*, ed. A. R. Waller and A. Glover, 13 vols. (London: Dent, 1902–6), vol. XI, pp. 456–508.

# 17

LAURA BROWN

# Pope and the other

The "other" has become a prominent theme in literary critical analysis. At the social and political level, its currency has been the result of two significant social and political events in the twentieth century: the clashes between colonizer and colonized in the 1940s and 50s, and the development of the new feminist movement in the 1970s. The rise of post-colonial studies and of feminist theory – the intellectual counterparts of these events – have profoundly influenced Anglo-American literary criticism of the late twentieth century. The "other" is the calling card of these critical paradigms. In relation to Western European literature, the concern with the "other" leads primarily to an attention to the representation of women or of indigenous or non-European peoples in literary texts. For instance, the passage on the "poor Indian" in the first epistle of Alexander Pope's *Essay on Man* stands out as an example of the status of native Americans in the early-eighteenth century imagination:

> Lo! the poor Indian, whose untutor'd mind
> Sees God in clouds, or hears him in the wind;
> His soul proud Science never taught to stray
> Far as the solar walk, or milky way;
> Yet simple Nature to his hope has giv'n,
> Behind the cloud-topt hill, an humbler heav'n;
> Some safer world in depth of woods embrac'd,
> Some happier island in the watry waste,
> Where slaves once more their native land behold,
> No fiends torment, nor Christians thirst for gold!
> To Be, contents his natural desire,
> He asks no Angel's wing, no Seraph's fire;
> But thinks, admitted to that equal sky,
> His faithful dog shall bear him company.
>
> (1, 99–112)

This passage is an encyclopedia of intersecting perspectives on indigenous peoples – a compendium of ideas of the "other" as understood through the modern critique of colonialism. Most generally, for contemporary readers the image of the "poor Indian" would bring to mind the sight of selected "natives" displayed in London and other European metropolitan centers as emissaries and "shows," popular curiosities that attracted growing audiences throughout the eighteenth century.[1] The currency of this image in literature is an indication of the visibility of the native "other" in these contexts. In addition, the image of the "poor Indian" would echo the representation of indigenous peoples in contemporary travel literature, a major publishing phenomenon with an extensive popular following in this period.[2] These travel narratives also often included proto-ethnographic accounts of the customs and manners of the people, in the same way that Pope here chooses to describe a quaint belief in canine afterlife as a peculiarity of his "poor Indian."

More specifically, the "poor Indian" is the object of an evaluative reversal here, in which the "poor," the "untutored," the uncivilized, and the "simple" human being is elevated to a position of special privilege, because he has direct access to a "natural" faith that European Christianity is implicitly denied. In this aspect, the passage evokes the long and complex debate about natural and revealed religion that developed in the seventeenth century, partially in response to the encounter with indigenous peoples around the world – peoples whose lack of access to the teachings of Christ, some thought, should not exclude them from salvation.

Furthermore, in suggesting that "proud Science" has led Europeans to "stray" from a more natural nobility, the description of this "poor Indian" points toward the idea of the "noble savage," which is most coherently defined by Rousseau later in the century in his *Second Discourse* (1756). By the second half of the eighteenth century, the sympathies of the savage or natural man, uncorrupted by civilization, become a model for European sensibility. The ironies of Pope's passage capture some of the complexities of this usage of indigenous peoples in the construction of European ideals of conduct and value: Pope's Indian is both admirable and pathetic. But the ironies inherent in this passage run even deeper. The Indian – a "slave" because of the practices of European colonialism – is also used implicitly to praise British imperialism. The allusions to slavery, "fiends," and "thirst for gold" that cause him to wish for a "safer" and "happier" fate, point directly to the cruelties of Spanish colonialism. For the British, Spain was considered to be the heartless and bloodthirsty colonial power, fortunately superseded in the eighteenth century by the benevolent, civilizing forces of British imperialism, which were coming to dominate the globe. According to this passage, to the extent that the "poor Indian" has truly suffered at the hands of the Spanish, his suffering is a testimony to the historical superiority of British global power.

Pope's Indian also raises a question about the relationship between Europeans and non-Europeans, and between human and non-human beings – a question fundamental to the European experience of the encounter with the "other" in the eighteenth century. The "poor Indian" foolishly, or innocently, thinks that his dog will accompany him to the heaven that his natural religion promises. The implied equality of human and non-human being, and even the specific question of whether dogs might accompany their masters or mistresses to heaven, are prominent topics in the debate that accompanied the rise of the life sciences in this period, in which the clear separation of man from beast gave way to a multifaceted discussion of differences and similarities between and among species. In keeping with these discussions, the idea of the chain of being – the influential classical and neoclassical conceptualization of the hierarchical ordering of the universe – was modified to include an increasingly fluid interpretation by which the gradations that separated beings on the chain were so minute or so gradual as to call distinctions into question, and elaborations upon the new systems of biological classification provided for hybrid creatures posited to stand in the interstices between the distinct classes that those systems defined.[3] The place of each being was thus potentially open to question in ways that could transcend hierarchy, or redefine it. One dimension of this discussion was the species debate, a significant, formative event in the development of modern ideas of racial inferiority, which raised the question of whether humans are divided into distinct species – and whether some species of human are inferior to others.[4] Meanwhile, the rise of pet-keeping in the eighteenth century encouraged some Europeans to believe that their companion animals were possessed of human traits, such as faithfulness, and inspired speculation about whether lapdogs had an afterlife.[5] The equality of the Indian and his dog thus signals a wide context of contemporary thought in which the indigenous non-European human being plays a major role, as inspiration and object.

In short, Pope's "poor Indian" demonstrates in a compact form the depth and breadth of the impact of the "other" on the eighteenth-century imagination. This richly developed portrait condenses a range of contemporary experiences arising from the historical situation of Pope's poem in early-eighteenth century England: the visibility of the non-European in the metropolitan centers of Europe, the prominence of representations of cultural encounter through travel and ethnographic writing, the inversion of the traditional hierarchy of the civilized over the "savage," the questioning of the assumptions of revealed religion, the contexts of colonial exploitation and slavery around the globe, the instabilities proposed by and within the systems generated by the new life sciences, and the rise of a new kind of relationship with and treatment of "companion animals." Pope's text at this point presents an integrated representation of a distinctive imaginative experience that we could define as a rich and pervasive engagement with alterity – an engagement that privileges the unfamiliar, the non-civilized, and the non-European, and that simultaneously evokes an inversion of traditional hierarchy, a destabilization of systems of order or continuity, and a questioning of fundamental assumptions of value and meaning. This engagement with alterity is one of the defining characteristics of the imaginative works of modernity.

Following the theoretical paradigms provided by post-colonial studies or feminist theory, literary critics have tended to understand this engagement with alterity exclusively in terms of the representation of "other" human beings. In the case of Pope, this perspective on "otherness" has generated, over the last two decades, a persistent and influential new focus on the alien, monstrous, disfigured, disabled, and especially the female in Pope's works. Thus many recent critical studies of Pope have sought to explicate his representations of women, especially in *The Dunciad* and *To a Lady*. They see anxieties about female fecundity, feminized modernity, and gender definition in various of his works; they explore Pope's relationships with and literary treatment of historical women, notably Lady Mary Wortley Montagu and Eliza Haywood; they track issues of monstrosity, disability, and bodily grotesquerie from Pope's own self-presentation to his poetic corpus; and they uncover attitudes towards new world slavery embedded within his works. The new Pope, by these lights, has a complex or contradictory, anxious or subtly sympathetic, appropriative or repressed relationship to women, marginalized individuals, and non-Europeans, and his works reveal the various ways in which the crafted form of Augustan verse depends upon the repression, incorporation, or irrepressibility of the "other."[6]

By now, the "other" is a very powerful tool for rereading Pope's poetry, and this tool has helped to highlight the prominence of alterity in his corpus. But our perception of the prevalence and even the nature of alterity – in Pope's poetry and in eighteenth-century literary culture more broadly – is limited by our primary category of analysis. The "other" is a habit of analysis that arises from a powerful tradition within modern philosophy. Post-colonial studies and feminist theory, especially as the latter is indebted to psychoanalysis, have schooled Anglo-American literary critics in the study of race and gender, and have trained us, in particular, to understand the engagement with alterity according to a rather rigorous epistemology that has its origins in the post-enlightenment critique of reason. The Enlightenment claim for the power and efficacy of reason led directly to a critique that took that power seriously, as a problem in itself. Central to the post-Enlightenment critique is the dichotomy between intelligence and its object, or between the knower and the known. Is the world of objects a reflection of consciousness? Do objects exist only as they are perceived by consciousness? These ideas were pursued in the German tradition by Hegel, whose influence is felt directly in modern post-colonial studies, and indirectly through the development of subsequent social, economic, and psychoanalytic theory.

Hegel constructs a system of thought around the dialectical relationship between subjective and objective, or between idea and nature. Self-consciousness is defined by its relationship to the natural world, and in particular by a relationship with another consciousness in that world, an "other" whose recognition gives self-consciousness existence. This system leads Hegel to the proposition of an inevitable struggle between two self-consciousnesses, one of which becomes the master and the other the slave. Marx, following Hegel, uses the subject/object dichotomy to develop the concept of alienated labour. Under capitalism, the object world is beyond the control of the world of men. The worker is estranged from his labour – the object world that he himself creates. As a result he becomes alien to himself and to other men; he becomes a slave of the object, because work constitutes his means of subsistence and thus his being. The worker thus estranges, or "others," himself from himself.

Modern psychoanalytic theory, the other major influence on post-colonial studies as well as on literary critical studies independently, brings a version of the subject/object dichotomy to bear on the psyche, and on gender, focusing on the constitution of the self in terms of the stages of its separation from the objects that surround it, specifically the mother. Following and revising Freud from a post-structuralist perspective, Lacan argues that the infant's separation from the mother generates the sense of "other" that is the necessary precondition for the development of selfhood. Then, seeing itself in the mirror, the child imagines that image of a coherent "other" as itself. In this way the idea of a self is based on the projection of an "other," which is a precondition for the entrance into language and culture.

Thus we inherit the idea of the "other," a term which has a complex history, but which we have come to use as a loosely constitutive category, conceived in a human form, which gives identity, meaning, and even existence to the subject, the knower, the master, the father, or the self. The "other" is assumed to be ever present – behind, within, or beneath any representation of power, autonomy, or individual identity, and it is the task of the literary critic to call attention to its presence or to explain its significance. Our use of the "other" in literary critical analysis today reflects this broadly influential structure of thought. But the concept of the "other" shapes and limits our approach, as well. Pope's poetry can help us step beyond some of those limits by providing a different model for our understanding of alterity – a model based in the imaginative experience of the period of European history when familiarity and convention, systems of hierarchy and order, and ideals of value and continuity were opened to revision and even revolution. In fact, eighteenth-century European history is marked by multiple, overlapping "revolutions," which shape its cultural productions. These changes range from the bourgeois political "revolutions" of mid-seventeenth century England and late eighteenth-century France, to the scientific "revolutions" of Newton and Linnaeus in physics and biology, the financial "revolution" and the rise of public credit and stock trading, the commercial "revolution" and the establishment of an economy based on consumption and an expanding retail market, and the rise of British imperialism and the corollary institutionalization of slavery. No wonder that the representation of an experience shaped by the encounter with the unfamiliar, the inversion of hierarchy, and the destabilization of order and value should be a repeated feature of eighteenth-century literary culture.

Pope's works can help us see the scope of that experience of alterity, and to understand that it is not restricted to the representation of the human form, although the common usage of the term "other" suggests that it must be. And eighteenth-century representations of alterity do not necessarily express a relationship of subordination, although again the "other" leads us to expect a dichotomy in which one side claims primacy over another. In Pope's works for instance, the "poor Indian" passage, in which alterity is depicted through the figure of a subordinate human being, is only one of a range of modes of alterity, or ways in which difference is imagined in this period. In order to explore that range, and for the purpose of argument here, we can distinguish four distinct modes. Though these are not restricted to the representation of a human figure, they do generate effects that can be compared directly with that of the "poor Indian" passage – an encounter with the unconventional, the unfamiliar, or the non-European, which raises fundamental questions about hierarchy, order, value, and meaning. If we let the "poor Indian" stand for the first mode of alterity – the one that focuses on the human figure – we can then distinguish three other, separate modes expressive of the same striking experience of alterity in Pope's works. The second is spatial – the representation of a landscape that is arranged, or colored in a way that directly challenges familiar structures of geographical order. The third is rhetorical – a linguistic structure that sets up an infinite regression, in which hierarchy is systematically repudiated. And the fourth is existential – representations of character in which conventional notions of identity are emptied of significance and replaced by an absence of being. These four modes give us access to a repertory of approaches to alterity that can deepen our understanding of the challenges to the conventional in Pope's works.

The most prominent example of the spatial mode – in which geography is the object of defamiliarization – occurs in the harlequinade scene from Book III of *The Dunciad*:

> Thence a new world to Nature's laws unknown,
> Breaks out refulgent, with a heav'n its own:
> Another Cynthia her new journey runs,
> And other planets circle other suns.
> The forests dance, the rivers upward rise,
> Whales sport in woods, and dolphins in the skies;
> And last, to give the whole creation grace,
> Lo! one vast Egg produces human race.
>
> (B text, III, 241–8)

The inverted landscape that this scene depicts opens another window into the diverse experience of alterity for the eighteenth-century reader. In his own note to this passage, Pope explains that this scene describes a stage farce, a recent popular drama that utilized extravagant machinery to depict a sorcerer's magical creation of a "new world." In the context of Pope's poem, this "new world" stands for the fundamental overturning of systems of order and value – an overturning generated by the coming of Dulness, the Queen of both emptiness and wild creation, who presides over the new, commodified culture of a capitalized printing industry.

This revolution is repeatedly represented in *The Dunciad* as an unfamiliar landscape, a "new world" with a specifically geographical content. For example, earlier in the poem, in the opening account of Dulness's kingdom in Book I, Pope describes the overturning of literary convention in the same geographical terms:

> She sees a Mob of Metaphors advance,
> Pleas'd with the madness of the mazy dance;
> How Tragedy and Comedy embrace;
> How Farce and Epic get a jumbled race;
> How Time himself stands still at her command,
> Realms shift their place, and Ocean turns to land.

Here gay Description Ægypt glads with show'rs,
Or gives to Zembla fruits, to Barca flow'rs;
Glitt'ring with ice here hoary hills are seen,
There painted vallies of eternal green.
In cold December fragrant chaplets blow,
And heavy harvests nod beneath the snow.

(B text, I, 67–78)

Like the "new world" of Book III, this landscape is characterized by a shifting movement of locations that should be still or stable, and by the inversion of geographical hierarchies, in which "Ocean turns to land" or "Whales sport in woods."

Hierarchy is called into question in other ways as well in these landscapes. The allusion to the "new world" in the passage from Book III is connected to the implications of modern astronomy. The trope of "other planets" and "other suns" specifically evokes the work of Galileo and the effects of the telescope and astronomical observation on the contemporary imagination. These images call traditional systems of astronomical order – moon, stars, and sun – into question, at the same time that they proliferate heavenly bodies – moons, "planets," and "suns" – in a way that destabilizes the singular supremacy of this world. And further, *The Dunciad*'s "new world" would also serve as a specific evocation of the geographical "new world" of the Americas, a focal point of imaginative engagement in this period. In associating this inverted geography with the Americas, these passages suggest that that object of European colonial expansion presents a landscape beyond familiar systems of order, where geographical relationships are unpredictable, and exotic creatures – whales and dolphins – are strangely displaced. Whales and dolphins themselves would have evoked the new products of trade and global exploration, and popular accounts of maritime travel and adventure.

Visually, both of these passages exploit a strong evocation of colour, and of foreground and background. The visualization of "refulgent" moons and stars, "glittering" ice, and "painted vallies" of a vivid green are central to this attractive effect, as are the representations of the components of a wide geographical panorama. In the passage from Book III the scene shifts from the "forests" here, to the "rivers" there, and to the "woods" and "skies" in other distinct areas of the scene; in the passage from Book I, the highlighted terms "Here" and "There" directly indicate the foreground and background of a painted landscape. These passages are ekphrastic: they use language to describe the "sister art" of painting. In these cases of ekphrasis, Pope's poetry depicts the familiar contemporary genre of landscape painting.

Ekphrasis plays an important role in several of Pope's major poems.[7] For instance, in his celebration of English imperialism, *Windsor-Forest*, ekphrasis supplies the means by which England is located at the center of a growing global empire. The poem uses a description of the landscape at the site of Windsor Castle to launch and substantiate its extended encomium on the *pax Britannica*. The opening lines render the effects of landscape painting:

> Here Hills and Vales, the Woodland and the Plain,
> Here Earth and Water seem to strive again . . .
> Here waving Groves a checquer'd Scene display,
> And part admit and part exclude the Day . . .
> There, interspers'd in Lawns and opening Glades,
> Thin Trees arise that shun each others Shades.
> Here in full Light the russet Plains extend;
> There wrapt in Clouds the blueish Hills ascend:
> Ev'n the wild Heath displays her Purple Dies,
> And 'midst the Desart fruitful Fields arise,
> That crown'd with tufted Trees and springing Corn,
> Like verdant Isles the sable Waste adorn . . .
> See *Pan* with Flocks, with Fruits *Pomona* crown'd,
> Here blushing *Flora* paints th'enamel'd Ground,
> Here *Ceres'* Gifts in waving Prospect stand,
> And nodding tempt the joyful Reaper's Hand.
>
> (11–40)

These lines from *Windsor-Forest* can be seen as a tame and orderly source for the inverted geographies that appear in *The Dunciad*. Pope's language in this earlier poem depicts the foreground and background of a visualized landscape with the same directives "here" and "there," and the same vivid images of a glittering "enamel'd Ground" and "verdant" fields that appear in *The Dunciad*.

Pope's ekphrasis in *The Dunciad*, then, takes up a set of images that are directly derived from contemporary nationalist and imperialist rhetoric, and that allude back to those familiar scenes and refigure them as an unfamiliar "new world." But the recasting of the ekphrastic representation of the fertile landscape of Britain as a radically unfamiliar and inverted geography in *The Dunciad* passages serves implicitly to destabilize the British landscape itself. Looking back on *Windsor-Forest* from the *The Dunciad*, we can see the strange features of the *The Dunciad*'s "new world" growing from hints provided initially in the imagery of the conventional scene of British nationalism. The displacement of land by ocean that we observed in the two *Dunciad* passages is suggested in *Windsor-Forest*'s image of "Earth and Water" striving for their proper place. Meanwhile the picture of the "fruitful Fields" floating like islands in an ocean-like plain contributes further to the suggestion of an implicit inversion even in the stable landscape of Windsor. The climatic paradoxes in the *The Dunciad* passage – the showers in Egypt and the fruits of Zembla – also seem anticipated in *Windsor-Forest*'s depiction of "fruitful Fields" arising in an uninhabited "Desart." Later in *Windsor-Forest*, the description of the river Loddon – a tributary of the Thames that stands for the triumphant power of British imperial expansion – contains the same strange hints of inversion:

> Oft in her Glass the musing Shepherd spies
> The headlong Mountains and the downward Skies,
> The watry Landskip of the pendant Woods,
> And absent Trees that tremble in the Floods;
> In the clear azure Gleam the Flocks are seen,
> And floating Forests paint the Waves with Green.
> Thro' the fair Scene rowl slow the lingring Streams,
> Then foaming pour along, and rush into the *Thames*.
>
> (211–18)

Here again, the geography of England – still "painted" with the colours of landscape art – has the same potential for a reversal of place, between ocean and land ("watry Landskip," "pendant Woods," and "floating Forests") as that of Dulness's "new world," and it displays the same tendency toward movement ("headlong," trembling, or "rushing") that is evident in the shifting, jumbled, mazy, or dancing activity of *The Dunciad*'s geography. From this perspective, even Pope's most conventional landscape painting seems slightly strange. In fact, for Pope, the depiction of a geographical setting apparently carries in itself the potential for the evocation of inversion, reversal, and unexpected movement – the features of spatial alterity. And, as we have seen in Book III, Pope refers to this inverted geography by the same name, the "new world," that identified the Americas in this period of imperial expansion, suggesting that this mode of geographical defamiliarization might be a way of registering the impact of that actual, alien landscape.

A clear example of another mode of alterity, distinct from the human or the spatial, occurs in a distinctive rhetorical structure located at the beginning of the second epistle of Pope's *Essay on Man*, in a passage that evokes the chain of being:

> Superior beings, when of late they saw
> A mortal Man unfold all Nature's law,
> Admir'd such wisdom in an earthly shape,
> And shew'd a NEWTON as we shew an Ape.
>
> (II, 31–4)

These lines posit a relationship that at first suggests an orderly hierarchy from apes to humans to angels, following the progressive upward trajectory of the chain of being. But it ultimately questions such orderly arrangements by placing the human in a relative position, in relation to which angels and apes are then defined. If humans are to angels as apes are to humans, then we must imagine a continuing regress in which apes are to humans as some other being is to apes, or angels are to some other being as humans are to angels. Such a regress makes the privileged position of humans or even angels purely relative, rather than absolute. Furthermore, as we have seen in relation to the "poor Indian" passage, the urban "show" alluded to here itself links apes and humans in a similar relativist fashion. "Natives" and apes were displayed interchangeably in this period, as equivalent objects of a kind of ecumenical global curiosity. To "show" a Newton, then – that is, to put a human being on display for money – is an allusion that links Newton, apes, and "natives." The linking of Newton and the ape, then, not only undercuts the hierarchy of the chain of being, but joins that subversion with an allusion to the species debate.

A hidden reversal of the same sort is effected in the rhetoric of the final passage of *Windsor-Forest*, when the new world comes home to England:

> Then Ships of uncouth Form shall stem the Tyde,
> And Feather'd People crowd my wealthy Side,
> And naked Youths and painted Chiefs admire
> Our Speech, our Colour, and our strange Attire!
> (403–6)

The contemporary scene to which Pope's passage refers is the experience of the visits of "native" princes or "chiefs" to London in this period – here most likely the embassy of the four Iroquois sachems, or the Indian Kings, that occurred in 1711, shortly before the publication of this poem. The historical experience of this visit was for many Londoners captured by the striking visual impact of the Indians in the "strange attire" provided them for the occasion. But, overturning the expectation of the admiration of the British populace at the attire of these visitors, Pope's lines place the European figure, instead of the Indians, in the position of object of amazement. The Indian Kings were to the people of London as, in these lines, the British are to the painted Chiefs. The analogy is at first circular – Londoners admire natives, just as natives admire Londoners. But it also follows the relativist model of Newton and the ape: the Indian Kings might admire some other beings as much as the Londoners admired them, or the British might admire some other beings as much as the painted chiefs admire them in *Windsor-Forest*'s utopian scene. The relativist result collapses Londoners and natives, in the same unfamiliar connection as Newton and the ape.

Placed in this context, the widespread use of zeugma that characterizes the rhetoric of Pope's *Rape of the Lock* can be seen as another means of generating the same alienating effect of relativism through the same structure of regress. Zeugma is the rhetorical device in which two incongruous parts of a sentence are linked together by a single verb. A well known example implicates the political world:

> Here *Britain*'s Statesmen oft the Fall foredoom
> Of Foreign Tyrants, and of Nymphs at home;
> Here Thou, Great *Anna*! whom three Realms obey,
> Doth sometimes Counsel take – and sometimes *Tea*.
>
> (III, 5–8)

Each of these two couplets works in the same way, and to the same end. Superimposing foreign policy and personal love affairs, or public political consultation and the private, decorative custom of the tea table reverses the conventional thinking that would see politics as an especially serious endeavour. But, like Newton and the ape, it also suggests a regress in which the statesmen or Anna is the fulcrum of a relativist scenario. Standing between counsel and tea, Queen Anne might make politics a trivial social event, but she might also make the tea table into serious politics. If tea can be as serious as counsel, then the orderly and hierarchical significance of the two terms – counsel above tea – is collapsed into a connection that levels the two in the same surprising and unfamiliar way as Newton and the ape. The same effect is created by the statesmen's relation to the tyrants and the nymphs. This rhetorical sequence of inversion and regress compactly reproduces the imaginative experience that we have seen elaborated in the much richer modes of human and spatial alterity. Here again, the effect is to undercut systems of order or hierarchy in a surprising moment of defamiliarization. But in this case language itself is complicit in representing alterity, through the role of the verb as the linking agent or fulcrum for this alienating effect; the formal regress of these passages points to a deeper defamiliarization – a strangeness that recent deconstructive theory would locate in the arbitrary nature of the linguistic sign.

The final example of alterity – the existential mode – extends this fundamental questioning of the human significance of language to a defamiliarization of human being. Indeed, this mode might also be understood through the post-structuralist argument that links the deconstruction of the unity of the word with that of the unity of being.[8] The existential mode is strongly evident in the representation of women in Pope's *Epistle to a Lady* and *The*

*Dunciad*. In these poems, the figure of the woman evokes an alternative mode of being, which calls conventions of character itself into question. In the opening lines of the *Epistle to a Lady*, a poem that seeks to account for the "Characters of Women," the definition of the female is proposed as a form of absence: "Most Women have no Characters at all" (2).The body of the poem depicts female character as constituted entirely by inconstancy, like Atossa who is "Scarce once herself, by turns all Womankind!" (116). Through its series of portraits, the poem extends this idea of changeableness or unknowability beyond variable character into the representation of a disappearance of the body as well as the soul. This effect is described in the passage near the end of the poem that generalizes about the "whole sex." "At last" when their youth is gone they take the form of true characterlessness:

> As Hags hold Sabbaths, less for joy than spight,
> So these their merry, miserable Night;
> Still round and round the Ghosts of Beauty glide,
> And haunt the places where their honour dy'd.
>
> (239–42)

These empty "Ghosts of Beauty" – living exemplars of an evacuated female being – call into question the existence of human being itself.

We can see the same state of non-being evoked in *The Dunciad* through the depiction of the Mighty Mother, Dulness. Like the "Ghosts of Beauty," Dulness is a form of female emptiness; daughter of "Chaos and eternal Night" (I, 12), she presides over "Emptiness" (I, 36), "nonsense" (I, 60), and namelessness (I, 56).Her power to overwhelm the order and value of modern culture, bringing "Universal Darkness" (IV, 655) to the world, arises directly and self-reflexively from her own non-being. The fogs and mists that surround Dulness visually express her absence – both from view and from being:

> All these, and more, the cloud-compelling Queen
> Beholds thro' fogs, that magnify the scene.
> She, tinsel'd o'er in robes of varying hues,
> With self-applause her wild creation views:
> Sees momentary monsters rise and fall,
> And with her own fools-colours gilds them all.
>
> (I, 79–84)

A kind of empty fog herself, in this passage Dulness's emptiness is represented as a lens that generates a vision of a "wild creation" – a "new world" of her own making. Dulness is a kind of ghost – surrounded by but also composed of clouds and fogs – who, as her "self-applause" indicates, exists only in and for herself, just as the "Ghosts of Beauty" are defined by their circular haunting of their own past. But significantly, this emptiness is the source of Dulness's "wild creation," and connects her absence with the defamiliarized landscapes of *The Dunciad*. In fact, the "scene" of "wild creation" that she is described as creating here is the perverse landscape of Egypt and Zembla where "Realms shift their place, and Ocean turns to land" (1, 72).

What do these modes of alterity tell us about the imaginative world of Pope's poetry? They show us the scope of its strangeness – a strangeness that can be embodied in a human form, laid out before us in a landscape, enacted through a rhetorical play on the relationships among words, or conceived as a character that is "no character at all." These modes of alterity are variously interconnected – especially through the cultural and geographical differences highlighted in European global expansion and exploitation, and through the new sciences' challenges to traditional structures of knowledge and belief. But despite these connections, alterity as we have explored it here does not convey a simple or single message: the "poor Indian" is both privileged and satirized, the "new world" of Dulness is both attractive and disturbing, the landscape of Britain is both a locus of power and a scene of disorder, the leveling of Londoners and natives or of Newton and the ape is both liberating and disturbing. And though we can trace the relevance of alterity to cultural encounter, intellectual and scientific innovation, religious freedom, imperialist ideology, racialist thought, and even animal liberation, none of these very significant political, intellectual, or social issues fully accounts for the representation of alterity in literary culture, or for any of the particular modes we have canvassed here. Though it is used to various specific political and social ends – in the eighteenth century and in the present day as well – alterity always stands apart from our uses of it. Strangeness, in Pope's writing and in general, seems to be an end in itself.

## NOTES

1. Richard D. Altick, *The Shows of London* (Cambridge, MA: Harvard University Press, 1978). For important studies in this area, see Further Reading, pp. 237–246.
2. Philip Edwards, *The Story of the Voyage: Sea Narratives in Eighteenth-Century England* (Cambridge: Cambridge University Press, 1994).
3. A. O. Lovejoy, *The Great Chain of Being: A Study of the History of an Idea* (Cambridge: Harvard University Press, 1953); Harriet Ritvo, *The Animal Estate: The English and Other Creatures in the Victorian Age* (Cambridge, MA: Harvard University Press, 1987); and *The Platypus and the Mermaid and Other Figments of the Classifying Imagination* (Cambridge, MA: Harvard University Press, 1997).
4. Harriet Ritvo, "Barring the Cross: Miscegenation and Purity in Eighteenth- and Nineteenth-Century Britain," in *Human, All Too Human*, ed., Diana Fuss (New York: Routledge, 1996), pp. 37–58.

5. Keith Thomas, *Man and the Natural World: A History of the Modern Sensibility* (New York: Pantheon, 1983).
6. For examples of major work on women see Further Reading, pp. 237–246 below. On monstrosity and Pope's own self-represented marginality see Further Reading, pp. 237–246 below. On slavery see Laura Brown, *Alexander Pope* (Oxford: Basil Blackwell, 1985), p. 40; Howard Erskine-Hill, "Pope and Slavery," in *Alexander Pope: World and Word*, ed. Howard Erskine-Hill (Oxford: Oxford University Press, 1998), pp. 37–9; and John Richardson, "Alexander Pope's 'Windsor-Forest': Its Context and Attitudes Toward Slavery," *Eighteenth-Century Studies* 35 (2001): pp. 1–17.
7. Jean Hagstrum, *The Sister Arts: The Tradition of Literary Pictorialism and English Poetry from Dryden to Gray* (Chicago: University of Chicago Press, 1958); Murray Krieger, *Ekphrasis: The Illusion of the Natural Sign* (Baltimore: Johns Hopkins University Press, 1992); James Heffernan, *Museum of Words: The Poetics of Ekphrasis from Homer to Ashbery* (Chicago: University of Chicago Press, 1993).
8. Jacques Derrida, *Of Grammatology*, trans. Gayatri Chakravorty Spivak (Baltimore: Johns Hopkins University Press, 1974).

# FURTHER READING

This list represents a selection from the vast library devoted to work on Pope. It is confined to full-length books, with a few exceptions. In addition, it emphasizes more recent work, and includes older studies only where they have withstood the test of time and retain their currency. For a more complete listing of earlier studies, see Kowalk, Lopez, and Tobin in the section on Bibliographical Works below.

## Reference

### Bibliographical works

Bedford E. G. and R. J. Dilligan, eds. *A Concordance to the Poems of Alexander Pope*. 2 vols. Detroit: Gale, 1974.

Griffith, R. H. *Alexander Pope: A Bibliography*. 2 vols. Austin: University of Texas Press, 1922–7. Not yet supplanted.

Foxon, D. F. *English Verse, 1701–1750: A Catalogue of Separately Printed Poems with Notes on Contemporary Collected Editions*. 2 vols. Cambridge: Cambridge University Press, 1975. Contains important listings of editions of Pope's poems.

Guerinot, J. V. *Pamphlet Attacks on Alexander Pope 1711–1744: A Descriptive Bibliography*. London: Methuen, 1969. Describes the wide range of hostile commentary published in Pope's lifetime.

Kowalk, W. *Alexander Pope: An Annotated Bibliography of Twentieth-Century Criticism 1900–1979*. Frankfurt: Peter Lang, 1981.

Lopez, C. L. *Alexander Pope: An Annotated Bibliography, 1945–1967*. Gainesville: University of Florida Press, 1970.

Tobin, J. E. *Alexander Pope: A List of Critical Studies Published from 1895 to 1944*. New York: Cosmopolitan Science and Art Service Co., 1945.

### Aids to study

Baines, P. *The Complete Critical Guide to Alexander Pope*. London: Routledge, 2000. Comprehensive survey of secondary material.

Barnard, J., ed. *Pope: The Critical Heritage*. London: Routledge, 1973. Charts the earlier phases of Pope's reception.

Berry, R. *A Pope Chronology*. Boston: G. K. Hall, 1988. The bare biographic facts, set out day by day.

Rogers, P. *The Alexander Pope Encyclopedia*. Westport, CT: Greenwood, 2004.

237

Wimsatt, W. K. *The Portraits of Alexander Pope*. New Haven: Yale University Press, 1965. Catalogues images of the poet, both portraits and caricatures.

### *Modern editions*
### Collected works

*The Twickenham Edition of the Works of Alexander Pope*. Ed. J. Butt *et al.* 11 vols. London: Methuen, 1938–68. The standard edition.
*The Prose Works of Alexander Pope*, vol. 1, *The Earlier Works 1711–1720*. Ed. N. Ault. Oxford: Blackwell, 1936. Vol. 2, *The Major Works 1725–1744*. Ed. R. Cowler. Hamden, CT: Archon, 1986.

### Selected works

*Literary Criticism of Alexander Pope*. Ed. B. A. Goldgar. Lincoln: University of Nebraska Press, 1965.
*Selected Prose of Alexander Pope*. Ed. P. Hammond. Cambridge: Cambridge University Press, 1987.

### Separate works

*The Art of Sinking in Poetry*. Ed. E. L. Steeves. New York: King's Crown Press, 1952.
*The Rape Observed: An Edition of Alexander Pope's Poem "The Rape of the Lock."* Ed. C. Tracy. Toronto: University of Toronto Press, 1974.
*The Rape of the Lock*. Ed. C. Wall. Boston: Bedford Books, 1998. Contains extensive collection of relevant documents.
*The Iliad*. Ed. S. Shankman. London: Penguin, 1996. With full introduction.
*The Dunciad in Four Books*. Ed. V. Rumbold. Harlow, Essex: Longman, 1999. A comprehensive edition, with exhaustive annotation.
*Pope's Dunciad of 1728: A History and Facsimile*. Ed. D. L. Vander Meulen. Charlottesville: University Press of Virginia, 1991. A text with bibliographical history.

### Collaborations

*The Memoirs of the Extraordinary Life, Works, and Discoveries of Martinus Scriblerus*. Ed. C. Kerby-Miller. New Haven: Yale University Press, 1950. Collaborative work by the Scriblerus group, with full introduction and notes.

### Manuscripts

*The Last and Greatest Art: Some Unpublished Poetical Manuscripts of Alexander Pope*. Ed. M. Mack. Newark: University of Delaware Press, 1984. Extensive collection of Pope's works surviving in manuscript.

### Letters

*The Correspondence of Alexander Pope*. Ed. G. Sherburn. 5 vols. Oxford: Clarendon, 1956. Standard edition.
*Alexander Pope: Selected Letters*. Ed. H. Erskine-Hill. Oxford: Oxford University Press, 2000. A generous selection.

## Biography

Mack, M. *Alexander Pope: A Life.* New Haven: Yale University Press, 1985. The fullest and most illuminating life.

Rosslyn, F. *Alexander Pope: A Literary Life.* London: Macmillan, 1990. A short introduction to Pope.

Sherburn G. *The Early Career of Alexander Pope.* Oxford: Clarendon, 1934. Remains an extremely valuable account of Pope's life up to 1727.

Spence, J. *Anecdotes, Observations, and Characters of Books and Men.* Ed. J. M. Osborn. 2 vols. Oxford: Clarendon, 1966. Invaluable source of Pope's autobiographic asides.

## Criticism

### Collections: published work

*Essential Articles for the Study of Alexander Pope.* Ed. M. Mack. Hamden, CT: Archon, rev edn, 1968. Contains many of the most historically influential studies on Pope.

*Alexander Pope: A Critical Anthology.* Ed. F. W. Bateson and N. A. Joukovsky. Harmondsworth: Penguin, 1972.

*Pope: Recent Essays by Several Hands.* Ed. M. Mack and J. A. Winn. Hamden, CT: Archon, 1980. Supplements the earlier *Essential Articles* (above).

*Pope.* Ed. B. Hammond. Harlow, Hertfordshire: Longman, 1996. Concentrates on modern and revisionist readings.

### Collections: new work

*Pope and His Contemporaries: Essays Presented to George Sherburn.* Ed. J. L. Clifford and L. A. Landa. Oxford: Clarendon, 1949. Contains some classic items.

*Writers and Their Background: Alexander Pope.* Ed. P. Dixon. London: G. Bell, 1972.

*The Art of Alexander Pope.* Ed. H. Erskine-Hill and A. Smith. London: Vision Press, 1979.

*The Enduring Legacy: Alexander Pope Tercentenary Essays.* Ed. G. S. Rousseau and P. Rogers. Cambridge: Cambridge University Press, 1988.

*Alexander Pope: Essays for the Tercentenary.* Ed. C. Nicholson. Aberdeen: Aberdeen University Press, 1988.

*Pope: New Contexts.* Ed. D. Fairer. Hemel Hempstead, Hertfordshire: Harvester, 1990. Emphasizes contemporary approaches.

*Alexander Pope: World and Word.* Ed. H. Erskine-Hill. Oxford: Oxford University Press, 1998.

### Monographs and essays: general

Bogel, F. V. *Acts of Knowledge: Pope's Later Poems.* Lewisburg: Bucknell University Press, 1981.

Damrosch, L. *The Imaginative World of Alexander Pope.* Berkeley: University of California Press, 1987.

Ferguson, R. *The Unbalanced Mind: Pope and the Rule of Passion.* Brighton: Harvester, 1986.

Griffin, D. H. *Alexander Pope: The Poet in the Poems*. Princeton: Princeton University Press, 1978.

Jackson, W. *Vision and Re-Vision in Alexander Pope*. Detroit: Wayne State University Press, 1983.

Morris, D. B. *Alexander Pope: The Genius of Sense*. Cambridge, MA: Harvard University Press, 1984.

Noggle, J. *The Skeptical Sublime: Aesthetic Ideology in Pope and the Tory Satirists*. Oxford: Oxford University Press, 2001.

Rogers, P. *Essays on Pope*. Cambridge: Cambridge University Press, 2006.

Russo, J. P. *Alexander Pope: Tradition and Identity*. Cambridge, MA: Harvard University Press, 1972.

## Studies of individual works

Leranbaum, M. *Alexander Pope's "Opus Magnum," 1729–1744*. Oxford: Clarendon, 1977.

Nuttall, A. D. *Pope's "Essay on Man."* London: Allen & Unwin, 1984.

Solomon, H. M. *The Rape of the Text: Reading and Misreading Pope's "Essay on Man."* Tuscaloosa: University of Alabama Press, 1993.

Aden, J. M. *Something like Horace: Studies in the Art and Allusion of Pope's Horatian Satires*. Nashville: Vanderbilt University Press, 1969.

Dixon, P. *The World of Pope's Satires: An Introduction to the "Epistles" and "Imitations of Horace."* London: Methuen, 1968.

Maresca, T. E. *Pope's Horatian Poems*. Columbus: Ohio State University Press, 1966.

Stack, F. *Pope and Horace: Studies in Imitation*. Cambridge: Cambridge University Press, 1985.

*More Solid Learning: New Perspectives on Alexander Pope's "Dunciad."* Ed. C. Ingrassia and C. N. Thomas. Lewisburg, PA: Bucknell University Press, 2000.

Williams, A. *Pope's "Dunciad": A Study of Its Meaning*. London: Methuen, 1955. A classic reading.

Winn, J. A. *A Window in the Bosom: The Letters of Alexander Pope*. Hamden, CT: Archon, 1977.

## Background and comparison

Brown, L. *Ends of Empire: Women and Ideology in Early Eighteenth-Century English Literature*. Ithaca: Cornell University Press, 1993.

Carretta, V. *The Snarling Muse: Verbal and Visual Political Satire from Pope to Churchill*. Philadelphia: University of Pennsylvania Press, 1983.

Doody, M. A. *The Daring Muse: Augustan Poetry Reconsidered*. Cambridge: Cambridge University Press, 1985.

Erskine-Hill, H. *The Poetry of Opposition and Revolution: Dryden to Wordsworth*. Oxford: Clarendon, 1996.

Hammond, B. *Professional Imaginative Writing in England, 1670–1740: "Hackney for Bread."* Oxford: Clarendon, 1997.

Ingram, A. *Intricate Laughter in the Satire of Swift and Pope*. Basingstoke: Macmillan, 1986.

Ingrassia, C. *Authorship, Commerce, and Gender in Early Eighteenth-Century England: A Culture of Paper Credit*. Cambridge: Cambridge University Press, 1998.

Jack, I. *Augustan Satire: Intention and Idiom in English Poetry, 1660–1750*. Oxford: Clarendon, 1952.

Kernan, A. *The Plot of Satire*. New Haven: Yale University Press, 1965.

Nokes, D. *Raillery and Rage: A Study of Eighteenth Century Satire*. Brighton: Harvester, 1987.

Rawson, C. *Order from Confusion Sprung: Studies in Eighteenth-Century Literature from Swift to Cowper*. London: Allen & Unwin, 1985.

*Satire and Sentiment, 1660–1830: Stress Points in the English Augustan Tradition*. Cambridge: Cambridge University Press, 1994.

Rawson, C. and J. Mezciems, eds. *Pope, Swift, and their Circle. The Yearbook of English Studies, Special Number*. London: Modern Humanities Research Association, 1988.

Rivers, I., ed. *Books and their Readers in Eighteenth-Century England: New Essays*. Leicester: Leicester University Press, 2001.

Rogers, P. *Eighteenth-Century Encounters: Studies in Literature and Society in the Age of Walpole*. Brighton: Harvester, 1985.

*Literature and Popular Culture in Eighteenth-Century England*. Brighton: Harvester, 1985.

Weinbrot, H. *The Formal Strain: Studies in Augustan Imitation and Satire*. Chicago: University of Chicago Press, 1969.

*Eighteenth-Century Satire: Essays on Text and Context from Dryden to Peter Pindar*. Cambridge: Cambridge University Press, 1988.

Woodman, T. *Politeness and Poetry in the Age of Pope*. Rutherford, NJ: Fairleigh Dickinson University Press, 1989.

*Particular topics*

## Self and world

Deutsch, H. *Resemblance and Disgrace: Alexander Pope and the Deformation of Culture*. Cambridge, MA: Harvard University Press, 1996.

Dickie, S. "Hilarity and Pitilessness in the Mid-Eighteenth Century: English Jestbook Humor." *Eighteenth-Century Studies* 37: 1 (2003): 1–22.

Mack, M. "'The Least Thing like a Man in England': Some Effects of Pope's Physical Disability on His Life and Literary Career." In *Collected in Himself: Essays Critical, Biographical, and Bibliographical on Pope and some of his Contemporaries*. Newark: University of Delaware Press, 1982: pp. 372–92.

Todd, D. *Imagining Monsters: Miscreations of the Self in Eighteenth-Century England*. Chicago: University of Chicago Press, 1995.

## Friends and enemies

Grundy, I. *Lady Mary Wortley Montagu: Comet of the Enlightenment*. Oxford: Oxford University Press, 1999.

Hammond, B. S. *Pope and Bolingbroke: A Study of Friendship and Influence*. Columbia: University of Missouri Press, 1984.

Nokes, D. *John Gay: A Profession of Friendship*. Oxford: Oxford University Press, 1995.

Rumbold, V. *Women's Place in Pope's World*. Cambridge: Cambridge University Press, 1989.

## Versification and voice

Sitter, J. E. *The Poetry of Pope's "Dunciad."* Minneapolis: University of Minnesota Press, 1971.
Spacks, P. M. *An Argument of Images: The Poetry of Alexander Pope*. Cambridge, MA: Harvard University Press, 1971.
Tillotson, G. *On the Poetry of Pope*. Oxford: Clarendon, 1938.

## Pope's Homer

Knight, D. *Pope and the Heroic Tradition*. New Haven: Yale University Press, 1951.
Shankman, S. *Pope's Iliad: Homer in the Age of Passion*. Princeton: Princeton University Press, 1983.
   *In Search of the Classic: Reconsidering the Greco-Roman Tradition, Homer to Valéry and Beyond*. University Park: Pennsylvania State University Press, 1994.
See also *The Twickenham Edition of the Works of Alexander Pope (above)*, VII–X.

## Pope and the classics

Brower, R. A. *Alexander Pope: The Poetry of Allusion*. Oxford: Clarendon, 1959.
Erskine-Hill, H. *The Augustan Idea in English Literature*. London: Edward Arnold, 1983.
Levine, J. M. *The Battle of the Books: History and Literature in the Augustan*. Ithaca, NY: Cornell University Press, 1991.
Weinbrot, H. D. *Alexander Pope and the Traditions of Formal Verse Satire*. Princeton: Princeton University Press, 1982.
   *Augustus Caesar in "Augustan" England: The Decline of a Classical Norm*. Princeton: Princeton University Press, 1978.

## Pope and the Elizabethans

Babb, L. "The Cave of Spleen." *Review of English Studies* 12 (1936): 165–76.
Beer, G. "'Our unnatural No-voice': The Heroic Epistle, Pope, and Women's Gothic." *Yearbook of English Studies* 12 (1982): 125–51.
Erskine-Hill, H. *The Augustan Idea in English Literature*. London: Edward Arnold, 1983.
Fairer, D. *Pope's Imagination*. Manchester: Manchester University Press, 1984.
Wasserman, E. R. *Elizabethan Poetry in the Eighteenth Century*. Urbana: University of Illinois Press, 1947.

## Pastoral and georgic

Chalker, J. *The English Georgic: A Study of the Development of a Form*. London: Routledge, 1969.
Rogers, P. *The Symbolic Design of Windsor-Forest: Iconography, Pageant, and Prophecy in Pope's Early Work*. Newark: University of Delaware Press, 2004.
   *Pope and the Destiny of the Stuarts: History, Politics, and Mythology in the Age of Queen Anne*. Oxford: Oxford University Press, 2005.

# Ideology

Barrell, J. "The Uses of Contradiction: Pope's 'Epistle to Bathurst.'" In *Poetry, Language and Politics*. Manchester: Manchester University Press, 1988: pp. 79–99.

Brown, L. *Ends of Empire: Women and Ideology in Early Eighteenth-century English Literature*. Ithaca, NY: Cornell University Press, 1993.

Gerrard, C. *The Patriot Opposition to Walpole: Poetry, Politics, and National Myth 1725–1742*. Oxford: Clarendon, 1994.

Hammond, B. S. *Pope and Bolingbroke: A Study of Friendship and Influence*. Columbia: University of Missouri Press, 1984.

Haydon, C. *Anti-Catholicism in Eighteenth-Century England, c.1714–80*. Manchester: Manchester University Press, 1993.

Kramnick, I. *Bolingbroke and his Circle: The Politics of Nostalgia in the Age of Walpole*. Cambridge, MA: Harvard University Press, 1968.

Monod, P. K. *Jacobitism and the English People, 1688–1788*. Cambridge: Cambridge University Press, 1989.

Skinner, Q. *Visions of Politics*. 3 vols. Cambridge: Cambridge University Press, 2002.

Young, B. W. *Religion and Enlightenment in Eighteenth-Century England: Theological Debate from Locke to Burke*. Oxford: Oxford University Press, 1998.

# Politics

Aden, J. M. *Pope's Once and Future Kings: Satire and Politics in the Early Career*. Knoxville: University of Tennessee Press, 1978.

Brooks-Davies, D. *Pope's "Dunciad" and the Queen of the Night: A Study of Emotional Jacobitism*. Manchester: Manchester University Press, 1985.

Cruickshanks, E. *Political Untouchables: The Tories and the '45*. London: Duckworth 1979.

Cruickshanks, E. and H. Erskine-Hill, *The Atterbury Plot*. London: Palgrave, 2004.
"The Waltham Black Act and Jacobitism." *Journal of British Studies* 24 (1985): 358–65.

Erskine-Hill, H. "Alexander Pope: The Political Poet in His Time." *Eighteenth-Century Studies* 15 (1981–82): 123–48.
"Pope and Civil Conflict." In *Enlightened Groves: Essays in Honour of Professor Zenzo Suzuki*. Eds. Eiichi Hara, Hiroshi Ozawa and Peter Robinson. Tokyo: Shohakusha, 1996.
*Poetry of Opposition and Revolution*. Oxford: Clarendon, 1996.

Gerrard, C. *The Patriot Opposition to Walpole: Poetry, Politics, and National Myth 1725–1742*. Oxford: Clarendon, 1994.

Goldgar, B. A. *Walpole and the Wits: The Relation of Politics to Literature, 1722–1742*. Lincoln: University of Nebraska Press, 1976.

Lenman, B. *Jacobite Risings in Britain 1689–1746*. London: Methuen, 1984.

Monod, P. K. *Jacobitism and the English People, 1688–1788*. Cambridge: Cambridge University Press, 1989.

Rogers, P. "The Waltham Blacks and the Black Act." *Historical Journal* 17 (1974): 465–86.
"Blacks and Poetry and Pope." In *Eighteenth-Century Encounters*. Brighton: Harvester, 1985: pp. 75–92.

Szechi, D. *Jacobitism and Tory Politics, 1710–14*. Edinburgh: J. Donald, 1984.
Thompson, E. P. *Whigs and Hunters: The Origin of the Black Act*. Harmondsworth: Penguin, 1975. A highly influential and contentious book.
Weinbrot, H. D. *Britannia's Issue: The Rise of British Literature from Dryden to Ossian*. Cambridge: Cambidge University Press, 1993.

## Crime and punishment

Baines, P. *The House of Forgery in Eighteenth-Century Britain*. Aldershot: Ashgate, 1999.
"'Earless on High': Satire and the Pillory in the Early Eighteenth Century." *Eighteenth-Century World* 1:1 (2003): 28–45.
"Theft and Poetry and Pope." In *Plagiarism in Early Modern England*. Ed. Paulina Kewes. Houndmills: Palgrave Macmillan, 2003: pp. 166–80.
Bell, I. *Literature and Crime in Augustan England*. London: Routledge, 1991.
Linebaugh, P. "The Ordinary of Newgate and his Account." In *Crime in England 1550–1800*. Ed. J. S. Cockburn. London: Methuen, 1977: pp. 246–69.
Reynolds, R. "Libels and Satires! Lawless Things Indeed!" *Eighteenth-Century Studies* 8 (1975): 475–7.
Rogers, P. "Pope and the Social Scene." In *Writers and their Background: Alexander Pope*. Ed. P. Dixon. London: G. Bell, 1972: pp. 101–42.
Sharpe, J. A. *Crime in Early Modern England*. Harlow: Longman, 1984.

## Landscapes and estates

Batey, M. *Alexander Pope: The Poet and the Landscape*. London: Barn Elms, 1999.
Brownell, M. R. *Alexander Pope and the Arts of Georgian England*. Oxford: Clarendon, 1978.
Hunt, J. D. *Garden and Grove: The Italian Renaissance Garden and the English Imagination: 1600–1750*. London: Dent, 1986.
Kelsall, M. *The Great Good Place: The Country House and English Literature*. Hemel Hempstead: Harvester Wheatsheaf, 1993.
Mack, M. *The Garden and the City: Retirement and Politics in the Later Poetry of Pope 1731–1743*. Toronto: University of Toronto Press, 1969. A key work, covering both landscape and politics.
Martin, P. *Pursuing Innocent Pleasures: The Gardening World of Alexander Pope*. Hamden, CT: Archon, 1984.

## Money

Carswell, J. *The South Sea Bubble*. Stanford: Stanford University Press, 1960.
Dickson, P. G. M. *The Financial Revolution in England*. New York: St. Martin's Press, 1967.
Erskine-Hill, H. *The Social Milieu of Alexander Pope: Lives, Example and the Poetic Response*. New Haven: Yale University Press, 1975.
Foxon, D. *Pope and the Early Eighteenth-Century Book Trade*. Ed. J. McLaverty. Oxford: Clarendon, 1991.
Nicholson, C. *Writing and the Rise of Finance*. Cambridge: Cambridge University Press, 1994.

# The book trade

Baines, P. and P. Rogers. *Edmund Curll, Bookseller.* Oxford: Clarendon, 2007.

Ezell, M. J. M. *Social Authorship and the Advent of Print.* Baltimore: Johns Hopkins University Press, 1999.

Foxon, D. *Pope and the Early Eighteenth-Century Book Trade.* Ed. J. McLaverty. Oxford: Clarendon, 1991. A book of central importance.

McLaverty, J. *Pope, Print, and Meaning.* Oxford: Oxford University Press, 2001.

Rogers, P. *Grub Street: Studies in a Subculture.* London: Methuen, 1972; abridged as *Hacks and Dunces: Pope, Swift, and Grub Street.* London: Methuen, 1980.

# Gender

Bowers, T. *The Politics of Motherhood: British Writing and Culture, 1680–1760.* Cambridge: Cambridge University Press, 1996.

Francus, M. "The Monstrous Mother: Reproductive Anxiety in Swift and Pope." *ELH* 61 (1994): 829–51.

Ingrassia, C. "Women Writing/Writing Women: Pope, Dulness, and 'Feminization' in the *Dunciad.*" *Eighteenth-Century Life* 14 (1990): 40–58.

Knellwolf, C. *A Contradiction Still: Representations of Women in the Poetry of Alexander Pope.* Manchester: Manchester University Press, 1998.

Nussbaum, F. *The Brink of All We Hate: English Satires on Women, 1660–1750.* Lexington: University of Kentucky Press, 1984.

Pollak, E. *The Poetics of Sexual Myth: Gender and Ideology in the Verse of Swift and Pope.* Chicago: University of Chicago Press, 1985.

Rumbold, V. *Women's Place in Pope's World.* Cambridge: Cambridge University Press, 1989.

Straub, K. *Sexual Suspects: Eighteenth-Century Players and Sexual Ideology.* Princeton: Princeton University Press, 1992.

Williams, C. D. *Pope, Homer, and Manliness: Some Aspects of Eighteenth-Century Classical Learning.* London: Routledge, 1993.

Zimbardo, R. A. *At Zero Point: Discourse, Culture, and Satire in Restoration England.* Lexington: University of Kentucky Press, 1998.

# Medicine and the body

Nicolson, M. H. and G. S. Rousseau. *"This Long Disease, My Life": Alexander Pope and the Sciences.* Princeton: Princeton University Press, 1968.

Rousseau, G. S. *Nervous Acts: Essays on Literature, Culture and Sensibility.* Basingstoke: Palgrave, 2004.

Stephanson, R. *The Yard of Wit: Male Creativity and Sexuality 1650–1750.* Philadelphia: University of Pennsylvania Press, 2004.

# The other

Barker, A. J. *The African Link: British Attitudes to the Negro in the Era of the Atlantic Slave Trade, 1550–1807.* London: Frank Cass, 1978.

Deutsch, H. *Resemblance and Disgrace: Alexander Pope and the Deformation of Culture.* Cambridge, MA: Harvard University Press, 1996.

Fabricant, C. "Defining Self and Others: Pope and Eighteenth-Century Gender Ideology." *Criticism* 39 (1997): 503–30.

Francus, M. "The Monstrous Mother: Reproductive Anxiety in Swift and Pope." *ELH* 61 (1994): 829–51.

Gubar, S. "The Female Monster in Augustan Satire." *Signs* 3 (1977): 380–94.

Stallybrass, P. and A. White. *The Politics and Poetics of Transgression*. Ithaca: Cornell University Press, 1986.

Todd, D. *Imagining Monsters: Miscreations of the Self in Eighteenth-Century England*. Chicago: University of Chicago Press, 1995.

Wheeler, R. *The Complexion of Race: Categories of Difference in Eighteenth-Century British Culture*. Philadelphia: University of Pennsylvania Press, 2000.

# INDEX

Main references are in bold type. AP = Alexander Pope.

Drayton, Michael (1563–1631), poet, 90, 93, 95, 108
Dryden, John (1631–1700), author, 1, 8, 38, 39, 50, 51, 82, 84, 89, 100, 110
Dublin (Ireland), 4, 5
dunces, 5, 23, 96, 153, 154, 158, 213

Easthampstead, Berkshire, 106, 114
Eden, 110
Empson, William (1906–84), critic, 2, 16
ekphrasis, 55, 229
Elizabeth I, Queen (1533–1603), 90, 98
Enlightenment, 9, 226
epic, 15, 67, 71, 92
Erasmus, Desiderius (1466–1536), humanist, 90, 97
estates, 10, 161–74
Euripides (c.485–406 BC), Greek dramatist, 80
Evans, Abel (1679–1737), poet, 122
Exchange Alley, London, 183

Fenton, Elijah (1683–1730), poet, 182, 190
Financial Revolution, 11, 176, 227
Fleet Ditch (London), 91, 100, 116
Fontenelle, Bernard Le Bovier de (1657–1757), French author, 108
Fortescue, William (1687–1749), lawyer and friend of AP, 10, 135, 136, 137–9, 140, 141–2
Foxon, David (1923–2001), scholar, 180, 189
French Revolution, 119

Galen (Claudius Galenus) (c.130–201 AD), physician, 93, 219
Garrick, David (1717–79), actor, 19–20
Garth, Sir Samuel (1661–1719), physician and poet, 218
Gay, John (1685–1732), author, 4, 7, 26–7, 28, 30, 31, 33, 35, 93, 113, 115, 136, 137, 139, 141, 152, 179, 188, 191, 212, 213
  The Beggar's Opera, 30; Polly, 30, 31; Trivia, 115, 189
George I, King (1660–1727), 70, 112, 114, 134
George II, King (1683–1760), 5, 31, 70, 83, 85, 134, 142, 143, 144, 146, 153
georgic, 110–12, 115
Gibbon, Edward (1737–94), historian, 82, 84
Gilliver, Lawton (c.1703–48), bookseller, 182, 194–6

Golden Age, 108, 125, 140
Gordon, Thomas (c.1691–1750), writer, 81, 146–7
Grand Tour, 73, 74
Grub Street, 11, 15, 16, 153, 155, 165, 169, 183, 191, 192, 193, 196
Grub-street Journal, 195

Hampton Court, Middlesex, 5, 52, 164
Hanoverian; accession, 4, 119
  Hanoverian regime, 82, 84, 86, 119, 134, 135, 162, 173
Harcourt, Simon, first Viscount (c.1661–1727), lawyer, 138, 155
Harley administration, 4, 112
Harley, Edward see Oxford, second Earl of
Harley, Robert see Oxford, first Earl of
Hartley, David (1705–57), doctor and philosopher, 218
Haywood, Eliza (c.1693–1756), writer, 117, 192–3, 207, 225
Hazlitt, William (1778–1830), critic, 220
Hearne, Thomas (1678–1735), antiquarian, 122
Hegel, Georg Wilhelm Friedrich (1770–1831), German philosopher, 226
Herrick, Robert (1591–1664), poet, 108, 168
Hervey, John Baron (1696–1743), courtier, 15, 18, 33, 99, 158, 202
Hobbes, Thomas (1588–1679), philosopher, 130
Homer (Greek poet), 4, 16, 26, 51, 59, 61, 63–74, 77, 78–9, 80, 85, 108, 214
  Iliad, 4, 55, 71, 74; Odyssey, 73
  see also Pope, works, translations
Hopkins, Gerard Manley (1844–89), poet, 39
Horace (Q. Horatius Flaccus) (65–8 BC), Roman poet, 6, 9, 18, 21, 67, 68, 69, 70, 76–7, 78, 81, 82, 83–4, 86, 98–100, 113, 140, 144, 145, 165, 166, 168, 173, 187, 202; see also Pope, works, Imitations of Horace
Houghton Hall (Norfolk), 165, 171
House of Lords, 31, 134, 136, 154, 195
Howard, Henrietta, Countess of Suffolk (c.1688–1767), courtier and friend of AP, 138, 162
Hughes, John (1677–1720), writer, 91

Indian kings, 232
Isle of Wight, Hampshire, 142

# Cambridge Companions to...

## AUTHORS

*Shakespearean Tragedy* edited by Claire McEachern

*Shakespeare's Poetry* edited by Patrick Cheney

*George Bernard Shaw* edited by Christopher Innes

*Shelley* edited by Timothy Morton

*Mary Shelley* edited by Esther Schor

*Sam Shepard* edited by Matthew C. Roudané

*Spenser* edited by Andrew Hadfield

*Wallace Stevens* edited by John N. Serio

*Tom Stoppard* edited by Katherine E. Kelly

*Harriet Beecher Stowe* edited by Cindy Weinstein

*Jonathan Swift* edited by Christopher Fox

*Henry David Thoreau* edited by Joel Myerson

*Tolstoy* edited by Donna Tussing Orwin

*Mark Twain* edited by Forrest G. Robinson

*Virgil* edited by Charles Martindale

*Edith Wharton* edited by Millicent Bell

*Walt Whitman* edited by Ezra Greenspan

*Oscar Wilde* edited by Peter Raby

*Tennessee Williams* edited by Matthew C. Roudané

*Mary Wollstonecraft* edited by Claudia L. Johnson

*Virginia Woolf* edited by Sue Roe and Susan Sellers

*Wordsworth* edited by Stephen Gill

*W. B. Yeats* edited by Marjorie Howes and John Kelly

*Zola* edited by Brian Nelson

## TOPICS

*The Actress* edited by Maggie B. Gale and John Stokes

*The African American Novel* edited by Maryemma Graham

*The African American Slave Narrative* edited by Audrey A. Fisch

*American Modernism* edited by Walter Kalaidjian

*American Realism and Naturalism* edited by Donald Pizer

*American Women Playwrights* edited by Brenda Murphy

*Australian Literature* edited by Elizabeth Webby

*British Romanticism* edited by Stuart Curran

*British Theatre, 1730–1830*, edited by Jane Moody and Daniel O'Quinn

*Canadian Literature* edited by Eva-Marie Kröller

*The Classic Russian Novel* edited by Malcolm V. Jones and Robin Feuer Miller

*Contemporary Irish Poetry* edited by Matthew Campbell

*Crime Fiction* edited by Martin Priestman

*The Eighteenth-Century Novel* edited by John Richetti

*Eighteenth-Century Poetry* edited by John Sitter

*English Literature, 1500–1600* edited by Arthur F. Kinney

*English Literature, 1650–1740* edited by Steven N. Zwicker

*English Literature, 1740–1830* edited by Thomas Keymer and Jon Mee

*English Poetry, Donne to Marvell* edited by Thomas N. Corns

*English Renaissance Drama* edited by A. R. Braunmuller and Michael Hattaway (second edition)

*English Restoration Theatre* edited by Deborah C. Payne Fisk

*Feminist Literary Theory* edited by Ellen Rooney

*The Fin de Siècle* edited by Gail Marshall

*The French Novel: from 1800 to the Present* edited by Timothy Unwin

*Gothic Fiction* edited by Jerrold E. Hogle

*Greek and Roman Theatre* edited by Marianne McDonald and J. Michael Walton

*Greek Tragedy* edited by P. E. Easterling

*The Harlem Renaissance* edited by George Hutchinson

*The Irish Novel* edited by John Wilson Foster

*The Italian Novel* edited by Peter Bondanella and Andrea Ciccarelli

*Jewish American Literature* edited by Hana Wirth-Nesher and Michael P. Kramer

*The Latin American Novel* edited by Efraín Kristal

*Literature of the First World War* edited by Vincent Sherry

*Literature on Screen* edited by Deborah Cartmell and Imelda Whelehan

*Medieval English Theatre* edited by Richard Beadle

*Medieval Romance* edited by Roberta L. Krueger

For EU product safety concerns, contact us at Calle de José Abascal, 56–1°,
28003 Madrid, Spain or eugpsr@cambridge.org.

www.ingramcontent.com/pod-product-compliance
Ingram Content Group UK Ltd.
Pitfield, Milton Keynes, MK11 3LW, UK
UKHW020334140625
459647UK00018B/2146